CW01263006

Buddhist Temples of Thailand

Buddhist Temples of Thailand

A Visual Journey Through Thailand's 40 Most Historic Wats

Text by Joe Cummings
Photography by Dan White

mc Marshall Cavendish
Editions

The Publisher acknowledges the sponsorship of Bangkok Glass Industry Co., Ltd and Boon Rawd Trading International Co., Ltd towards the publication of this book.

Project Editors: Greg Lowe (Thailand), Melvin Neo (Singapore)
Designer: Mark Soo/Shy Designs
All photos by Dan White except pages 60 (Madison Images), 58-59, 61, 88-89 (Luca Tettoni), 175 (Tourism Authority of Thailand)

© 2010 Marshall Cavendish International (Asia) Private Limited

Published by Marshall Cavendish Editions
An imprint of Marshall Cavendish International (Asia) Private Limited
A member of Times Publishing Limited

All rights reserved

No part of this publication may be reproduced, stored in a retrieval system or transmitted, in any form or by any means, electronic, mechanical, photocopying, recording or otherwise, without the prior permission of the copyright owner. Request for permission should be addressed to the Publisher, Marshall Cavendish International (Asia) Private Limited, 1 New Industrial Road, Singapore 536196. Tel: (65) 6213 9300, fax: (65) 6285 4871. E-mail: genref@sg.marshallcavendish.com. Website: www.marshallcavendish.com/genref

The publisher makes no representation or warranties with respect to the contents of this book, and specifically disclaims any implied warranties or merchantability or fitness for any particular purpose, and shall in no events be liable for any loss of profit or any other commercial damage, including but not limited to special, incidental, consequential, or other damages.

Other Marshall Cavendish Offices
Marshall Cavendish International. PO Box 65829, London EC1P 1NY, UK • Marshall Cavendish Corporation. 99 White Plains Road, Tarrytown NY 10591-9001, USA • Marshall Cavendish International (Thailand) Co Ltd. 253 Asoke, 12th Flr, Sukhumvit 21 Road, Klongtoey Nua, Wattana, Bangkok 10110, Thailand • Marshall Cavendish (Malaysia) Sdn Bhd, Times Subang, Lot 46, Subang Hi-Tech Industrial Park, Batu Tiga, 40000 Shah Alam, Selangor Darul Ehsan, Malaysia

Marshall Cavendish is a trademark of Times Publishing Limited

National Library Board Singapore Cataloguing in Publication Data
Cummings, Joe.
Buddhist temples of Thailand : a visual journey through Thailand's 40 most historic wats / text by Joe Cummings ; photography by Dan White. – Singapore : Marshall Cavendish Editions, c2010.
p. cm.
ISBN-13 : 978-981-261-857-3

1. Buddhist temples – Thailand – History. 2. Buddhist art – Thailand. 3. Buddhist architecture – Thailand.
4. Thailand – Religious life and customs. I. White, Dan. II. Title.

BQ6336
294.343509593 — dc22   OCN476633272

Printed in Singapore by KWF Printing Co Ltd

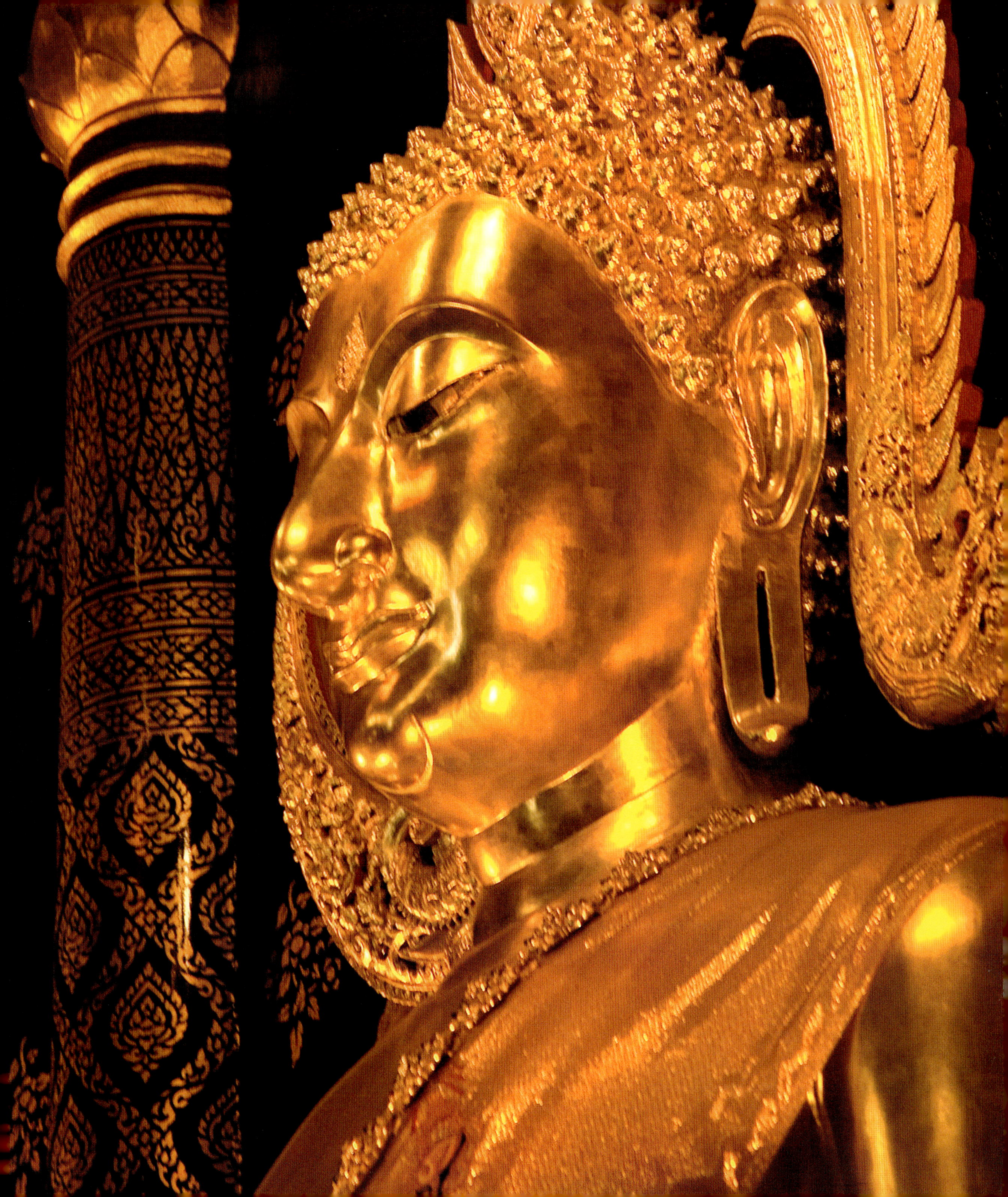

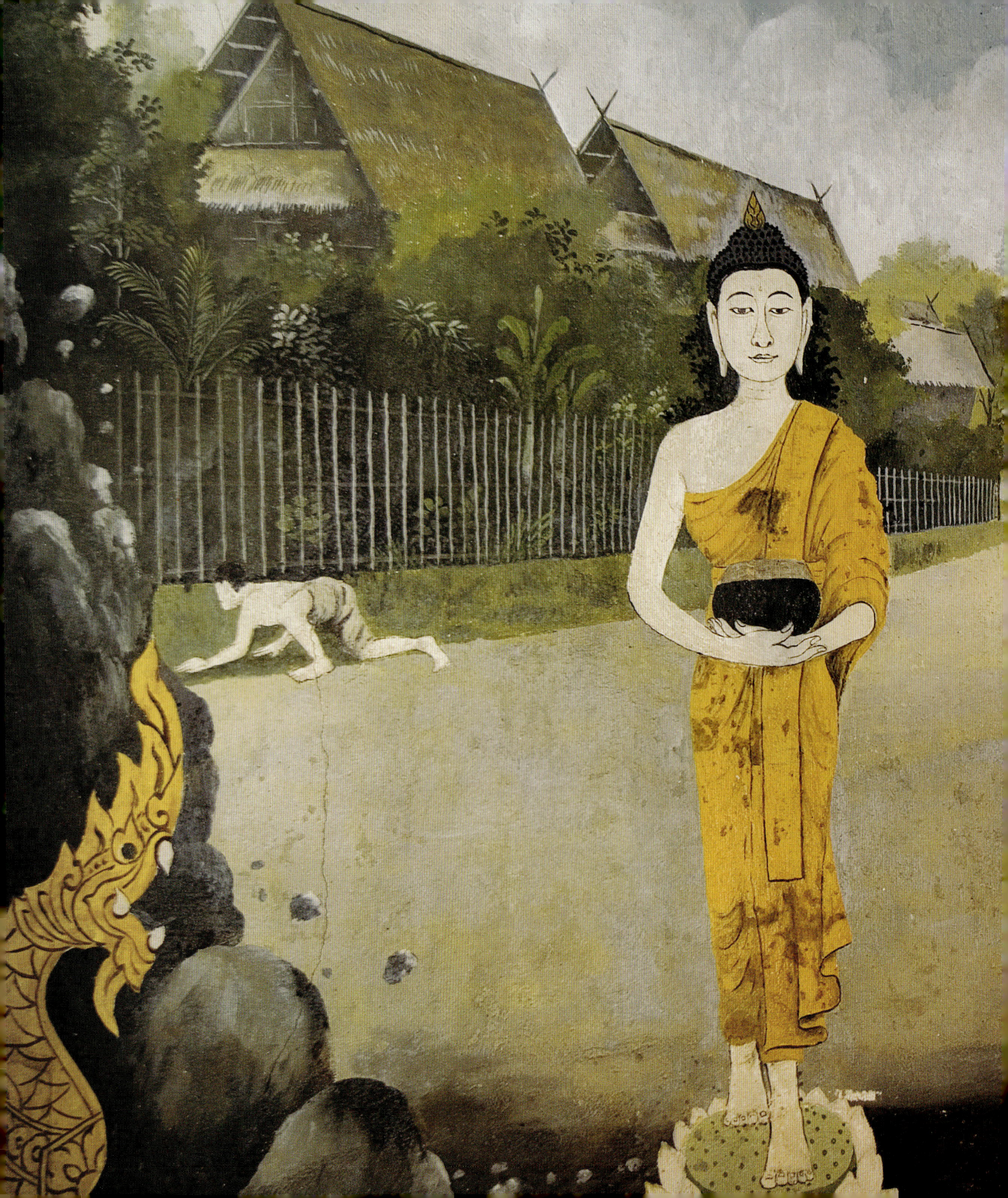

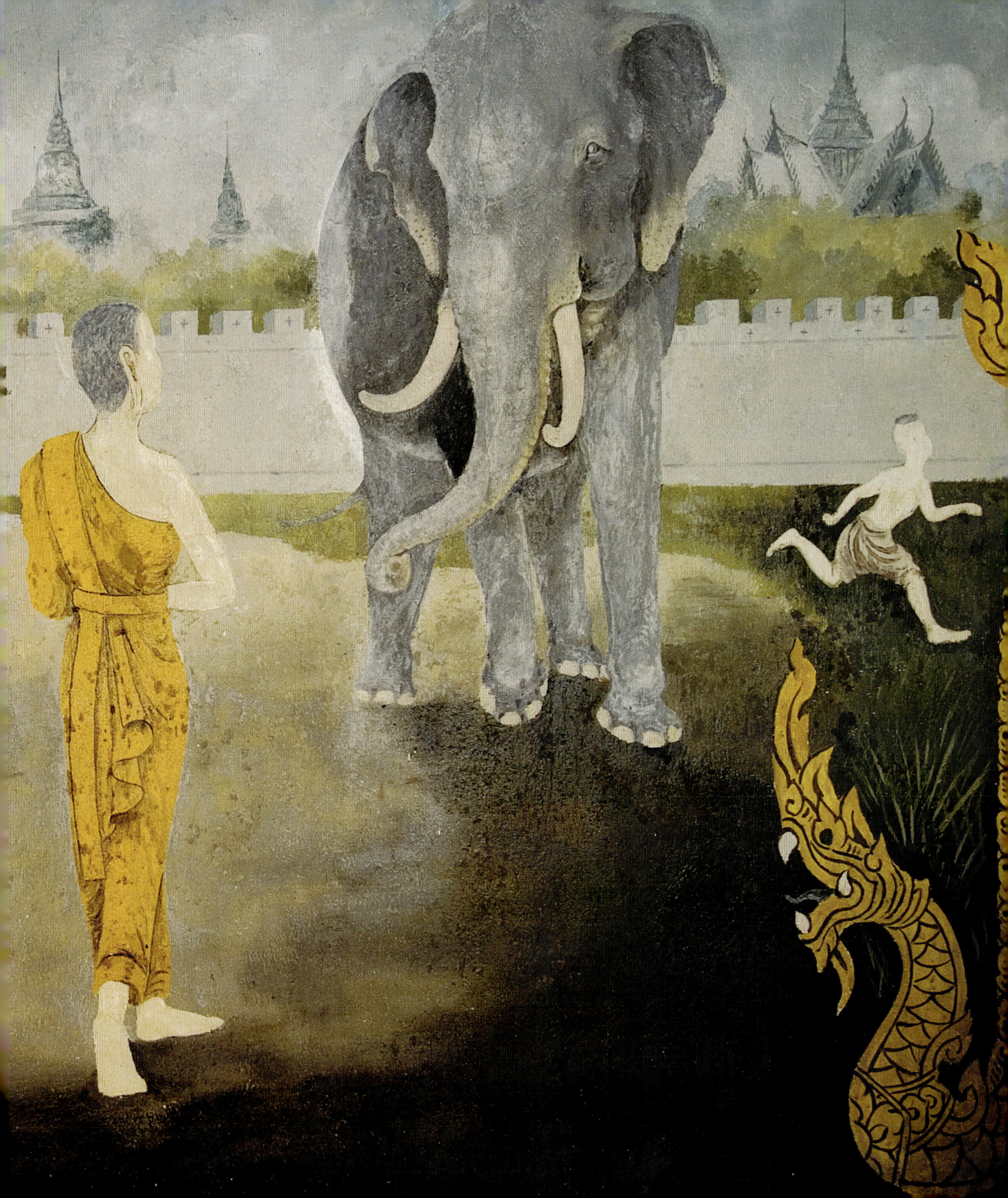

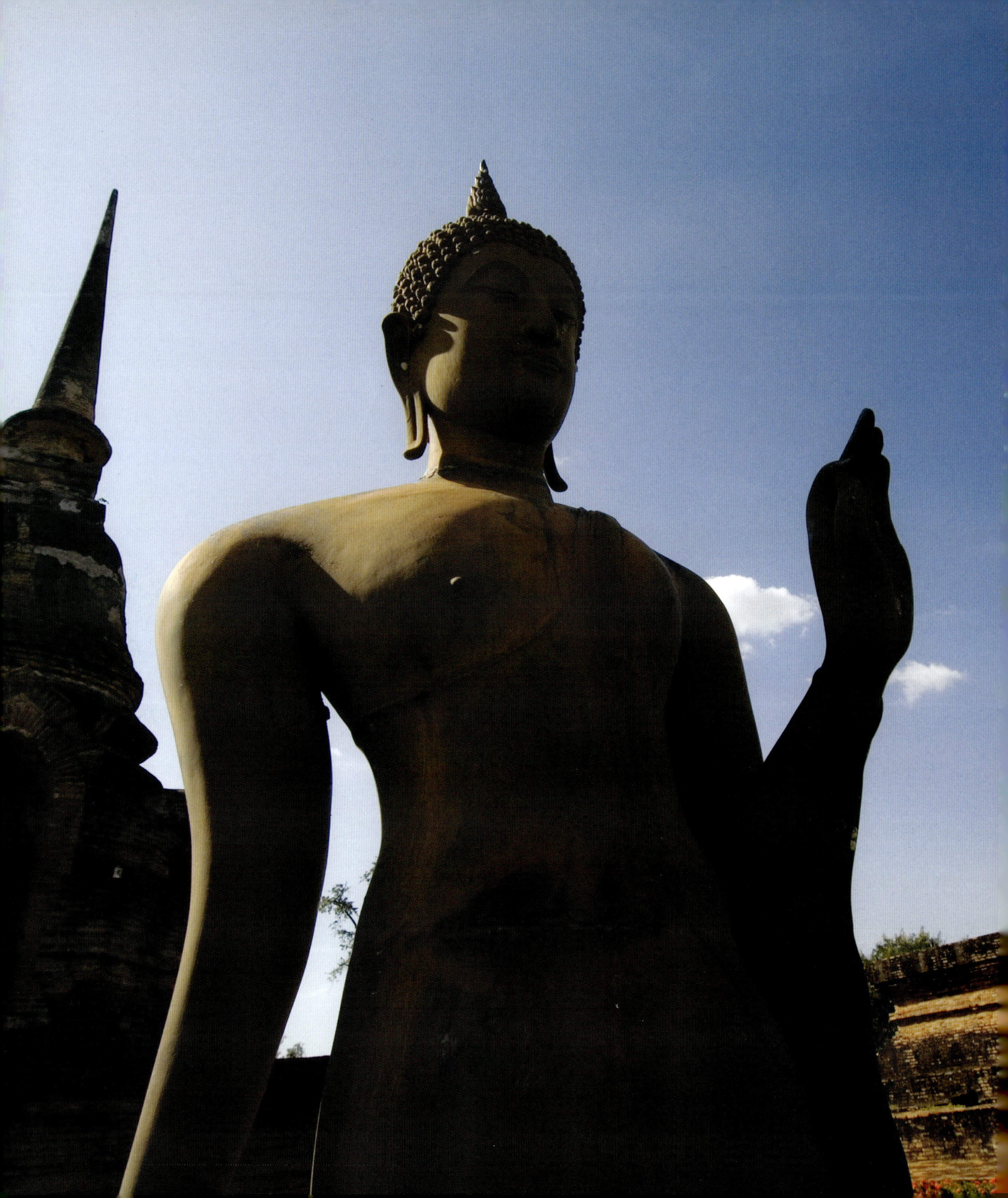

Contents

INTRODUCTION

12   Forewords

18   Eras and Empires: Power, Buddhism and the Evolution of *Wats* in Thailand

26   Ancient Structures, Form and Function: The *Wat's* Role in Everyday Life

34   A Day In The Life: The *Wat's* Role in Thai Buddhist Society

Contents

THE TEMPLES

BANGKOK

50	Wat Phra Chetuphon (Wat Pho), Ratanakosin style
58	Wat Phra Si Ratana Satsadaram (Wat Phra Kaew) Ratanakosin style
62	Wat Saket, Ratanakosin style
66	Wat Suthat, Ratanakosin style
70	Wat Molilokkayaram, Ratanakosin style
74	Wat Arun, Ratanakosin style
80	Wat Suan Phlu, Ratanakosin style
84	Wat Daowadeungsaram, Ratanakosin style
88	Wat Benchamabophit, Ratanakosin style
92	Wat Dusitaram, Ratanakosin style

AYUTHAYA & CENTRAL THAILAND

98	Wat Yai Chaimongkhon, Ayuthaya style
104	Wat Na Phra Men, Ayuthaya style
108	Wat Yai Suwannaram, Phetchaburi, Ayuthaya style
112	Wat Ko Kaew Sutharam, Phetchaburi, Ayuthaya style
116	Wat Phra Dhammakaya Pathum Thani, Contemporary style

NORTHERN THAILAND

126	Wat Phra Sing Chiang Mai, Lanna style
132	Wat Phra That Doi Suthep Chiang Mai, Lanna style
136	Wat Umong Suan Phutthatham, Chiang Mai, Lanna style
142	Wat Ton Kwen Chiang Mai, Lanna/Tai Lü style
146	Wat Phra Kaew Don Tao Lampang, Lanna/Shan style
150	Wat Pongsanuk Lampang, Lanna/Shan style
154	Wat Si Rong Meuang Lampang, Lanna/Shan style
158	Wat Phra That Lampang Luang, Lampang Lanna/Tai Lü style
164	Wat Lai Hin Lampang, Lanna/Tai Lü style
168	Wat Sasanachotikaram (Wat Pa Fang), Lampang, Lanna/Shan/Pa-O style

NORTHERN THAILAND (continued)

172	Wat Phra That Hariphunchai Lamphun, Lanna style
176	Wat Chom Sawan Phrae, Lanna/Shan style
180	Wat Phra Si Ratana Mahathat, Phitsanulok, Sukhothai style
186	Wat Mahathat, Sukhothai, Sukhothai period
194	Wat Chao Chan, Si Satchanalai, Angkor/Sukhothai style
198	Wat Phra That Chae Haeng, Nan, Lanna/Tai Lü style
204	Wat Phumin, Nan, Lanna/Tai Lü style
212	Wat Phra That Chang Kham, Nan, Lanna/Tai Lü style
216	Wat Hua Khuang, Nan, Lanna/Tai Lü/Nan style
220	Wat Jong Klang, Mae Hong Son, Shan style

NORTHEAST THAILAND

226	Prasat Hin Khao Phanom Rung, Prasat Hin Khao Phanom Rung Historical Park, Buriram Angkor style
232	Prasat Hin Phimai, Prasat Hin Phimai Historical Park, Nakhon Ratchasima, Angkor style
238	Wat Phra That Phanom, That Phanom, Nakhon Phanom, Lao style
242	Wat Chedi Khiri Wihan, (Wat Phu Thok) Nong Khai, Contemporary provincial style

SOUTHERN THAILAND

248	Wat Phra Mahathat, Nakhon Si Thammarat, Nakhon Si Thammarat style

FURTHER READING

255	Further Reading

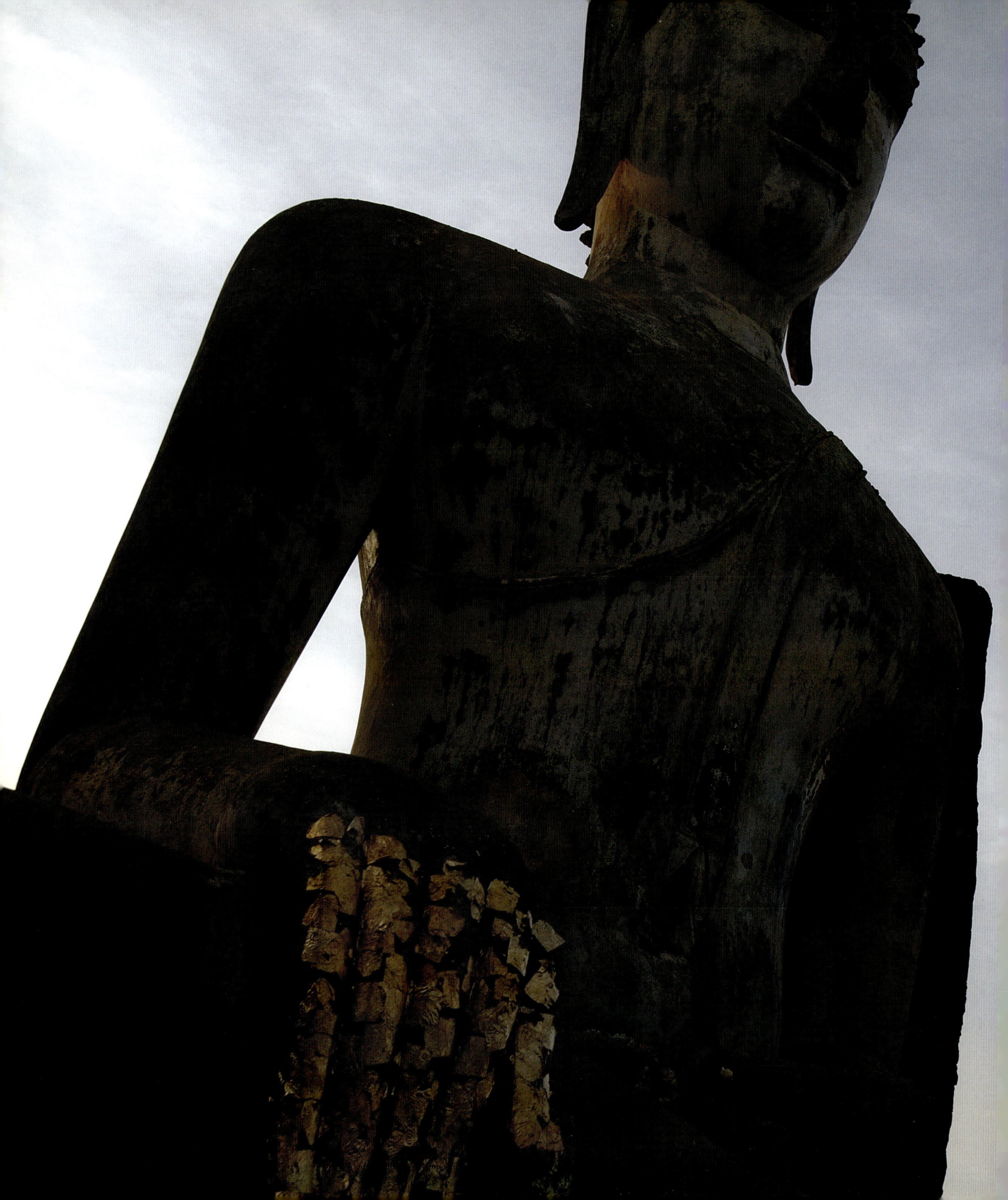

Foreword

Greg Lowe

This book, in many ways, was born from frustration. After eight years living in Thailand, a fair portion of which had been spent working in the local publishing and bookselling industry, I still had not found a single title that covered both the history and regional diversity of one of the country's most iconic structures — the Buddhist temple.

There were books exploring temples (*wat* in Thai) in Bangkok and Chiang Mai, and the ruins of Ayuthaya and Sukhothai. Some delved into Buddhism's role in Thai culture, while others cast light on temple traditions in a broader context. But there was no single offering that attempted to encapsulate the development of Buddhism in Thailand and its interplay with the rise and fall of empires and their respective temple-building programmes. There was nothing that took this historical thread and showed how it remained deeply interwoven in the very fabric of everyday life in Thailand.

A conversation with Joe Cummings — a Southeast Asian art-history expert with 30 years' experience writing travel books on the region — confirmed that he too had found no such book, despite extensive research on the subject. He *would* like to write one, however, he said.

There was a gap in the market, a hole to be plugged. Frustration transformed into action. We were on.

The initial challenge was setting the criteria for temple selection. First, we decided that all the *wats* should be historically significant due to their distinctive art and architecture. Where possible, they should be active living temples — in Thailand a *wat* is only really a *wat* if occupied by five or more monks. But these rules could bend to avoid missing some of the country's best known and most significant sites such as Wat Phra Kaew in Bangkok and Wat Mahathat in Sukhothai.

Fortunately, Joe has a near unfathomable knowledge of such things and he produced a list of 40 temples that fit the bill. No mean feat considering Thailand has more than 31,000 temples dotted across the country.

Logistics was the next challenge. There was a four-month window from late-November 2008 to early-April 2009 when the weather and light would be optimal. Photographer Dan White, a keen motorcyclist, set out on an epic 12,000-km road trip, a journey which would make him one of a select few to have visited so many of these temples, let alone shoot them.

Dan's experience as a photojournalist and writer has enabled him to develop a repertoire of skills to face seemingly impossible challenges. These would prove useful: not only would he have to ride along treacherous roads half shutter-blind and fighting off the self-repeating Buddha images that were forever burned onto his retina, he would often arrive at a location to find the temple's doors locked and have to use his seven words of Thai and a host of gestures to gain entry. He succeeded on all occasions but one.

Next, it was down to designer Mark Soo to sift through more than 6,000 images and select the final cut and then structure and lay out the book. Mark's ability to remain calm, at least on the surface, during times of stress provided an anchor that kept the project on track.

Thanks also to Panaikorn Chartikavanij and Lalitya Rangsit, who provided an essential sounding board for ideas. And our sponsors Bangkok Glass Industry and Singha Corporation who had the vision to support this project.

Now we have the end result. The first book to cover Thailand's 40 most historic temples, and one that is comprised entirely of commissioned photography save for five pictures. The book breaks ground by bringing together the history of temple development, the *wat's* continual role in daily life and a collection of popular temples and rare, hidden gems. It breaks ground again with Joe's original research, which for the first time sheds light on elements such as the intricate carvings on the eastern *gopura* at Phanom Rung.

We hope this book inspires you to visit some of these magnificent cultural sites.

Foreword

Joe Cummings

From the gilt grandeur of Bangkok's royal *wats* to the candied teak of northern Lanna temples and the virtual sermons carved in stone at northeastern Angkor-era *prasat hin*, Thailand's Buddhist monasteries have, along with the celebrated cuisine, become part of the nation's cultural legacy. For over three decades I've been privileged to contemplate the Buddhist art and architecture of Thailand, and beyond that, to experience a living temple culture. Along with learning about the *wat's* varied forms and functions, I've been touched by the everyday wisdom of the *buddhadharma*.

Although such wisdom is not confined within monastery walls, for me the *wat* institution — part of a lineage dating back to India's first Buddhist monasteries nearly 2000 years ago — serves as a tangible and ubiquitous reminder that I'm not alone in appreciating the teachings of Gautama Buddha. When I'm away from Thailand or its Buddhist neighbours in Southeast Asia for more than a few weeks, I miss the easy solace afforded by a stroll amid the stupas, open chapels and chanting monks.

One reason many of us have became so hooked on temple-hopping in Thailand no doubt springs from the fact that the monuments are simply so accessible. Like your neighbourhood 7-eleven, *wats* aren't closed on weekends or full moon days. You don't have to be Buddhist to enter, and in even the strictest religious settings they're open to all, regardless of race, nationality, gender or social class.

Somerset Maugham, the English writer whose works spanned both the 19th and 20th centuries, published two famous comments on the Buddhist temples of Thailand. "They are unlike anything in the world, so that you are taken aback, and you cannot fit them into the scheme of the things you know," he opined. "It makes you laugh with delight to think that anything so fantastic could exist on this sombre earth." The other, less flattering impression, written while he was coming down with malaria in Bangkok in 1923: "The *wats* oppressed me by their garish magnificence, making my head ache."

The numbers alone put a strain on one's imagination. According to Thailand's Department of Religious Affairs, there were a total of 40,717 registered *wats* in the country as of 2004, of which roughly 34,000 were functioning monasteries, that is, occupied by Buddhist monks.

The 40 temples featured encapsulate the major styles and eras in terms of political history, art and architecture. A number of the selections are iconic, whether in terms of Thai nationhood or as attractions for foreign visitors. Most of them are the finest examples of their era, while the remainder boast noteworthy artistic innovation.

Many people have mentored and inspired me along the Thai temple trail, of which I'd like to single out three. Professor Joanna Williams gave me the basic skills for conducting original research in art history, and taught me how to cultivate the background knowledge to make use of those skills. His Serene Highness Prince Subhadris Diskul, the finest art historian Thailand has ever produced, offered encouraging words of advice and has inspired me more than any other Thai scholar. Finally without the writings of Buddhadasa Bhikkhu, I would never have come to Thailand in the first place.

Once you're on the temple trail, you may find you can't stop. At first you're in awe of the history, the design and the details. In a short while, they may start to look all the same. But after you've walked inside 10, or 20, or 50, you begin to notice the myriad differences between even the most similar. You develop preferences and then, in a few years, abandon them. Along the way you pick up on the *wat's* social dimension, which adds considerable depth to one's appreciation.

I hope you enjoy the journey as much as we have.

Foreword

Dan White

This book started for me with a list. Assignments often do. Greg Lowe, the initiator of this project, and Joe Cummings the author and well-known Thailand expert, sent over the photographic shoot list for me to follow. Some of the names I knew — places I had worked before. Most I had never heard of.

I looked at the maps and worked out the routes and the roads. This was to become more than a series of photoshoots. Looking at the obscure and diverse nature of the locations I realised it was best to approach it as one long motorcycle trip. For those who enjoy motorcycle touring, Thailand is something special. With piles of camera kit strapped onto a smallish, but very reliable locally assembled Kawasaki cruiser, I set off from Bangkok to Mae Hong Son via the stunning border road over the rugged hills from Mae Sot. Then from Chiang Mai to Nan, via Lampang, and on past the lake at Phayao. On again down huge eight-lane highways and up dusty tracks, past southern beaches of pristine tropical sand. From the furthest northern points where hill tribe people cultivate rice and tea on steeply stepped mountain paddies, to the deepest south where the fishermen of Songkhla speak harshly and quickly as they mend their nets in small, rough commercial ports on plastic-bag strewn beaches. Then on to Isan, the heart of the country in many ways, over sugar palm and rice-field covered flatlands. In all it took 12,000 km of motorcycling to cover every location on the list.

The list became a voyage of historical discovery. Starting with the first location, the well-known wonders of Wat Mahathat in Sukhothai, the second location I was sent to was 60 km from the main temple sites — Wat Chao Chan. It took some finding. I eventually found myself driving down a heavily wooded, jungle path miles from the main temple complexes and historical parks. I arrived in a clearing. It was utterly Khmer. The bright afternoon sunshine flooded through the trees creating javelins of light silhouetting a structure that was unmistakably straight from the heart of Angkor — all these hundreds of miles north of Angkor Wat itself or the exquisite satellite temples of Phimai or Phanom Rung. A deserted outpost of a long-gone empire seemingly lost in the woods. All that history packed into this tiny, atmospheric, leafy and deserted place.

I never knew what Joe had in store for me next. Nan in the far north of Thailand remains a treasure trove of the most beautiful architecture and fascinating traditional culture. More hidden gems around Chiang Mai and Lampang — places that even many locals have never heard of such as Wat Lai Hin or Wat Ton Kwen. Fading, elegant and exquisite testaments to craftsmen and priests from a distant era, the details were often spellbinding. The tiny delicate relief sculptures of a greedy cat tracking a clueless and possibly doomed bird on a gate to a place that initially seemed crumbling. A faded painting in a far corner of Buddha in his last moments.

Isan is a place of historical wonder and robustly welcoming hospitality. Thai, Lao, and Khmer all mixed up in a hotch-potch of architecture, rural kindness and fiery, fiery food. That Phanom, and the Angkor-style temples in Khorat and Buriram remain dramatic testaments to the flow of empire and the skill of ancient architects.

Bangkok is home to some of the world's most spectacular religious buildings. The list, however, revealed other lesser known treasures. In small crumbling structures down hidden lanes, locked ordination halls contain ancient murals, lost statues and amazing light.

Thailand is a country where people flock from all over the world to enjoy famously splendid historical treasures. Not everyone realises, however, what other riches are hidden or unknown — from north to south and east to west. Enjoy.

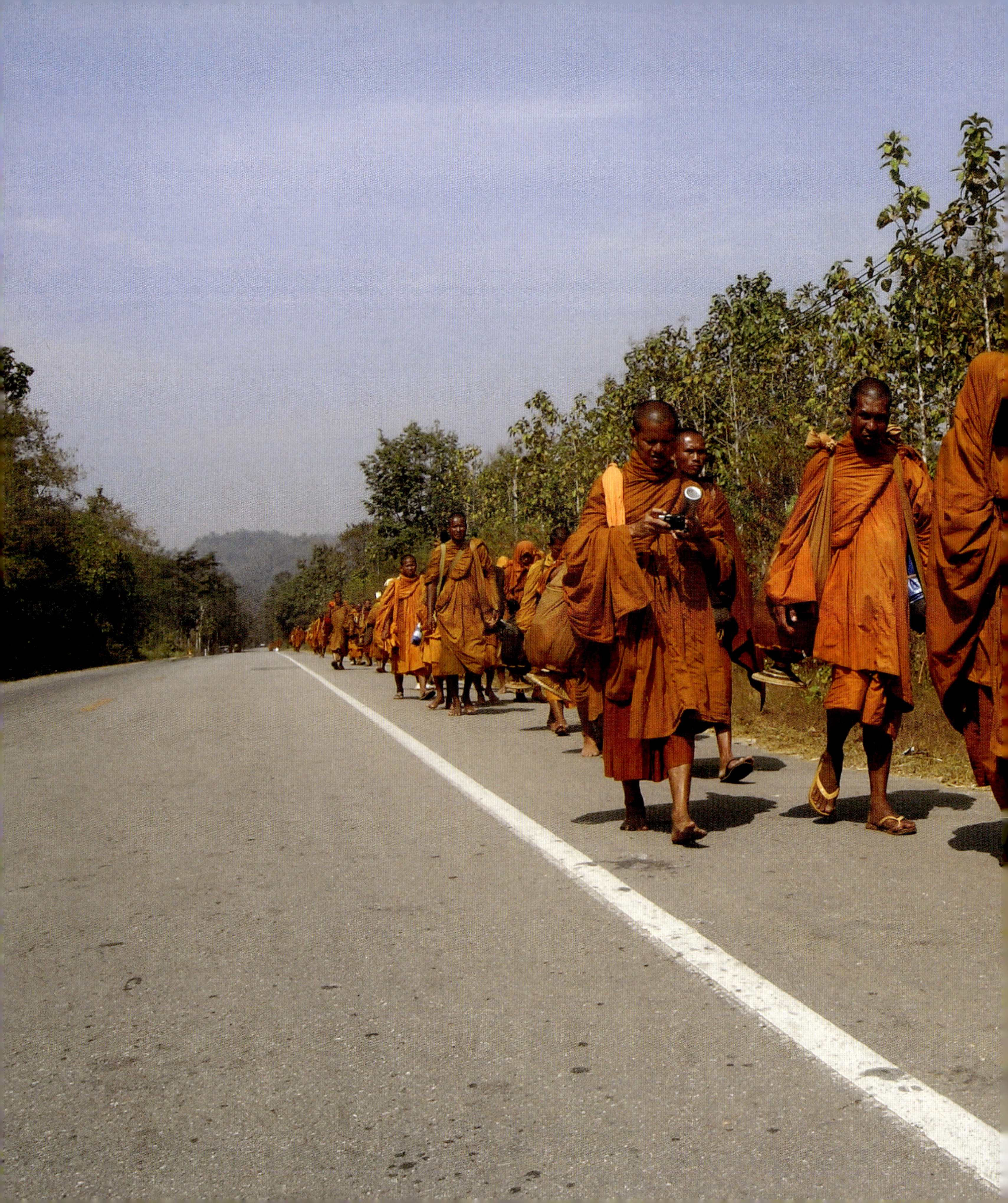

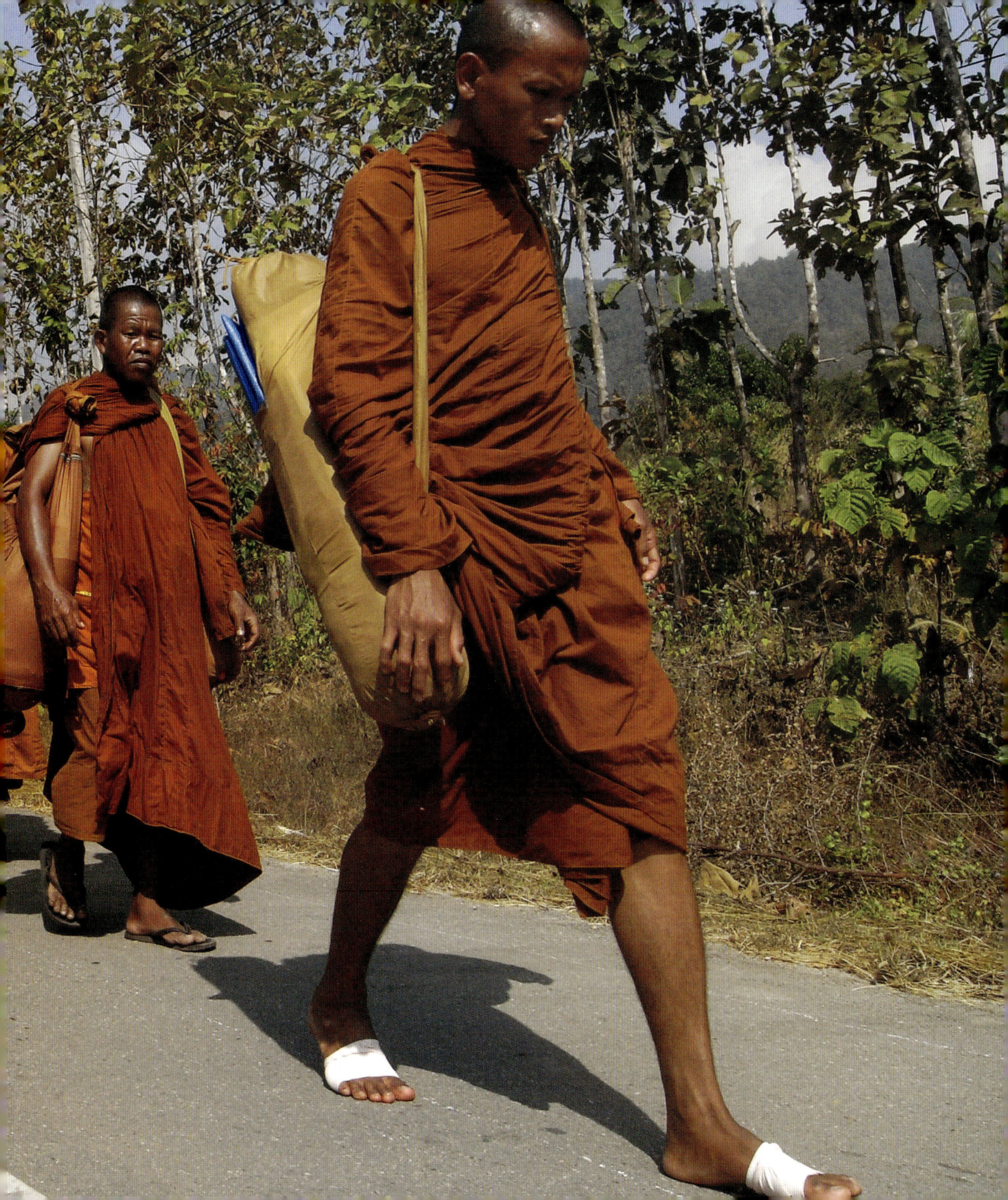

Eras and Empires
Power, Buddhism and the Evolution of Wats in Thailand

Around the 1st century AD, according to Cambodian legend, an Indian noble called Kaundinya arrived on the shores of mainland Southeast Asia as commanded in a dream. Wielding a sacred lance, he conquered the new land and married Soma, a half-human, half-serpent Cambodian queen. Together, they are said to have established a kingdom along the southern reach of the Mekong River. Although the facts are obscured by myth, this story — of which there are several regional variations — symbolises a general truth accepted by scholars today, that Indian immigrants to Southeast Asia in the early centuries of the first Christian millennium intermarried with the natives and created a new culture.

This culture laid Indian religion and art over indigenous custom in a way that fused the two traditions into one. Perhaps much as 'Westernisation' — not to mention the influences of nearby Japan, China and Korea — affects Southeast Asia today, the 'Indianisation' of Asia west of the Annamite Mountains franchised Shiva and Buddha.

The Chinese, who were the first and only outsiders to write about this era in Southeast Asian history, knew the kingdom as Funan. Essentially no architecture from the Funan empire remains, but since Hinduism appears to have dominated Funan, it's unlikely any Buddhist monuments were erected.

Thai chronicles assert that during the 3rd century BC, India's King Ashoka sent Buddhist missionaries east to a land called Suvarnabhumi (Golden Land). Suvarnabhumi was a loose collection of principalities based in an impressively fertile area stretching from southern Myanmar, across central Thailand, and into western Cambodia. If these early Buddhist visitors sponsored or inspired temple construction, none has ever been verifiably documented, despite regional legends claiming that certain present-day architecture — such as Thailand's Phra Pathom Chedi — were built over monuments dating to this period. However there seems little doubt that by the 1st century AD, Buddhism had accompanied Indian traders to mainland Southeast Asia. As the religion became accepted locally, shrines, stupas, temples and monasteries followed.

As an important commercial relay point between India and Cambodia to the west and east, and between China and the Malay-Indonesian archipelago to the south, the area now occupied by the Thai nation was criss-crossed with religious and cultural influences from many differing sources. Between the 6th and 11th centuries, the Mon of central Thailand adapted an array of Indian styles — principally Gupta — to produce Buddhist art, of which today remains a broad selection of portable art objects such as Buddha figures and votive tablets. Inscriptions left behind by this sophisticated Mon Buddhist kingdom called Buddhist art Dvaravati, a name borrowed from the Indian epic *Mahabharata*.

The Dvaravati Mon no doubt built temples, but none remain even partially standing today. Another Mon kingdom called Hariphunchai, however, flourished in northern Thailand from the 11th to 13th centuries and left behind several Buddhist monuments, including the unique, stepped-pyramid style Chedi Kukut. This stupa bears a striking resemblance to the Satmahal Prasada in Polonnaruwa, Sri Lanka.

Expanding Khmer influence in the region partially absorbed Mon culture, and the Angkor Empire eventually annexed central Thailand's Mon homelands. Between the 9th and 13th centuries, the empire's emissaries built Angkor-style Hindu monuments in what is now northeastern Thailand and as far west as Lopburi and Kanchanaburi.

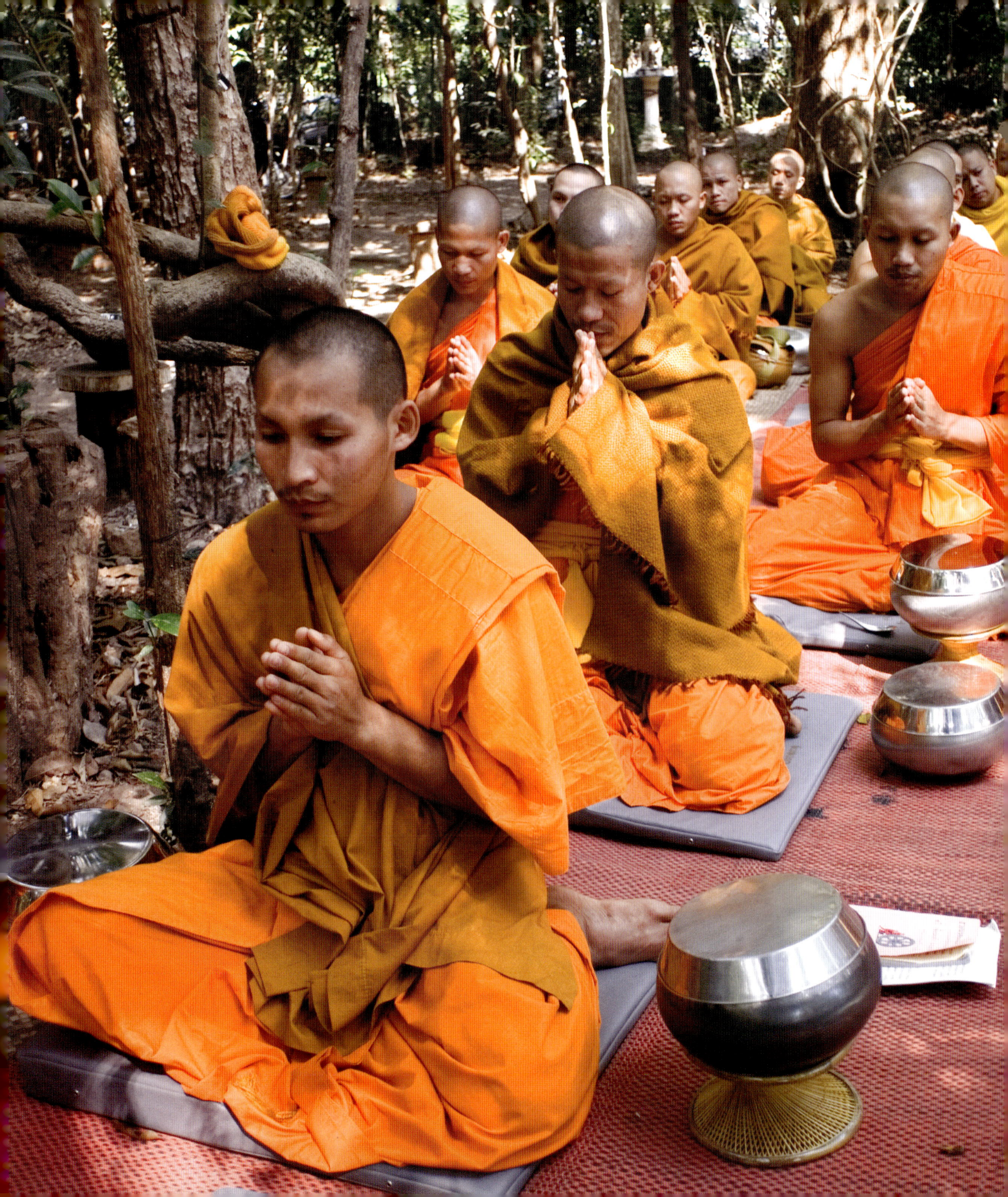

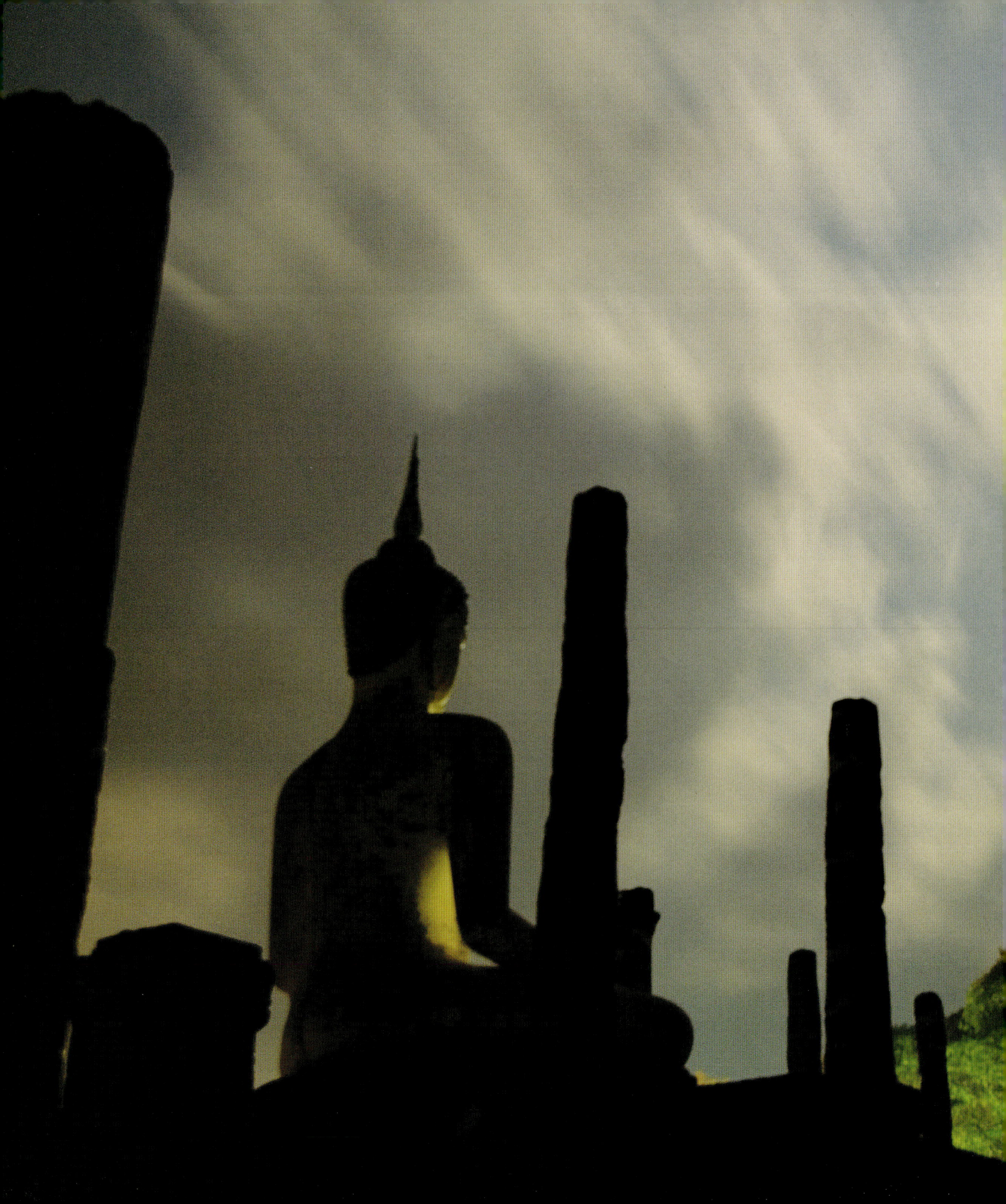

Page 19: Monks from Wat U Mong, Chiang Mai, chant in a wooded area of the *wat* compound.

Left: Temple ruins at Sukhothai.

Above: An enormous seated Buddha at Wat Si Chum, Sukhothai.

Right: Ayuthaya architects combined northern Thai, Shan, Burmese, Sri Lankan and Khmer motifs and techniques to produce Thailand's most elaborate stupas, such as this one at Wat Yai Chaimongkhon.

Page 24: The octagonal Lanna-style stupa at Wat Phra That Doi Suthep is regilded frequently.

Meanwhile Buddhist art in southern Thailand was dominated by the Sailendra and Srivijaya kingdoms of the Thai-Malay Peninsula, Java and Sumatra. Phra Borom That, in the southern Thai town of Chaiya (thought to have been a regional Srivijaya capital from the 8th to 10th centuries), strongly resembles the Buddhist *chandis* of central Java.

Around this same time in the far north of Thailand, Thai tribes — whether indigenous or migrant has yet to be definitively established — gathered together in ever-stronger city states called *meuang*. The decline of Angkor in the mid-13th century allowed these principalities to unite to create the Sukhothai kingdom in the lower north.

Later the chieftains of Sukhothai seized Hariphunchai from the Mon, and in 1296 joined with rulers in other Tai states, including Luang Prabang and Vientiane, to form Lan Na Thai (literally 'million Thai rice fields'), today often referred to simply as Lanna. During the Sukhothai and Lanna periods the Thais built a multitude of monasteries throughout northern Thailand, many of which are today considered masterpieces of Thai Buddhist architecture.

A more powerful Thai kingdom called Ayuthaya developed in the Chao Phraya River basin to the south, and in 1376 Sukhothai was folded into the burgeoning Ayuthaya empire, along with Hanthawady or Pegu (Bago in today's Myanmar). After taking over

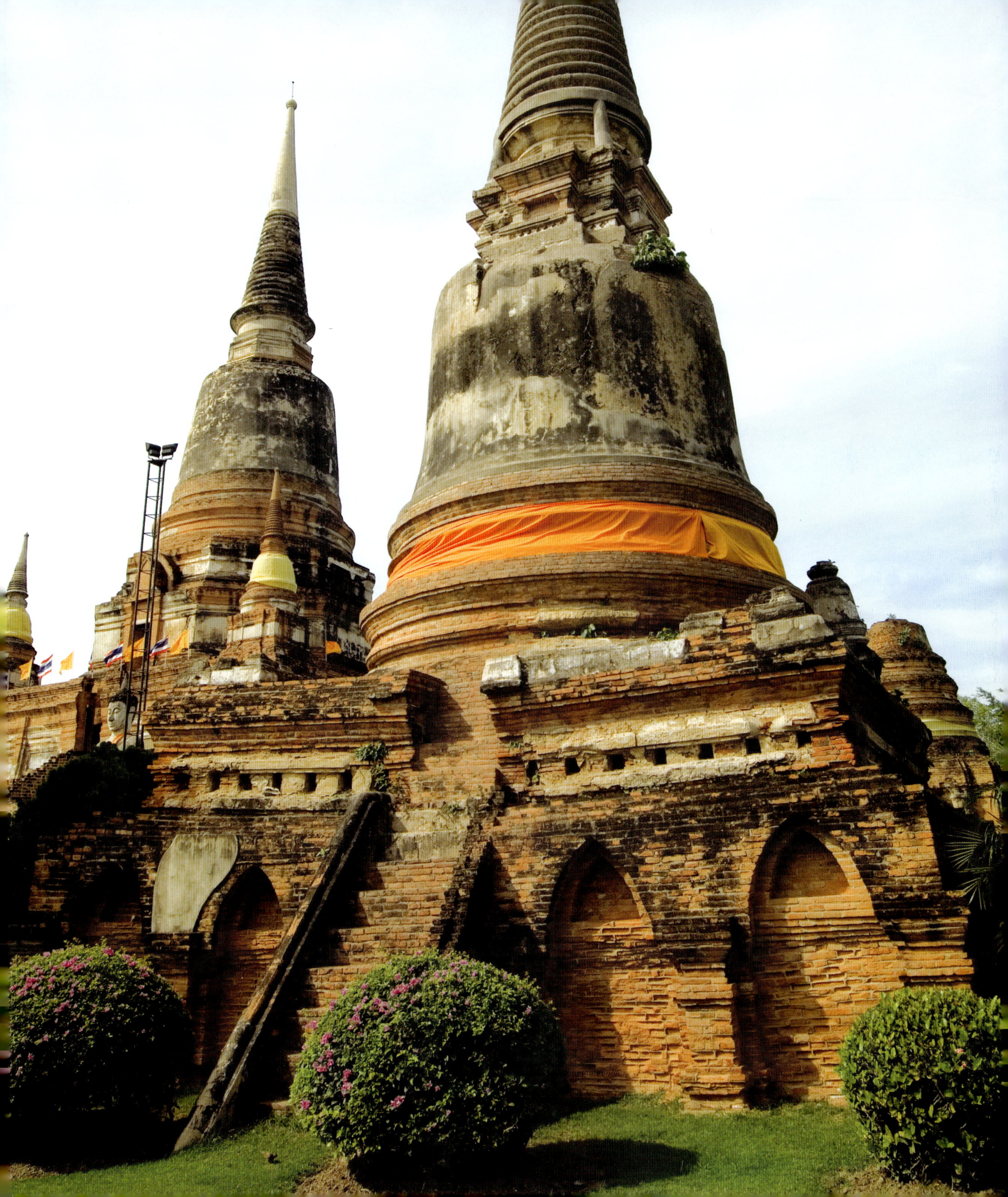

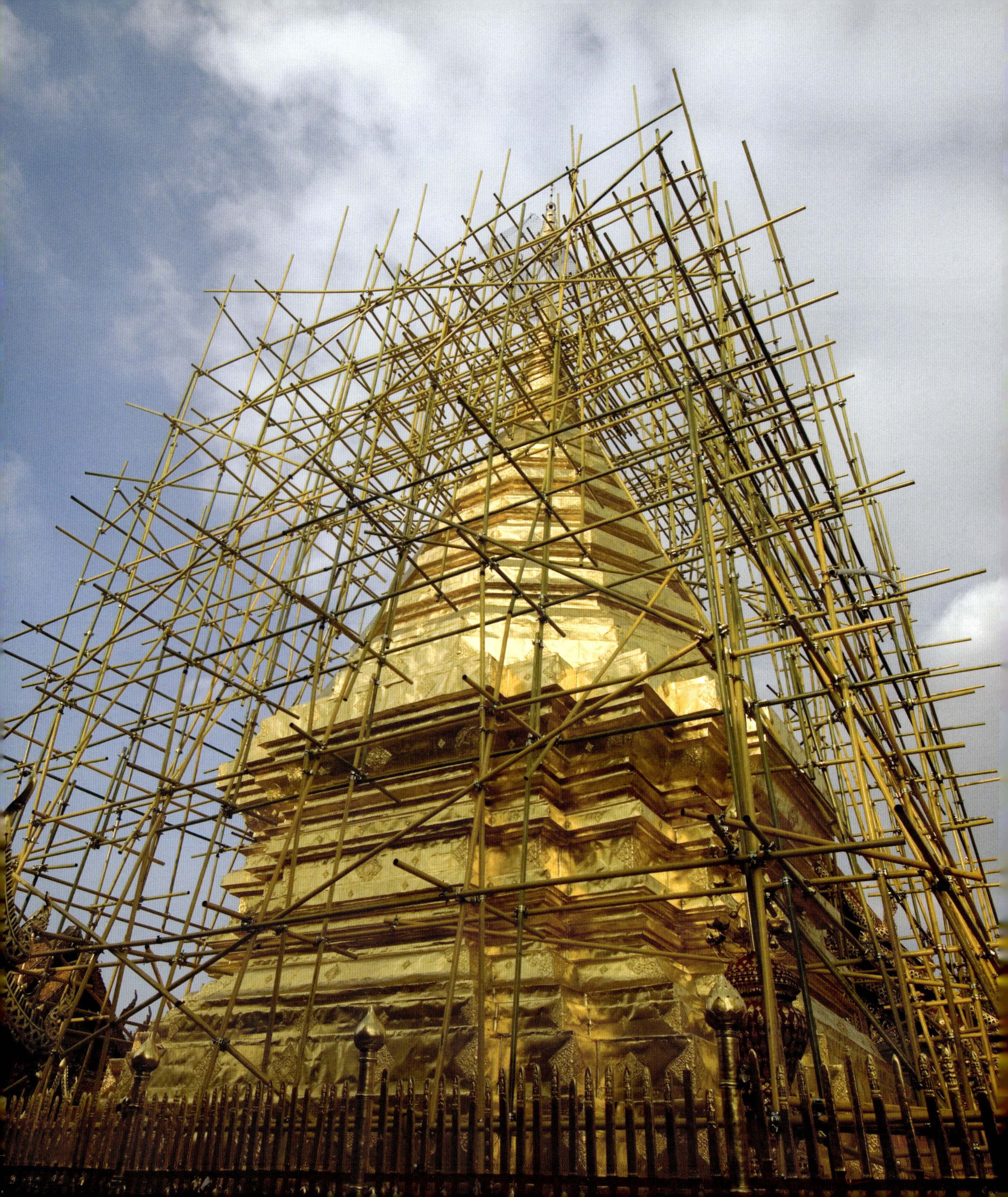

former Khmer strongholds in U Thong and Lopburi, Ayuthaya's rulers annexed Angkor in 1451. Although much of Angkor court culture was adopted by the Thais at Ayuthaya, the Thai monarchs abandoned the *devaraja* (god-king) concept of divine kingship and professed the Ashokan idea that legitimate kings should be *dhammaraja* (dhamma-king) who rule in accordance with Buddhist dharma.

During its 417-year rule, the Ayuthaya Empire became a crucible for all of the Southeast Asian Buddhist cultures it had come into contact with. Shrines and monasteries multiplied even more than at Sukhothai, as Ayuthaya's architects combined northern Thai, Shan, Burmese and especially Khmer motifs and techniques to produce the most elaborate Buddhist sculpture and architecture that Thai culture has seen before or since.

The Burmese invaded Ayuthaya in 1765 and after two years of warfare, left the capital in ruins, but the Thais quickly recuperated and founded a new capital farther south along the Chao Phraya River in 1769. Thailand's current royal lineage, the Chakri dynasty, dates to the founding of Bangkok in 1782, when Wat Phra Kaew, Wat Pho and several other royal-sponsored monasteries were constructed. Although this era in Thai art history is referred to as Ratanakosin (after the name of Bangkok's early royal district), temple architecture followed late Ayuthaya models with only minor adaptations.

Once Thailand moved from an absolute to a constitutional monarchy in 1932, the royal coffers could no longer support the continuous construction of monasteries, which under their self-supporting status have tended to lack the degree of innovation seen in previous centuries. Dynastic upheavals, which no doubt contributed to artistic change, have also been noticeably absent since 1782.

Inspiration and Dedication

Monastery construction allows sponsors to sacrifice some portion of their wealth for the propagation of the faith. By the time Mahayana Buddhism had developed in Asia, such financial sacrifice had become codified as *dana* or selfless giving, considered the first of the 10 *paramita* or 'perfections' in Buddhism. Full accomplishment of each *paramita* came to be considered a prerequisite for the attainment of Buddhahood. Mahayana Buddhism's Saddharma Pundarika Sutra asserted that 'even little boys who, in playing, erect here and there heaps of sand with the intention of dedicating them as stupas' are on the path to liberation.

Ostensibly such generosity and self sacrifice was not for one's own liberation from worldly bondage but for the salvation of all humankind – the bodhisattva ideal in Mahayana and Vajrayana Buddhism. Epigraphs found on Buddhist monuments often dedicate the *puñña* (religious merit) earned from their construction so that 'all beings may be happy' or attain Buddhahood. In everyday folk Buddhism, however, Thai Buddhists often speak of temple-building as a sure way to be reincarnated into a better spiritual position in a future lifetime.

Royal Sponsorship

Early on in Asia, kings, queens and other royalty became among the biggest temple patrons. Legend says that King Ashoka, considered India's first Buddhist monarch, ordered the construction of 84,000 shrines and stupas throughout Buddhist Asia in the 3rd century BC. Although it seems highly unlikely such a quantity of Buddhist monuments were raised during Ashoka's reign, there is little doubt he initiated a tradition of royal sponsorship that has spanned over two millennia, and that continues to this day in modern Asia.

The *dharmmaraja*, on the other hand, ruled by supporting and sustaining dharma or Buddhist law, and if he failed to do so he lost his legitimacy. Inspired by Buddhist ethics, India's King Ashoka developed a political vision that included vast public works. Ascribed to King Anawrahta, a 12th century stupa inscription in Bagan reads, 'Greed, hate, delusion, rooted all in self. O may they die, whenever born in me. Won not by oppression, may my wealth remain'. King Ramkhamhaeng of Thailand's Sukhothai kingdom was said to have met with his subjects on almost a daily basis to hear their complaints about his administration. True or not, the fact that these legends live on in the minds of the Thais indicates a weather change in social perceptions from pre-Buddhist to Buddhist polities.

ANCIENT STRUCTURES, FORM AND FUNCTION
THE WAT'S ROLE IN EVERYDAY LIFE

It is thought that in the early centuries BC, following the death of Gautama Buddha, monks wandered from village to village, depending on the support of lay Buddhists without establishing any residential centres specifically for the monks. As Theravada Buddhism grew exponentially in India, Sri Lanka and Southeast Asia, however, the numbers of monks and nuns increased to a point where Buddhist leaders agreed it would be better to confine the monastic community in a particular place during the annual monsoons, in order to prevent them from damaging young rice and vegetable crops, and to keep the monks safe from being stranded in stormy weather.

The first monastic rains retreats took place quite simply in forests or parks donated by the lay community. These retreat settlements gradually evolved into full-fledged monasteries serving both as residences for monks and nuns and as centres of learning and meditation for local peasants.

ORDER OF CONSTRUCTION
STUPA

The first step in dedicating a spot to the Sangha or Buddhist community, and the single most important Buddhist architecture dating back to India and Sri Lanka, is the stupa. These roughly conical, solid monuments tapering to a ringed spire remain the first and most sacred architectural component to be established at any *wat*.

The oldest standing stupas in Thailand, erected in Chiang Mai, Chiang Rai, Chiang Saen, Lamphun and Lampang, featured large octagonal bases topped with slender superstructures probably influenced by Shan stupa architecture. Later stupas at Sukhothai, Si Satchanalai and Kamphaeng Phet, mixed Khmer influences — such as the blunt, corncob-shaped *prang* (modelled after Angkor-style shrine towers) — with such native innovations as lotus bud-shaped finials.

Historically the psychological power of the Buddhist stupa may have evolved out of the ancient animistic notion that some inseparable link exists between life forms and their physical components, even after death. Funerals and funerary monuments the world over perpetuate this belief, but the stupa evolved into far more than an expanded tombstone. Originally conceived to commemorate the Buddha's bodily remains, it eventually came to represent the teacher's living philosophy. Thus the Buddhist stupa, like the Christian crucifix, fully transcended its initial function as a death symbol.

Buddhist commentaries recognised three kinds of stupas (*chetiya* in Pali; *jedi* or chedi in Thai). The *dhatu chetiya* contains corporeal relics of the Buddha or an arahant, while the *paribhotta chetiya* enshrined objects the Buddha had used during his lifetime. *Dharma chetiya* contained scriptural formulae, particularly a summary of the law of causation or *pratitya samutpada*. Thus in everyday parlance, anything interred in a stupa is generally referred to as *dhatu* (Thai: *thaat*) or 'element'. Materials selected for interment are usually sealed inside a small canister,

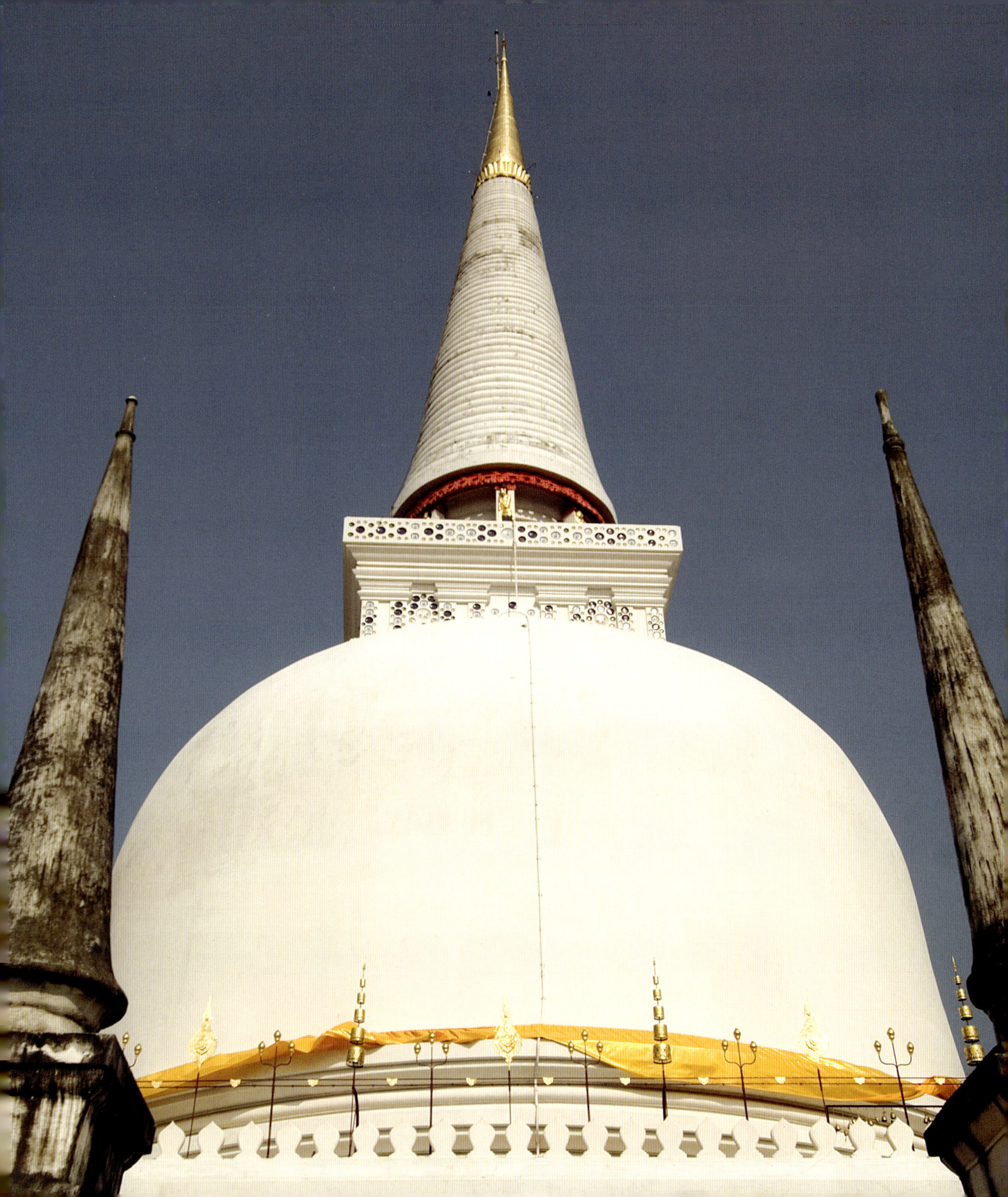

Page 27: A Sinhalese-influenced stupa at Wat Phra Mahathat, Nakhon Si Thammarat.
Above: Wihan at Wat Thai Yo.
Right: Uposatha (bot) at Wat Dusitaram.

box or casket. At this level of perception, the *dhatu* – Buddha relics or items empowered by magico-religious ritual, including miniature stupas, Buddha images or prayer scrolls – act as spiritual seed to 'impregnate' and bring spiritual life to the masonry. The most common Sanskrit term for the stupa's main dome – *anda* or 'egg' – reinforces this idea of cosmic reproduction.

In addition to a codification of varying iconographies, floor plans and vertical order and composition of architectural elements, stupa construction requires a rigid set of ceremonial activities, from start to finish.

Wihan & Bot

Once a stupa is established, the next structure to be built is the *vihara* (Thai: *wihan*), a roofed chapel where Buddhist devotees can meditate and listen to learned monks lecture on *buddhadharma* (Buddhist philosophy). The rectangular floor plan is studded with thick pillars – in northern Thailand often made from solid teak logs, elsewhere of brick or cement – which support a lofty roof, often layered in tiers of three or more.

Once a stupa and chapel are in place, the next structure of importance to erect is the monastic

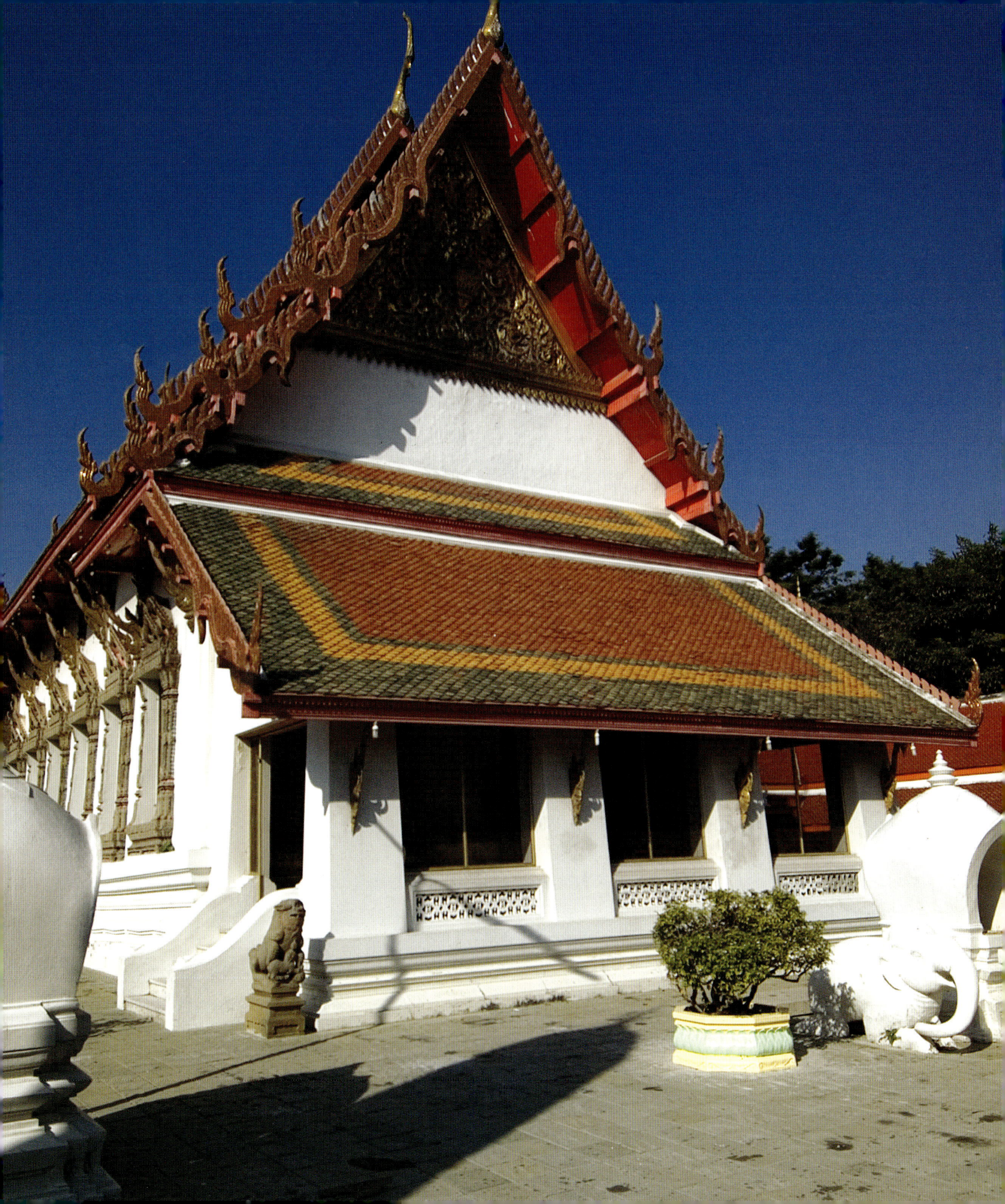

Above: Monastic quarters at Wat Thai Yo, Songkhla.

ordination hall (Pali: *uposatha*; Thai: *bot*). Often smaller than the *wihan*, the *bot* is the only building within which it is permissible to ordain laymen as *samanera* (novice monks following 10 precepts) or *bhikkhu* (fully ordained monks following 227 precepts). The rituals involved with building and consecrating an ordination hall are almost as complex as for the building of a stupa.

The most key features are the eight *sima* (boundary stones) that form a rectangle outside and around the building. Traditionally carved from stone in the shape of a stylised banyan tree leaf (symbolising the enlightenment of the historical Buddha seated beneath a banyan), three of the markers stand along each of the two long sides of the rectangular *bot*, with two markers along each of the two shorter sides.

Buried beneath each *sima*, invisible to the casual visitor, is a heavy iron ball known in Thai as *luuk nimit* (sign-ball). Resembling cannonballs of ancient warfare, the *luuk nimit* have been individually consecrated and ritually buried in lengthy ceremonies known as *fang luuk nimit* (burying the sign-balls). Until these balls have been properly interred, no ordination may take place within the perimeter.

The Mountain & The Triangle

Throughout the Thai Buddhist *wat*, the most significant geometric shape found is the triangle, whether speaking of the low-swept *wihan* roofs or the elevation of the stupa. In Hindu-Buddhist cosmology a mountain called Meru sits at the centre of the universe, and two-dimensional renderings of the mythical land form — in temple murals and illustrated Buddhist manuscripts, for example — show a complex of triangles. Surrounding Mount Meru, the universe unfolds in concentric circles or squares representing seven continents alternating with cosmic oceans. Beyond the seventh continent stretches an infinite ocean interrupted solely by four 'corner' continents, one of which is Jambudvipa, the only mythical terrain inhabited by humans. Viewed from above, the scheme looks very much like a mandala, the circular diagrams created by Buddhist artists as an object for meditation.

Some stupas, such as the great *chedi* at Wat Arun in Bangkok are consciously designed to imitate the Meru model, with a tall central stupa surrounded by four satellite stupas. Social organisation in Southeast Asian city states imitated a similar pattern, with a central ruling group at the centre, surrounded by satellite states and often referred to as a 'mandala'. Royal palace architecture, too, often followed this model.

According to Buckminster Fuller, and to eminent Thai architect Sumet Jumsai, oceanic cultures brought triangle-based architecture with them. The triangle extended from the three-way palm leaf thatch found throughout coastal Asia to inland stupa architecture. As Jumsai wrote in his intriguing and highly speculative work *Naga*:

"In contrast to the rectangle or square which is collapsible, the triangle is rigid. But in its rigidity, the triangle has to be able to sustain both compression and tension along its sides, so that push on one is neutralised by pull on another . . . [it is] the strongest structural system known, not only in physics but also in molecular physics.

"A seemingly static masonry monument is thus in reality a dynamic structure held together in constant compression and tension."

The stupa exploits the triangle's tensile strength in much the same way that an Amerindian wigwam does, expanding the two-dimensional triangle into three-dimensional space via a circle, thus producing a cone. The triangle also plays a predominant role in figures of the meditating Buddha. The head and body form a vertical triangle, while the folded legs and bottom of the spine describe a horizontal one.

Above: Wooden bargeboards carved and decorated to represent the *naga* (water serpent deity) were common in Tai Lü and Lanna temples.

OTHER STRUCTURES

Following the stupa, *wihan* and *bot*, other buildings may be constructed in any order demanded by need, as donations allow. Typically as the *wat* community waits for a quorum of monks (at least five monks must be present for an ordination to take place), it depends on visiting monks for ceremonies and teachings.

To shade gatherings of monks and laypeople, various roofed, open-sided pavilions known in Thai as *sala* (from the Portuguese *sala*) may be constructed. More stupas — usually smaller than the original, principal stupa — may be erected, along with walls to mark the monastery grounds and a principal entrance gate.

As a quorum of monks is reached it becomes necessary to provide living quarters (Thai: *kuti*). These can vary in style tremendously, from small wooden huts barely large enough for a narrow bed in rural wats, to multi-storey air-conditioned apartments in Bangkok.

As the community grows, structures whose purposes are strictly ceremonial will gradually fill the grounds, including lofty bell towers (for signalling wake-up and meals) and drum towers (to call monks for regular chanting).

A scripture hall (*ho trai*) or library to hold the *Tipitaka* (Pali Buddhist scriptures) will usually be added at one point. Up until 50 years ago or so, these would take the form of a wooden or brick building raised on high stilts planted in a lotus pond, in an effort to keep out palm leaf-devouring vermin. Nowadays new *ho trai* are more often established in multi-purpose buildings at ground level.

In a nod to Thailand's pre-Buddhist tradition of animism, most monasteries have at least one shrine dedicated to land spirits (*phra phum*), to which daily offerings of food and beverage are made.

Schools were once a major part of any urban wat and even many rural *wats*. While a larger number of monasteries around Thailand still have schools operating on their grounds, they are now under the auspices of the government's education ministry rather than the Buddhist community.

Most other additions to the monastery compound are placed for convenience (washrooms, laundry rooms, kitchens) or for beauty (trees, rock gardens, lotus ponds).

Cardinal Orientation

Despite political and aesthetic differences from era to era, certain overall design commonalties are shared among the otherwise varying architectural traditions. Among the most important of these is a determination of the cardinal directions, usually achieved by planting a pole or pillar upright on the chosen site and observing the sun's shadow between sunrise and sunset to demarcate a north-south line. A line that exactly bisects the north-south axis provides an east-west line, thus commanding the four main compass directions. By bisecting these right angles, ordinal directions (intermediate compass points) may be determined as demanded by architectural design or iconographical placement.

East takes on the most important directional orientation in most temples because the Buddha was said to have been facing east beneath the Bodhi tree when he attained enlightenment. Hence you will usually find the most important Buddha image in a temple facing east. The main entrance of the *wihan* will, of course, face east as well.

Glossary

Bargeboard	Carved wooden beams that frame roof gables atop *bot* and *wihan*
Bodhisattva	A term used to refer to the Buddha during the period before he became the Buddha, including his previous lives; Buddhist saint
Bodhi tree	'tree of enlightenment', ie banyan tree (*ficus religiosa*), a common feature in Buddhist monastery grounds.
Bot	See ubosotha
Brahman	Pertaining to Brahmanism, an ancient religious tradition in India and the predecessor of both Hinduism and Buddhism (not to be confused with `Brahmin', the priestly class in India's caste system)
Chedi	From Pali *chetiya*; see stupa
Gopura	Term borrowed from Hindu architecture to refer to entrance pavilions in Angkor-period temple complexes
Ho rakhang	Bell tower
Ho trai	Library where the *Tipitaka* (Buddhist canon) is stored
Isan	Northeastern Thailand; from the Sanskrit name for the medieval kingdom Isana, which encompassed parts of Cambodia and northeastern Thailand
Jataka	Stories of the Buddha's previous lives, often depicted in monastery murals or bas-reliefs
Ku	Small stupa that is partially hollow and open; sometimes found inside northern Thai *wihan* instead of a traditional Buddha altar
Kuti	Monk's dwelling; meditation hut
Mondop	From Sanskrit *mandapa*; square, spired building in a *wat*
Prang	Khmer-style tower or stupa
Prasat	Ornate temple structure with a cruciform ground plan and spire
Sala	Open-sided, roofed meeting hall or resting place (from Portuguese *sala*, 'room')
Sema	Also *sima*; boundary stones used to consecrate ground used for monastic ordinations
Stupa	Sealed, conical-shaped shrine containing Buddhist relics and constructed in a geometric configuration that symbolises a preservation of the Buddhadharma
Thewada	From Sanskrit *devata*; angel or divine being
Ubosotha	Consecrated hall where laymen are ordained as novice monks or full monks
Wat	Buddhist monastery
Wihan	Sanctuary and assembly hall used for ceremonies involving both monks and laypeople; contains the monastery's principal Buddha image

A Day in the Life

The Wat's Role in Thai Buddhist Society

The primary purpose of Buddhist monasteries in Thailand is to ordain and train Buddhist monks in the Vinaya (monastic discipline) so that they can put Buddhist dharma into practice. A secondary aim is for the monks to serve the Buddhist community at large, firstly as examples of the positive results attained through dharma practice, secondly to impart Buddhist teachings to laypeople and lastly to perform ceremonies associated with important life transitions, including births, weddings, funerals and house and shop consecrations.

Around 95 per cent of Thai citizens claim to be Buddhists, most of whom follow Lankavamsa, a lineage within Theravada Buddhism originally received from Sri Lanka during the Sukhothai period. Since the Sukhothai era (13th-15th centuries), Thailand has maintained an unbroken monastic ordination lineage, the only country in the Theravada world to have done so. Thai men are expected to shave their heads and don monastic robes temporarily at least once in their lives. Some enter the monkhood twice, first as 10-vow novices in their pre-teen or teen years and again as fully ordained, 227-vow monks sometime after the age of 20. Temporary ordination is thought to accumulate significant merit for one's parents.

Monks depend on the faithful for their daily meals, collected during early morning alms-rounds in which monks walk the streets of the neighbourhood nearest their monastery and accept food offerings placed into their black-lacquered bowls by laypeople kneeling along the roadside. Called *pintabaht* in Thai, the monk's morning alms round is a monumentally charitable act that offers laypeople another opportunity to make merit. Laypeople may also visit monasteries to make ritual offerings — a lotus bud or jasmine garland, a yellow candle and three incense sticks — to Buddhist shrines inside the compound. Food may be offered directly to monks as well, and cash can be left in donation boxes placed near altars or entryways around the monastery compound.

Thai Buddhists believe that temple offerings accumulate spiritual merit that will help them accomplish arduous tasks, solve domestic problems or bolster their health. There is no mandatory day of the week when Thai Buddhists are expected to make temple visits. Instead, they visit the *wat* whenever they feel the need to make merit, most often on *wan phra* (monk days), which occur every 7th or 8th day depending on phases of the moon. They may also go to a temple to make merit for themselves on auspicious occasions, such as birthdays, the new year or Buddhist holidays such as Visakha Puja (celebrating the birth, enlightenment and passing away of the Buddha) or Asalha Puja (celebrating an occasion when a thousand monks spontaneously gathered to hear the Buddha speak). On such festival days, *wats* may organise *ngaan wat* (temple fairs), typically noisy, carnival-like events featuring live music, games and food booths over a period of two or more days.

Thais also visit *wats* in order to practise meditation, to listen to monks chanting *sutta* (Buddhist scripture) or to attend dharma talks by the abbot or other respected monks. Visitors may also seek counsel from individual monks or nuns regarding life problems.

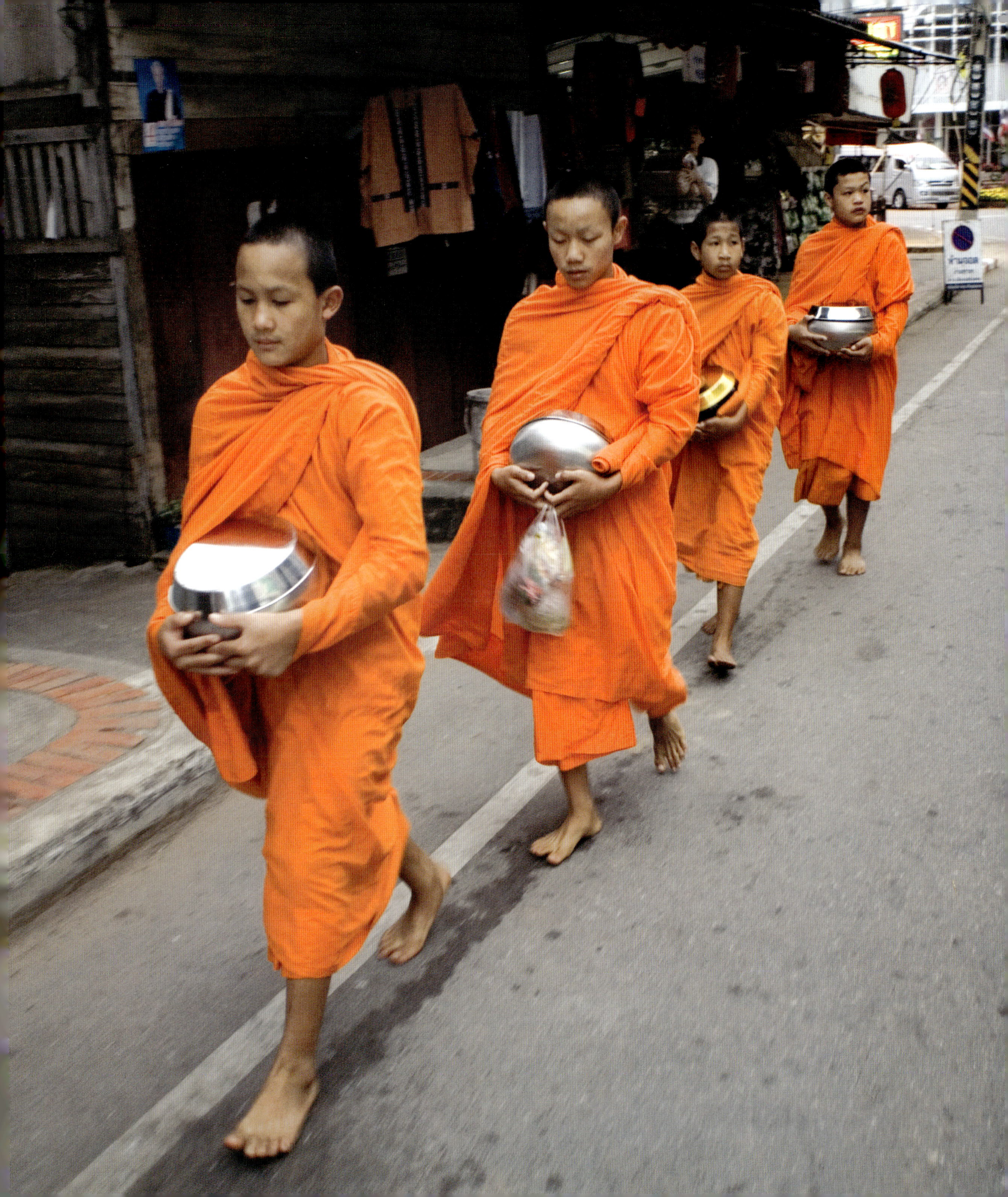

36 Buddhist Temples of Thailand

Page 35: Monks trod the early morning streets to perform the daily *pintabaht* (alms-collecting).

Far left: In a rural area of Isan, novices pause to chant blessings for a woman offering almsfood.

Left: A monk reaffirms his monastic precepts before an elder monk, a ritual performed fortnightly.

Below: Out-of-town monks take photos while visiting Wat Phra That Doi Suthep.

A Day in the Life 37

38 Buddhist Temples of Thailand

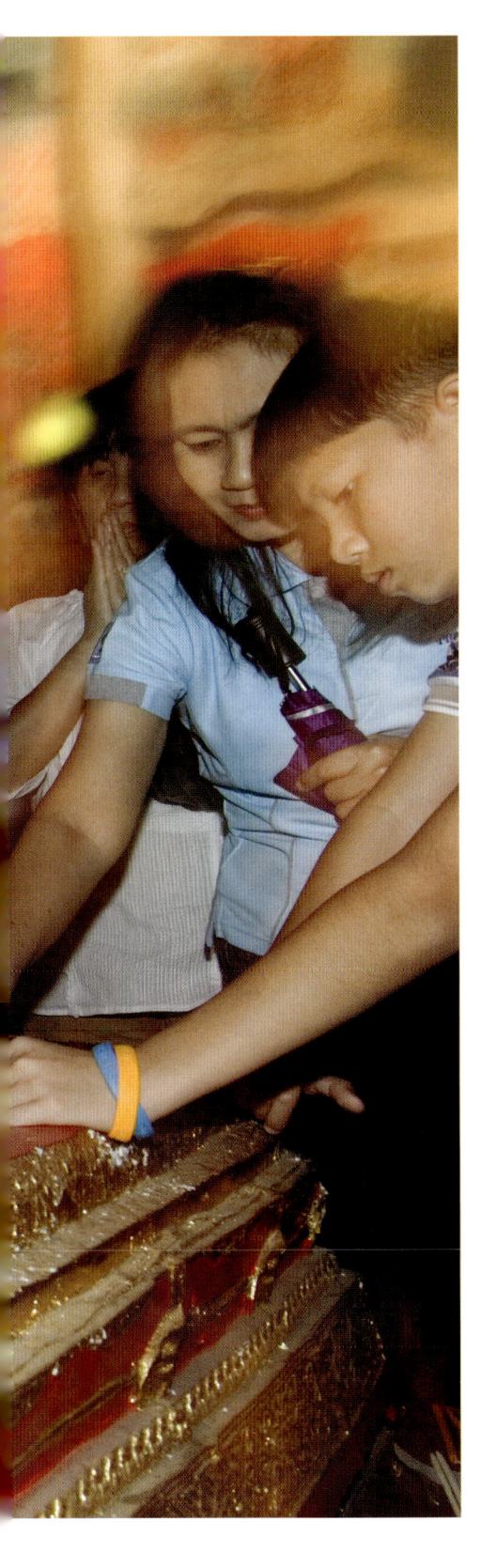

Left: At a Buddha footprint shrine at Wat Phumin, Nan, laypeople make wishes while standing coin offerings on their edges, in the belief that the intention of the offering will be more efficiently received by the shrine.

Above: Following northern Thai custom, a couple perform the traditional *seup chadaa* (life-extending) ceremony at Wat Phra That Chae Haeng, Nan, using a roll of string blessed by monks.

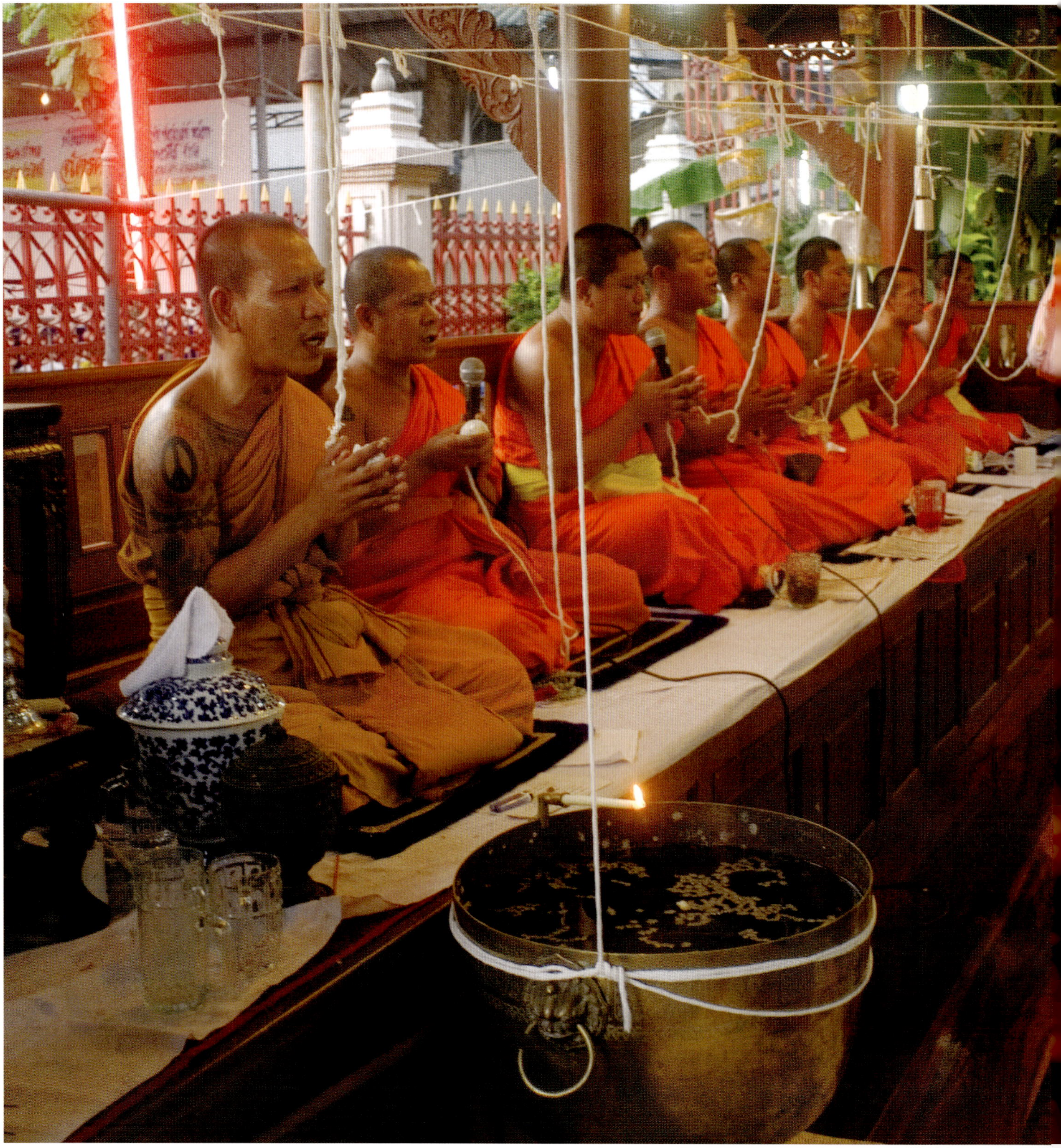

Left and above: Monks at Wat Intharawihan, Bangkok, create *nam mon* (holy water) by linking *sai sin* (blessed string) between themselves, the *wat* and a vat of water into which candlewax is dripped.

42   Buddhist Temples of Thailand

Left: Temple fair at Wat Indrawiharn, Bangkok.

44 Buddhist Temples of Thailand

Left: Fortune-telling is a popular pastime at some temples.

Right: Votive coins to be purchased for offering at shrines within the *wat*.

Below: Laypeople make offerings and pray at the feet of a giant standing Buddha image at Wat Intharawihan.

Far right: Ngaan wat (temple fairs) offer entertainment and recreation to temple devotees, while raising funds for the monastery.

A Day in the Life 47

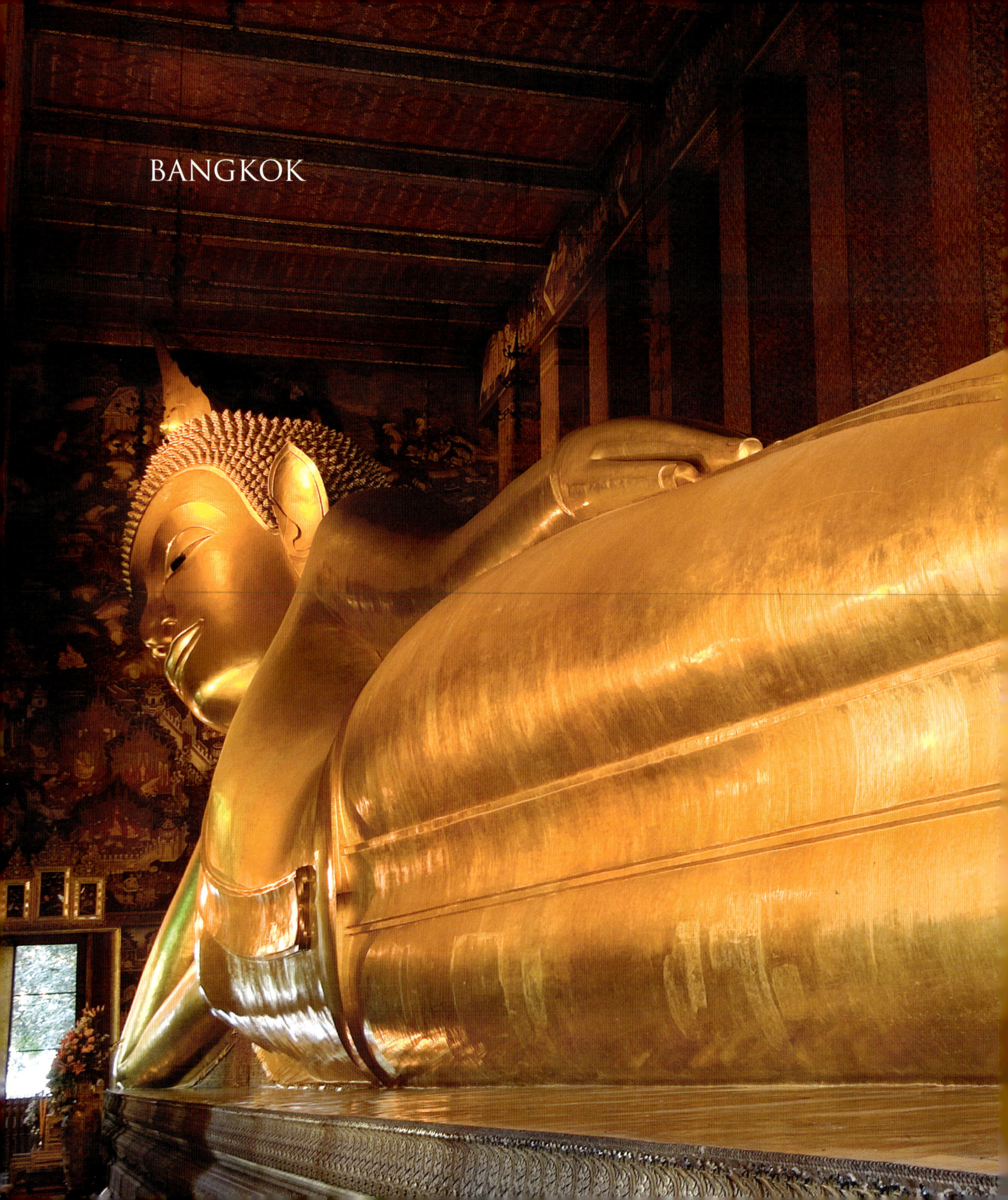

BANGKOK

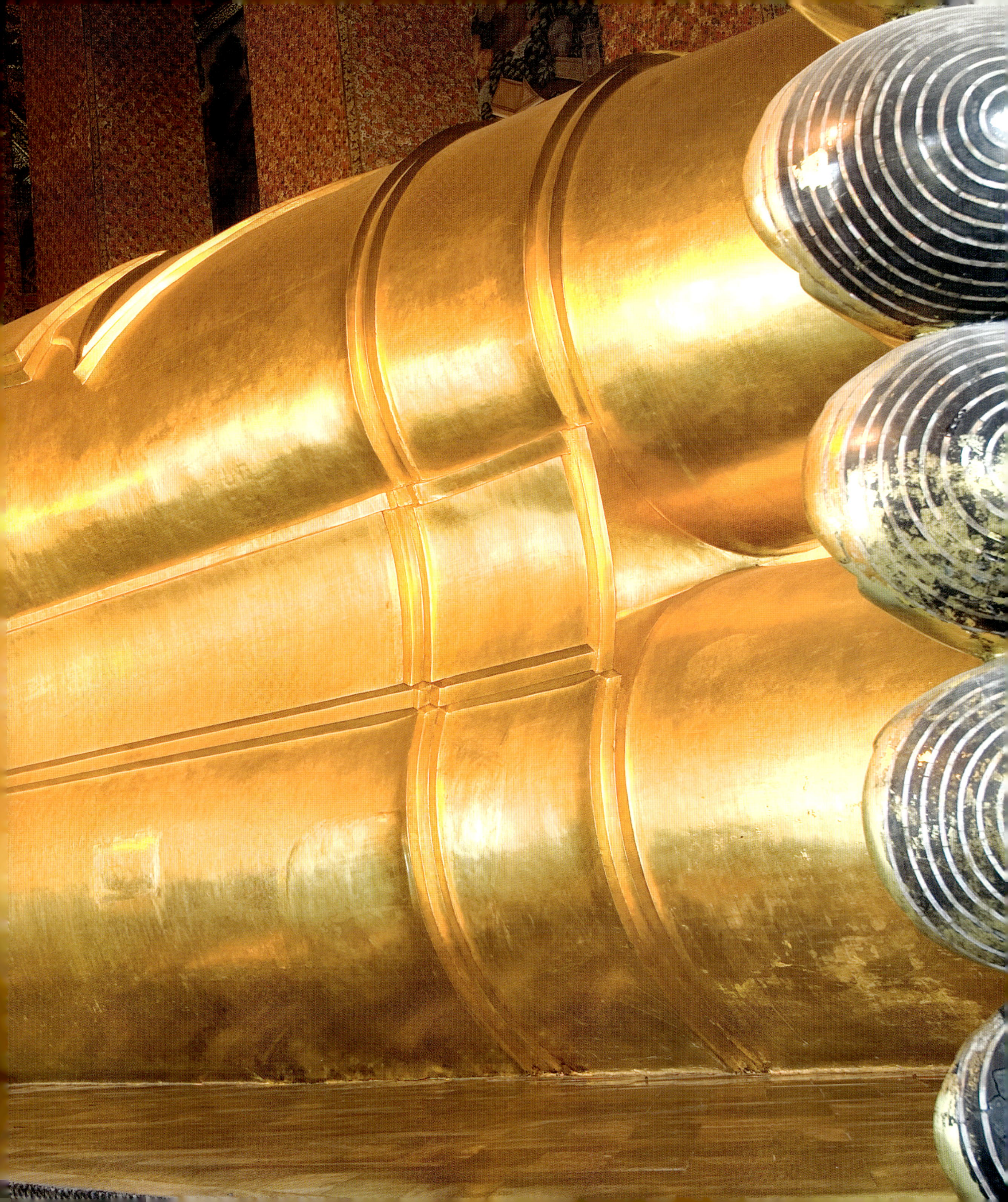

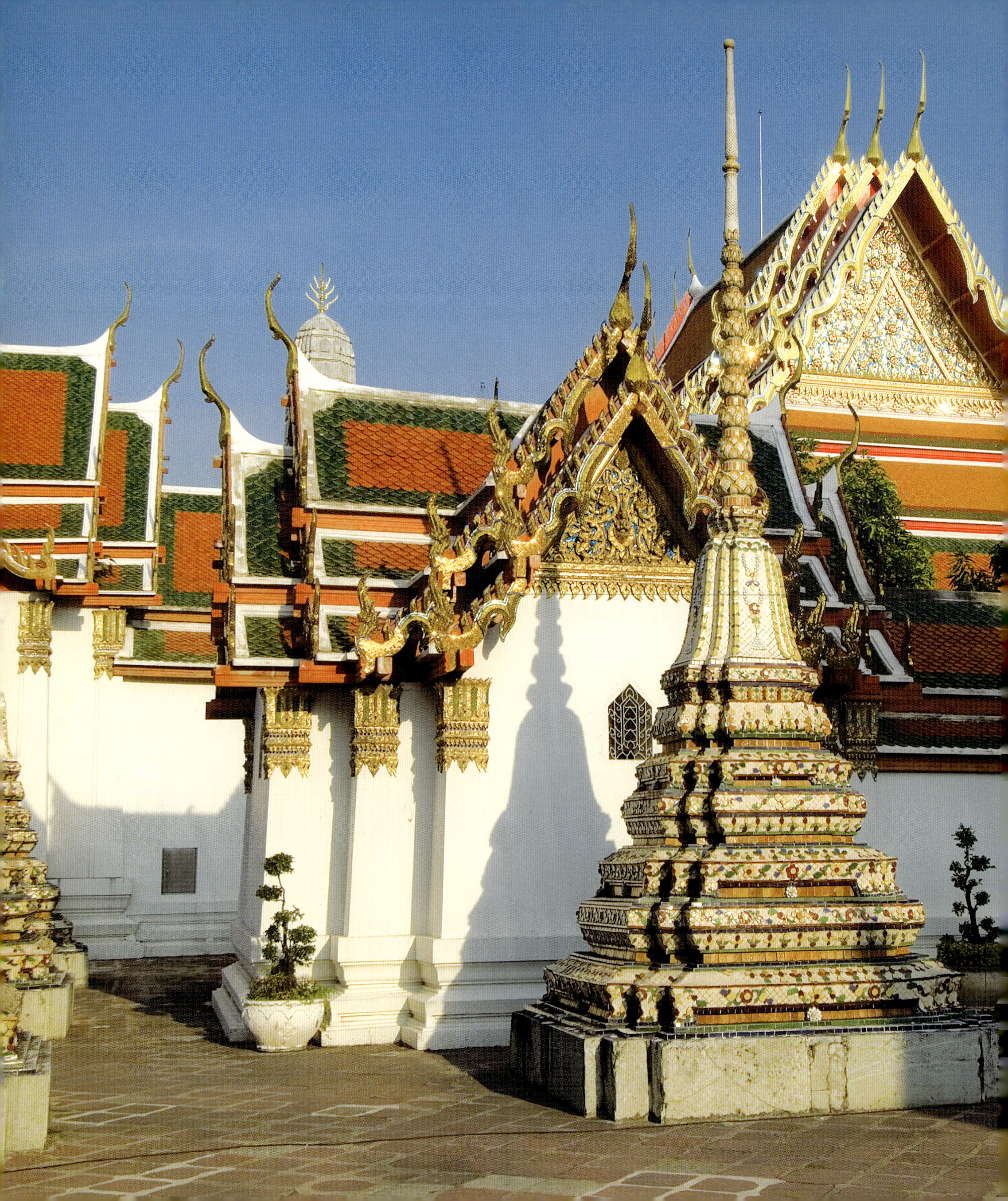

Wat Phra Chetuphon (Wat Pho)

Bangkok

Bangkok's oldest and largest monastery occupies 25 acres adjacent to the Grand Palace and is near the Tha Tian river pier, in the historic royal Ko Ratanakosin district. The grounds are divided into two separate cloistered compounds divided by Soi Chetuphon. Tourists typically visit only the northern compound, where a world-famous reclining Buddha and massage school are located, along with the main *wihan* and *bot*. Across the *soi*, the much less-visited southern compound contains monks' residences and a secular school.

By order of Rama I, construction on Wat Phra Chetuphon began in 1789 and was completed 16 years later. An earlier 16th century temple called Wat Photharam occupied the same site and was partially incorporated into the newer project. The short name for the original temple, Wat Pho, remains the most common moniker for its replacement.

The new monastery served as a centre for traditional Thai medical knowledge. A large series of marble slabs were inscribed with medical texts, including herbal remedy formulae, and installed in the northern temple pavilions. In 2008, the plaques were listed by the United Nations Educational, Scientific and Cultural Organization's (UNESCO) Memory of the World Programme, which recognises the preservation of valuable cultural archives around the world.

Pages 48-49: The world-famous 46-metre long reclining Buddha at Wat Phra Chetuphon.

Left: A cloister and *wihan*, along with a few funerary stupas, at Bangkok's oldest Buddhist monastery, Wat Phra Chetuphon.

Pages 52-53: A close-up of a mural scene at Wat Phra Chetuphon, depicting 18th century royal court life.

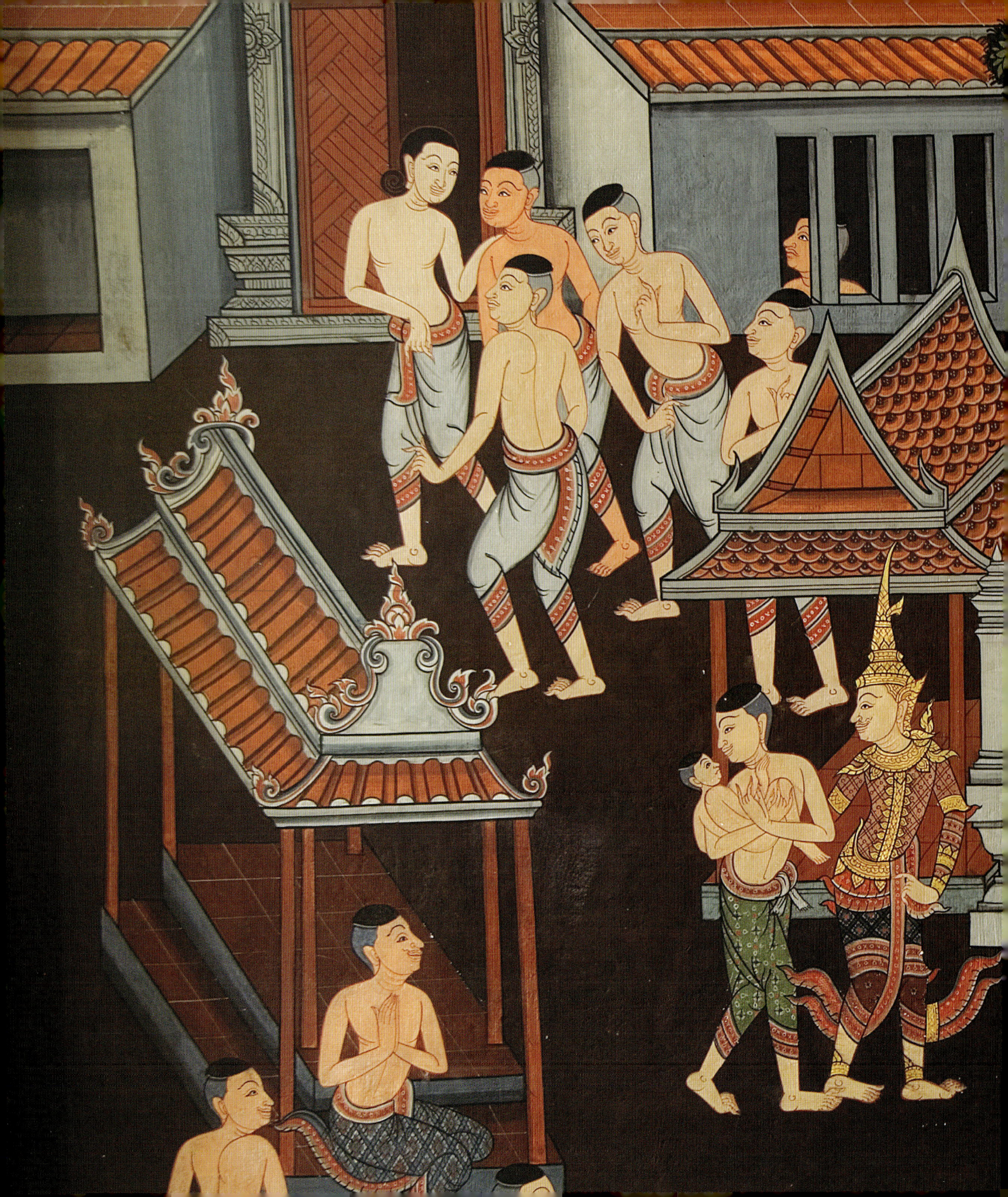

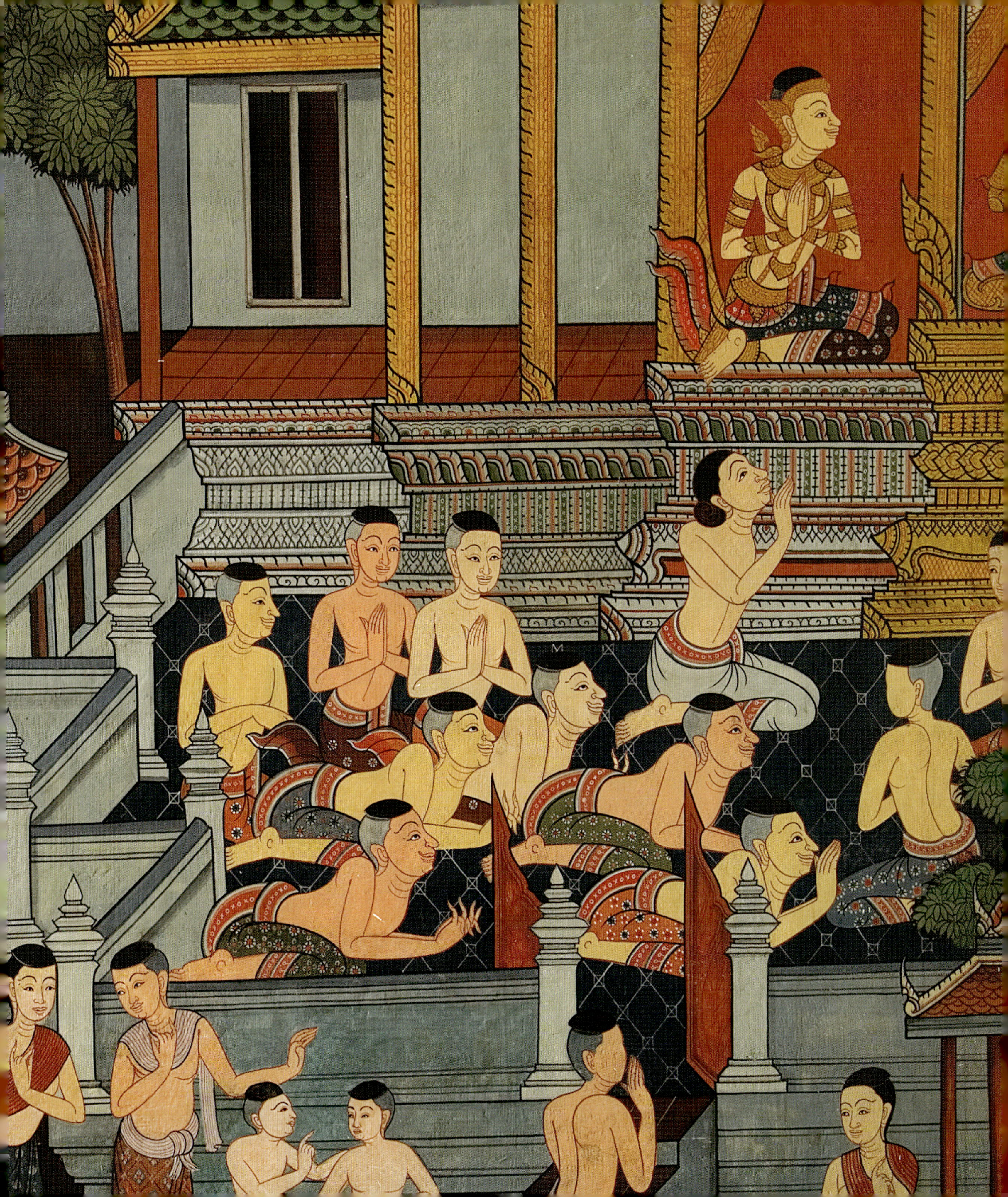

Pundits erected stone statues of ascetics practising therapeutic massage and yoga postures in the northern compound, and established a training centre for traditional Thai massage that is still in operation. The massage teaching component of the programme has moved to a nearby location outside the monastery, but trainees still practise massage inside the compound. Because of this early focus on education, Thais today refer to Wat Pho as Bangkok's first university.

One of Rama II's sons, Prince Poramanuchit, excelled in poetry and took up residence in the southern compound in order to compose verse and teach literature. He later ordained as a monk, remaining in robes the rest of his life and rising to the rank of *Sangharaja* (Supreme Patriarch of Thai Buddhism).

Many Buddha images from abandoned temples in Ayuthaya and other parts of Thailand were brought here, and today Wat Pho boasts over a thousand Buddha images, more than any other monastery in Thailand. The most famous, Phra Phuttha Saiyat, is a reclining Buddha that measures 46 metres long and 15 metres high. Built during the Third Regnum, of brick encased in plaster and then gilded, the colossal image illustrates the Buddha's passing into *parinibbana* (final nirvana) upon death. The soles of the figure's feet feature inlaid mother-of-pearl designs representing the 108 different auspicious characteristics of a Buddha.

In front of the pavilion containing the reclining Buddha stand four large stupas, decorated with glazed porcelain and enshrining the ashes of the first four Chakri kings. Ninety-one other stupas can be found throughout the compound.

The interior walls of the *bot* feature *Jataka* murals painted in the Third Regnum and elegant window panels adorned with *lai rot nam* ('washed with water,' gold designs applied to black lacquer) depicting Thai folk tales. The lower exterior wall of the *bot* is lined with 152 marble bas reliefs carved with scenes from the *Ramakien,* the Thai version of the Indian *Ramayana* epic.

Two *wihan* adjacent to the *bot* contain large, exquisite gilded bronze Buddhas, respectively named Phra Jinnarat and Phra Jinachi, both from Sukhothai. The majestic *phra rabiang* (cloister galleries) extending between these and two other *wihan* are lined with 394 gilded Buddha images.

Above: An artist restores the vibrant *lai kham* — gold leaf designs on lacquer — inside the reclining Buddha chapel at Wat Phra Chetuphon.

Right: An original Sukhothai bronze sitting Buddha at Wat Phra Chetuphon.

Pages 56-57: Stupas in the Ratanakosin era were heavily decorated with fragments of colourful Chinese porcelain.

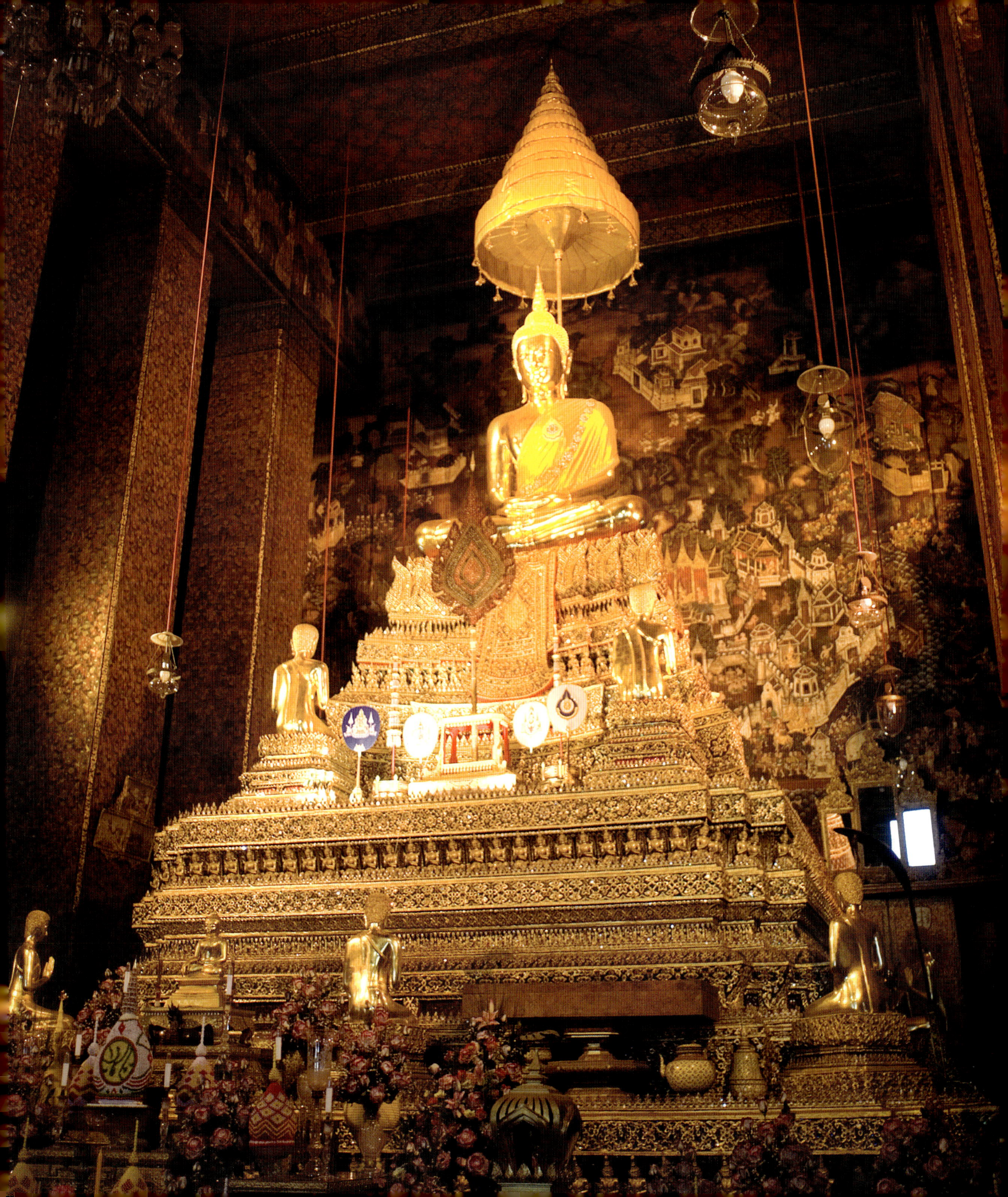

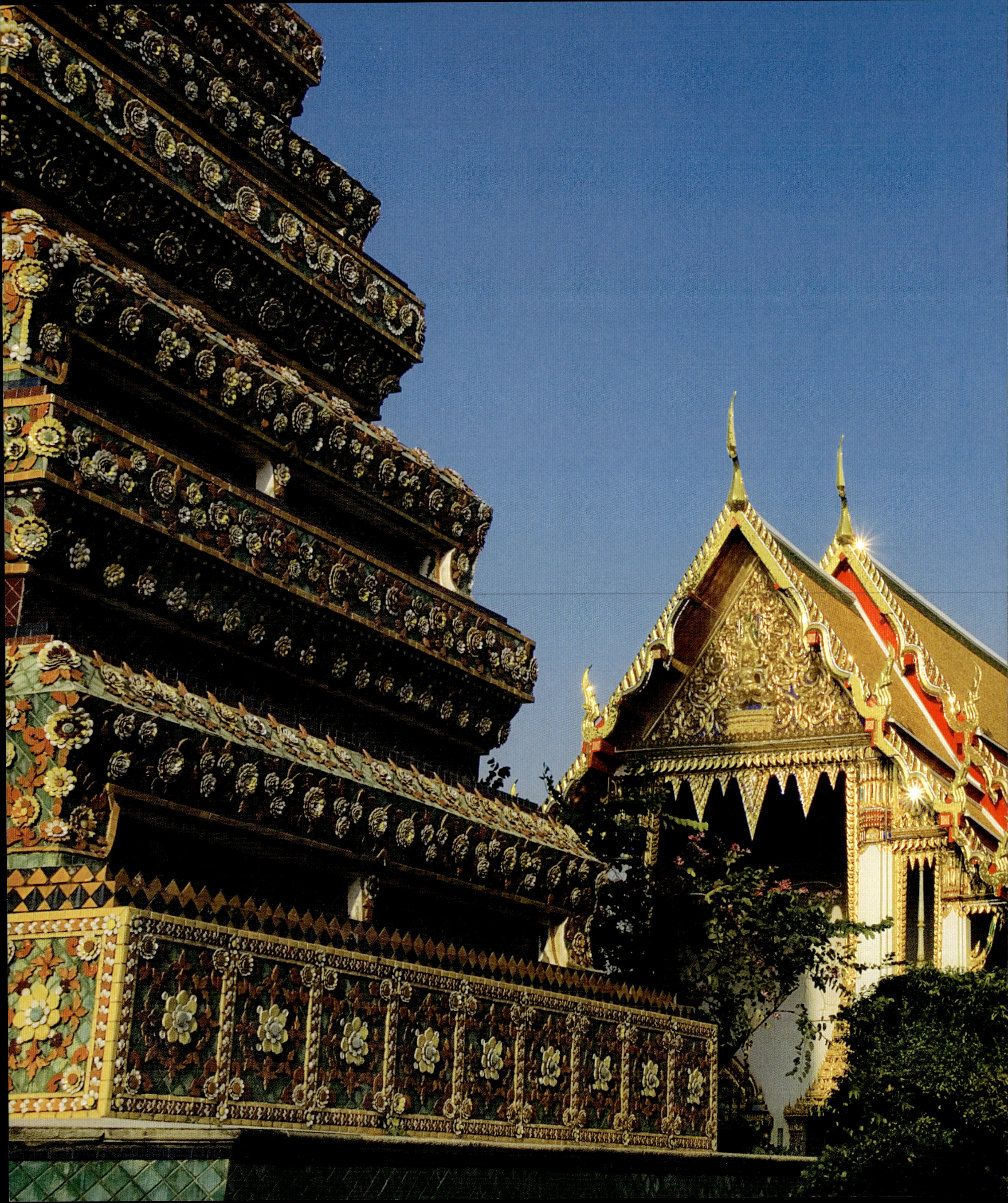

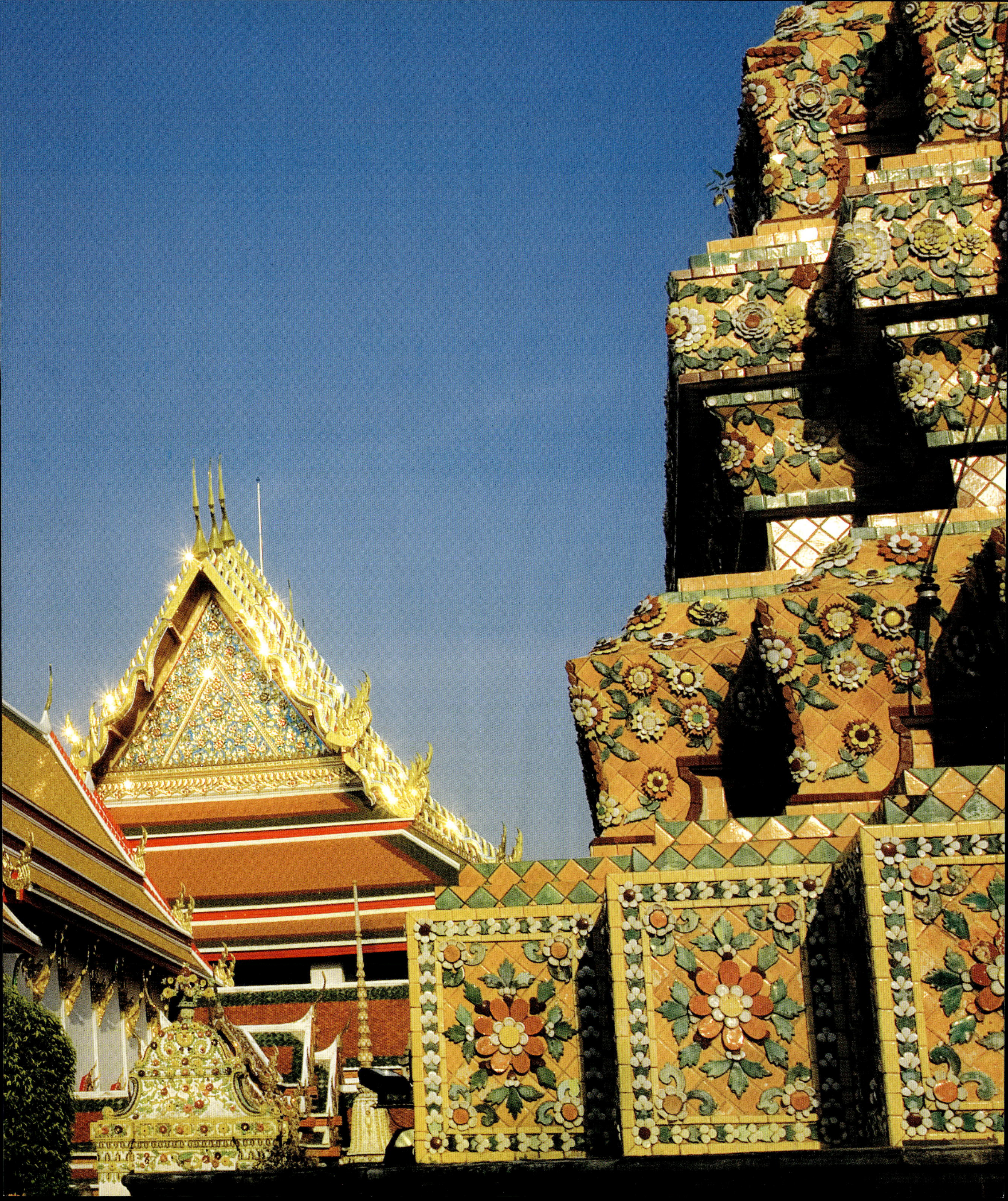

Wat Phra Si Ratana Satsadaram (Wat Phra Kaew)

BANGKOK

When Bangkok succeeded Thonburi as the capital of the kingdom of Siam in 1782, Indian astrologers and high-ranking Buddhist monks were brought in to select and consecrate grounds for a royal palace and a royal monastery. They chose a riverside settlement known as Bang Makok (the source of the abbreviated name 'Bangkok'), and after the hallowed zone was marked off with carved stone pillars, engineers added a system of linked canals to create a royal 'island' known as Ko Ratanakosin. Siam's most talented architects and artisans then weighed in, creating majestic edifices designed to astound all who ventured into the new capital. The 1785 completion of Wat Phra Kaew (Monastery of the Gem Buddha), along with the adjacent Grand Palace, transformed humble Bang Makok into a glittering glory whose scale and intricacy continue to make a lasting impression.

Inside lofty brick-and-stucco walls, the million-square-metre grounds collect together over a hundred buildings dedicated to the fusing of the monarchy and Buddhism as the main pillars of Thai sovereignty. Inside the *bot*, the tallest of the temple buildings, roofed with gleaming orange and green tiles and supported by pillars encrusted with blue mosaics and carved, gilded plaster, sits Phra Kaew, the kingdom's holiest Buddha image. The significance of the 66-centimentre tall image – perched atop a high pedestal overlooking the ebb and flow of visiting worshippers – extends beyond Buddhism to encompass a talismanic protection of the kingdom.

Although nicknamed the 'Emerald Buddha' because of its deep green hue, Phra Kaew is carved from nephrite, a type of jade. Stylistically the image clearly belongs to 13th-14th century Lanna, despite legends saying it was sculpted in India and brought to Siam from Ceylon. An apocryphal tale says it was once covered with plaster and gold leaf and kept in the niche of a stupa in Chiang Rai, and that while

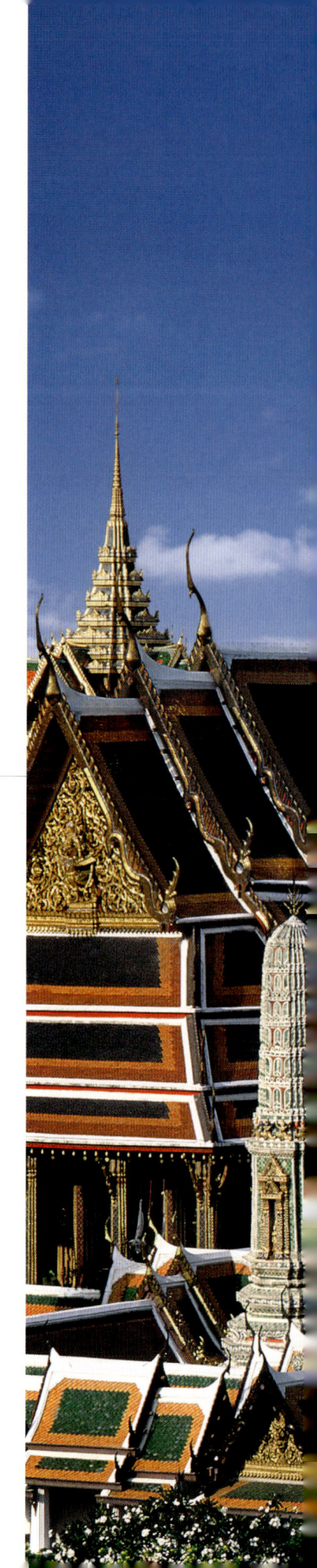

58 Buddhist Temples of Thailand

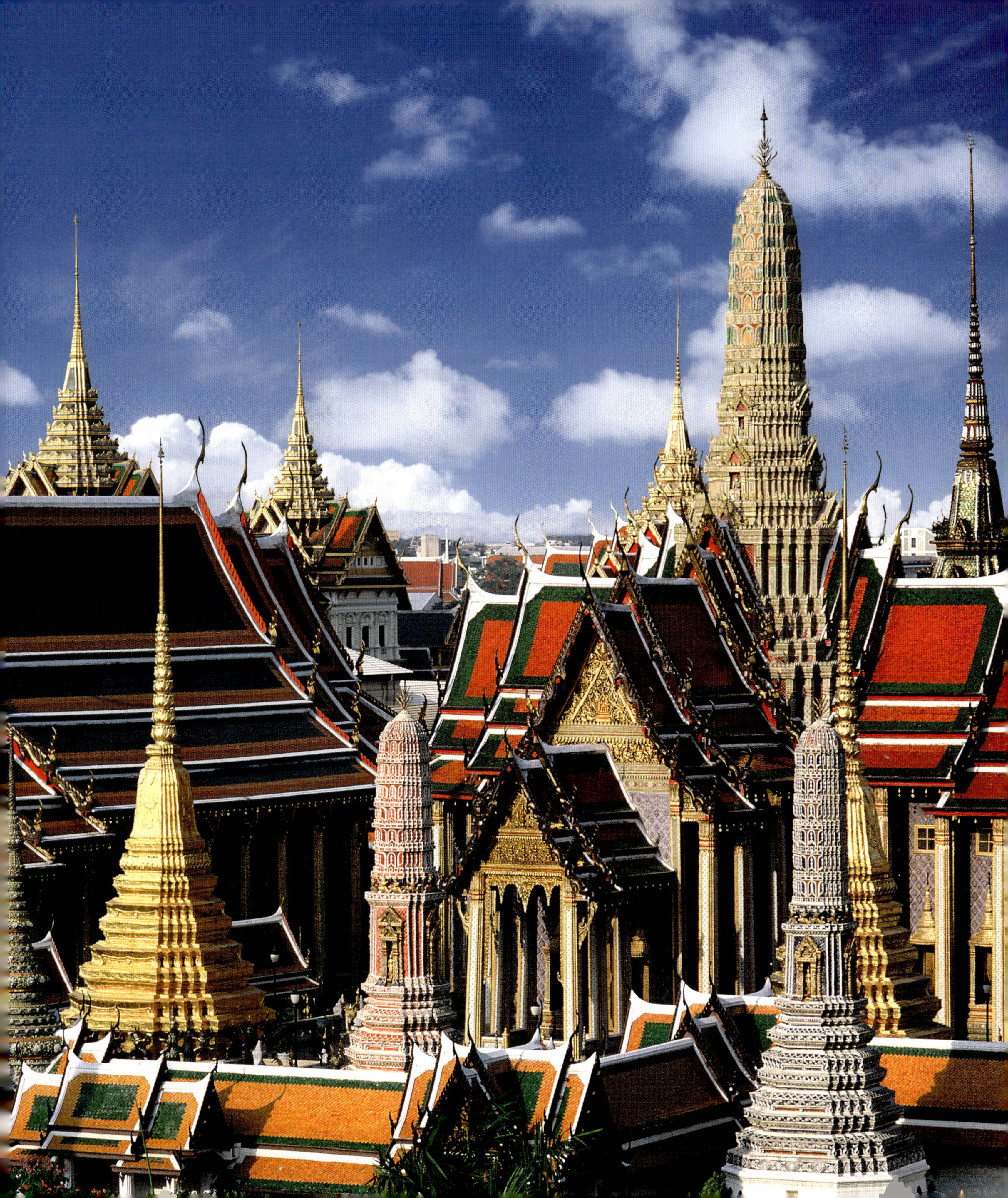

Pages 58-59: Wat Phra Kaew, the first royal temple built when Siam's capital was moved to Bangkok.

Above: The large compound at Wat Phra Kaew is filled with stupas, chapels and cloisters.

Right: Wat Phra Kaew's 'Jewel Buddha', the centrepiece of the temple, is displayed inside a richly ornamented cabinet.

the image was being moved after a storm damaged the stupa, the plaster fell away to reveal the jade. Afterwards Phra Kaew was kept in Lampang for 32 years before being moved to Chiang Mai, from where it was transferred to Luang Prabang, Laos in the mid-16th century. When Luang Prabang came under Vientiane rule, the image was taken to Vientiane, where it remained until Siam waged war against Laos 200 years later and the image was brought to Bangkok.

A cloister adjacent to the *bot* is painted with deeply hued 18th century murals depicting the *Ramakien* in a series of 178 panels. The murals have undergone several restorations, including a major one finished in time for Bangkok's 1982 bicentennial.

The remainder of the temple compound is occupied by extremely colourful *wihan* and *sala* roofed with polished orange and green tiles and supported by mosaic-encrusted pillars and rich marble pediments, along with several similarly adorned stupas.

Attached to the temple complex, the Grand Palace served as the principal royal residence until the early-20th century, when the Thai royal family moved to the newer Chitrlada Palace elsewhere in the capital. Parts of the palace are open to the public as a museum.

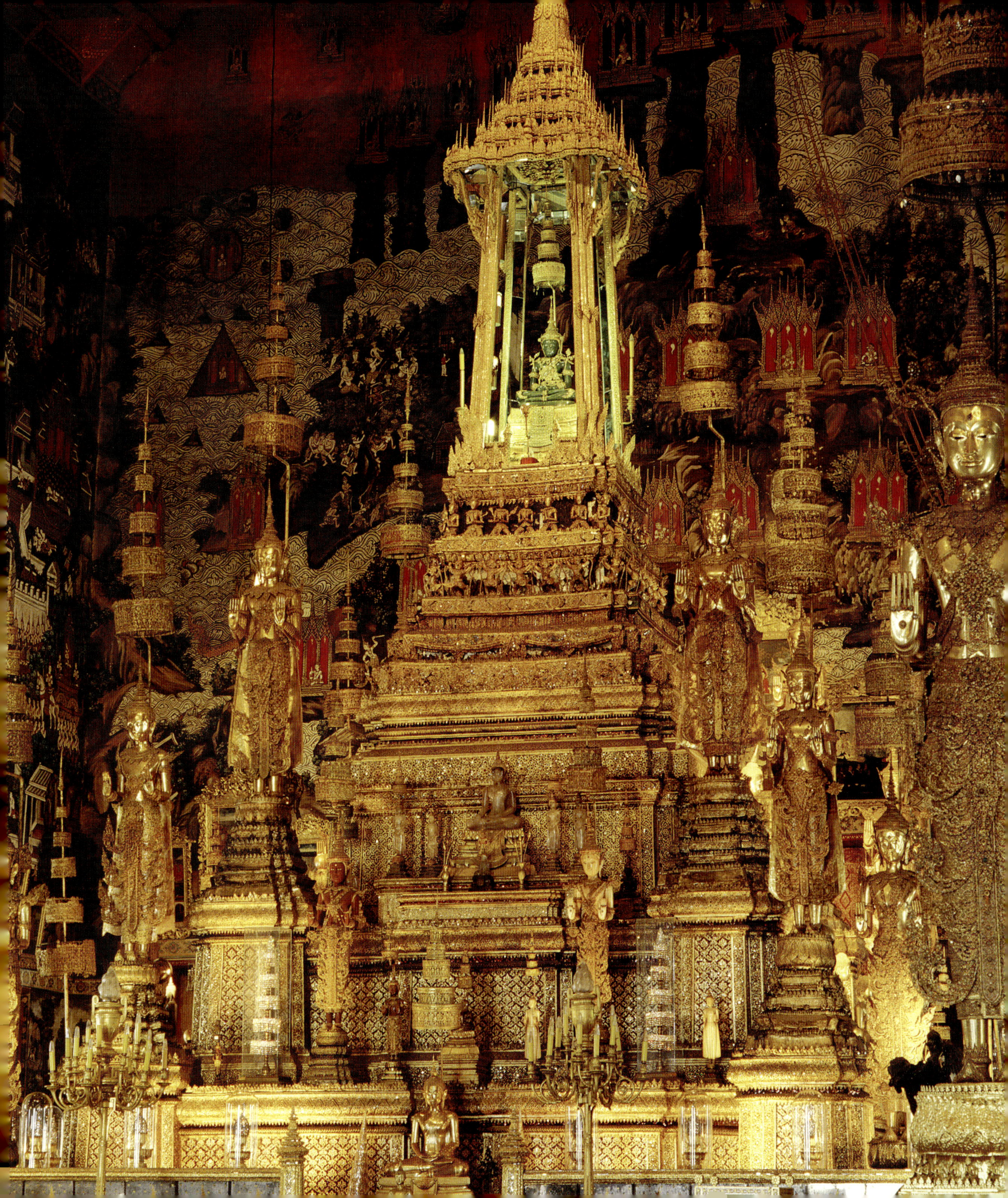

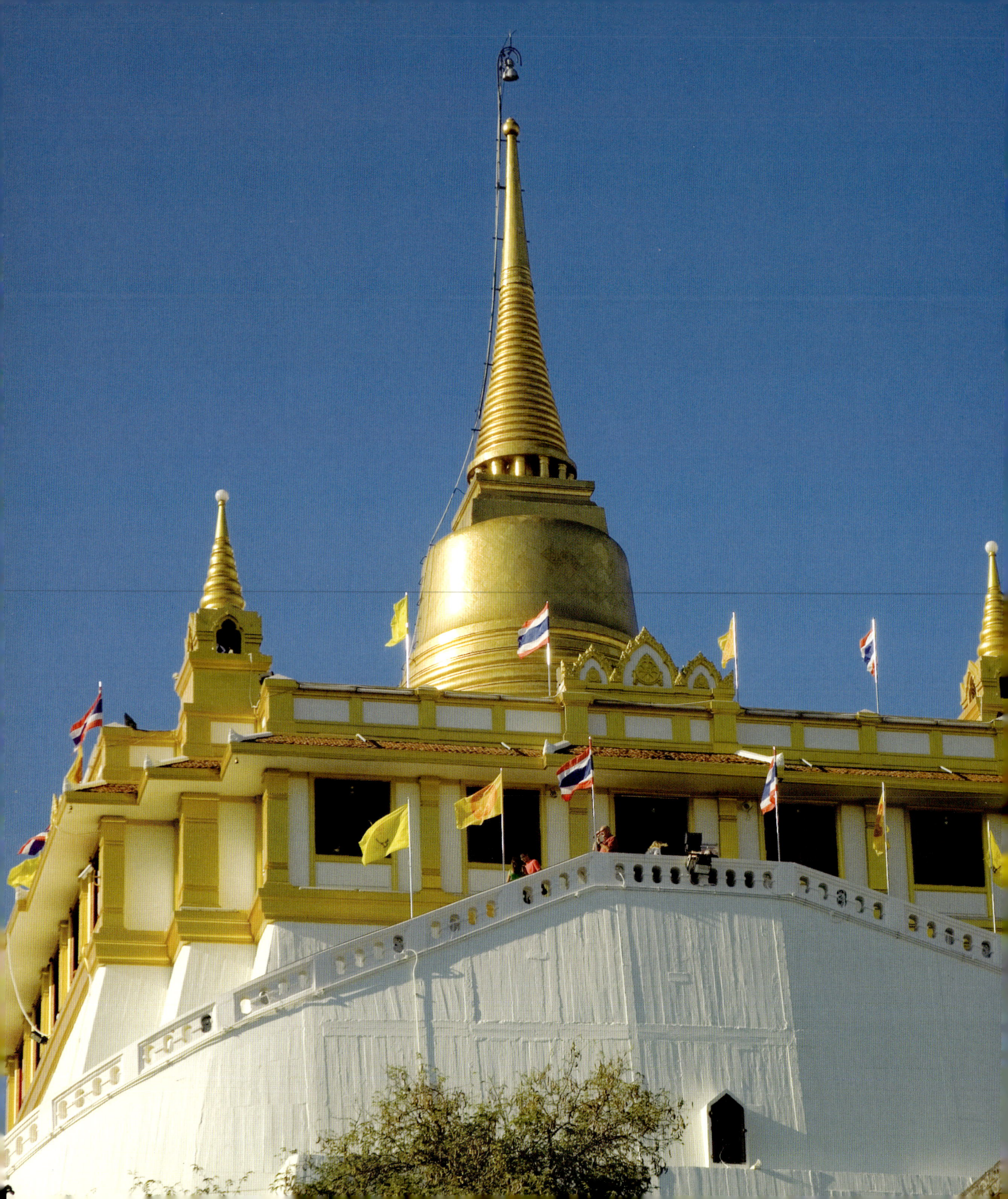

Wat Saket

Bangkok

Built during the Ayuthaya era and originally called Wat Sakae, this temple was restored under Rama I (1782-1809). The king renamed the temple Wat Saket — Hairwashing Monastery — after he held a royal hairwashing ceremony following a trip to Cambodia. Standing just outside the perimeters of the royal district of Ko Ratanakosin, Wat Saket initially served primarily as a centre for cremation ceremonies, which were not permitted inside the walled district. During a plague in the reign of Rama II, 30,000 bodies were cremated here.

The stately *bot*, which dates to the Rama I era, is surrounded by *sema* (ordination markers) housed in stone structures meant to resemble elephant howdahs. They are considered masterpieces of Ratanakosin art of this kind. Murals inside the *bot* were originally painted under Rama III and restored under Rama VII. The wooden *ho trai* (Tripitika tower) features nicely carved door and window panels.

Wat Saket's most famous structure is an artificial hill known as the Golden Mount. It was created when a large stupa under construction by Rama III collapsed because the soft, marshy ground would not support it. The resulting mud-and-brick hill was left to sprout weeds until Rama IV crowned the hill with a small stupa. The king also had the hill reinforced with a thousand teak logs to keep it from collapsing again. The stupa was rebuilt towards the end of the 19th century by Rama V when the Viceroy of India, Lord Curzon, made a gift of a Buddha relic excavated in India. A concrete cap was added to the artificial hill during World War II to prevent further erosion.

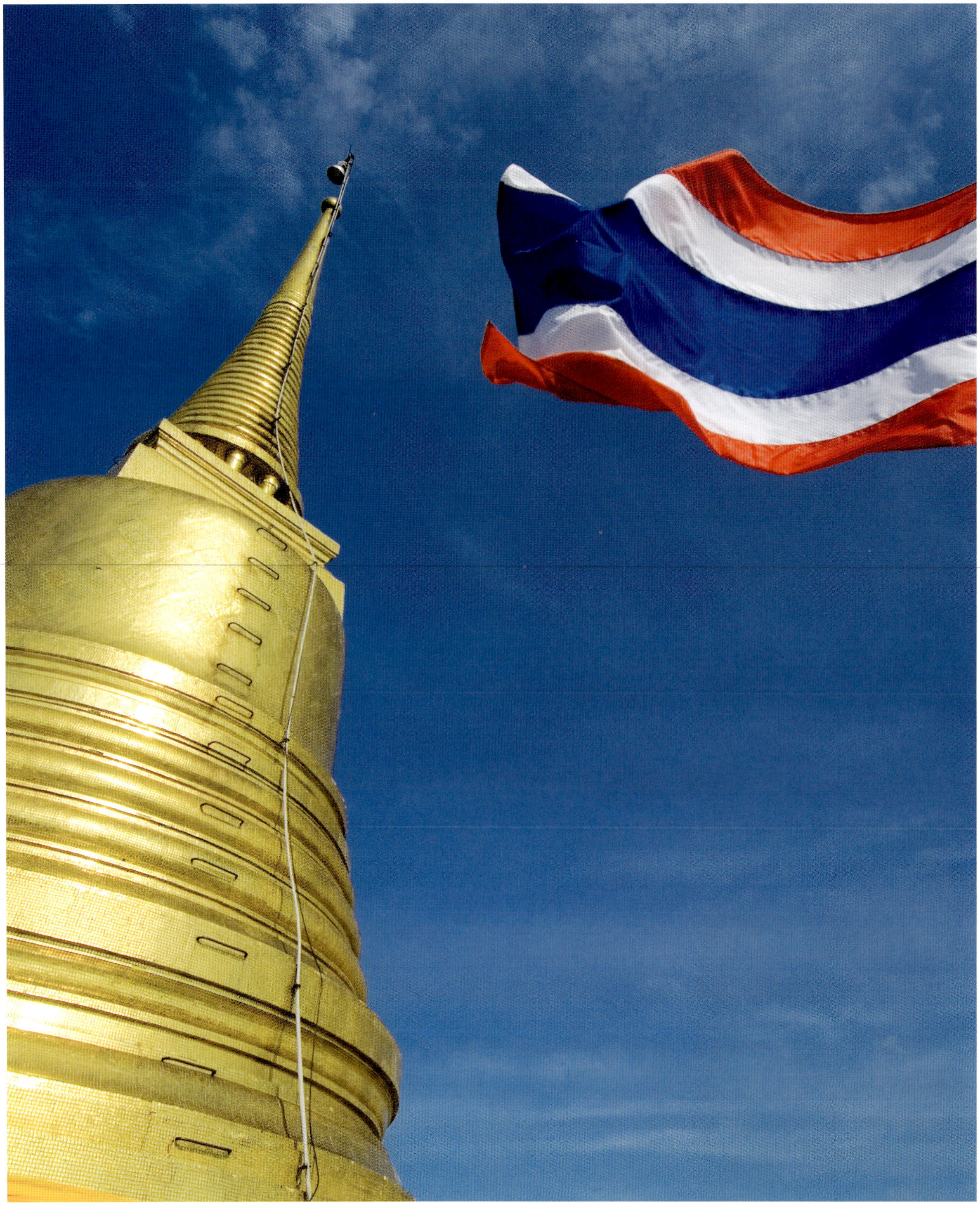

It has become a custom for Bangkok residents to commemorate deceased relatives by adding small shrines or plaques to the un-cemented base of the Golden Mount amidst the remaining jumble of bricks and vegetation. Visitors may climb to the stupa at the top of the mount via a stairway that spirals up and around its sides. The terrace at the summit provides a 360-degree view of Bangkok, including Wat Phra Kaew and the Grand Palace, Wat Ratchanadda and the Democracy Monument.

During the annual Loy Krathong Festival (late October to mid-November, depending on the lunar calendar), Wat Saket hosts Bangkok's largest temple fair for nine days. Temple devotees wrap the Golden Mount in auspicious red cloth, set up hundreds of foodstalls and arrange theatrical and musical performances. The festival culminates in an inspiring candlelight procession up the Golden Mount.

Pages 62-63: Phu Khao Thong — the Golden Mount.
Left: The gilded stupa atop the Golden Mount.
Above: A night view of the Golden Mount, with Mahakan Fort in the foreground.

Wat Suthat

Bangkok

Soon after his coronation in 1782, Rama I ordered the construction of Wat Suthat, intended to be the main royally sanctioned monastery in Bangkok. Construction and expansion continued through the reigns of Rama II (1809-24) and Rama III (1824-51), and today the *wat* encompasses 10 acres and bears the kingdom's highest royal temple grade, Rachavoramahavihan.

Wat Suthat's principle Buddha image, brought by river from Sukhothai's abandoned Wat Si Ratana Mahathat, is the largest Sukhothai-era bronze image in Thailand. When the Buddha arrived in the new capital, Rama I walked barefoot in the streets alongside his subjects for seven days while the image was paraded around the city. Called Phra Si Sakyamuni, the eight-metre high, 13th century image is enshrined in the temple's main *wihan*, one of the oldest Ratanakosin-era religious structures in Bangkok. Following the mysterious death of Rama VIII in 1946, the young monarch's ashes were interred in the base of the Phra Si Sakyamuni.

The *wihan's* wooden doors were carved and painted by several artisans, including King Rama II himself, and the extensive *Jataka* murals adorning the interior walls represent exemplary Ratanakosin style in its blend of Thai classical art and European influence. The *wihan* columns are painted with early Bangkok scenes, including the arrival of Westerners in the 19th century.

Two Brahmanist shrines close to the temple – the Thewa Sathan dedicated to Shiva and located northwest of Wat Suthat, and the smaller San Jao Phitsanu dedicated to Vishnu and found to the east – play special roles in Thai spiritual beliefs. Here Brahman priests perform daily and annual rituals that are believed to promote animistic protection for the kingdom. These same priests preside over the annual Royal Ploughing Ceremony on the Sanam Luang grounds in May.

66 Buddhist Temples of Thailand

Region: Bangkok

A giant ceremonial swing, assembled from huge teak logs and covered in red lacquer, stands in front of the *wat*. Known in Thai as Sao Ching-Cha, the lofty apparatus was once the focus of an important annual ceremony associated with rice farming. A special pavilion was built into Wat Suthat's north walk as a vantage point from which Rama IV could watch the ceremonies. The royal minister of rice, presiding over hundreds of Brahman court astrologers, would lead processions through the district to the swing, where teams of men would swing in ever-heightening arcs in an effort to reach a bag of gold suspended from a 15-metre high bamboo pole. Some participants swung as high as 30 metres into the air. Many died trying to grab the coins, and in 1932 the dangerous swing ceremony was discontinued. The swing still stands in its original spot, and Brahman priests still preside over an annual rice harvest thanksgiving ceremony in December.

Pages 66-67: A neat row of Buddha images line the cloister at Wat Suthat. Note the faded remains of mural paintings on the wall.

Left: Phra Si Sakyamuni, the largest Sukhothai bronze Buddha in the world, was brought to Bangkok from Sukhothai in the late-18th century.

Above: The wihan at Wat Suthat is one of the oldest Ratanakosin religious structures in Bangkok.

Below: The *wihan's* wooden doors were carved and painted by several artisans, including King Rama II himself.

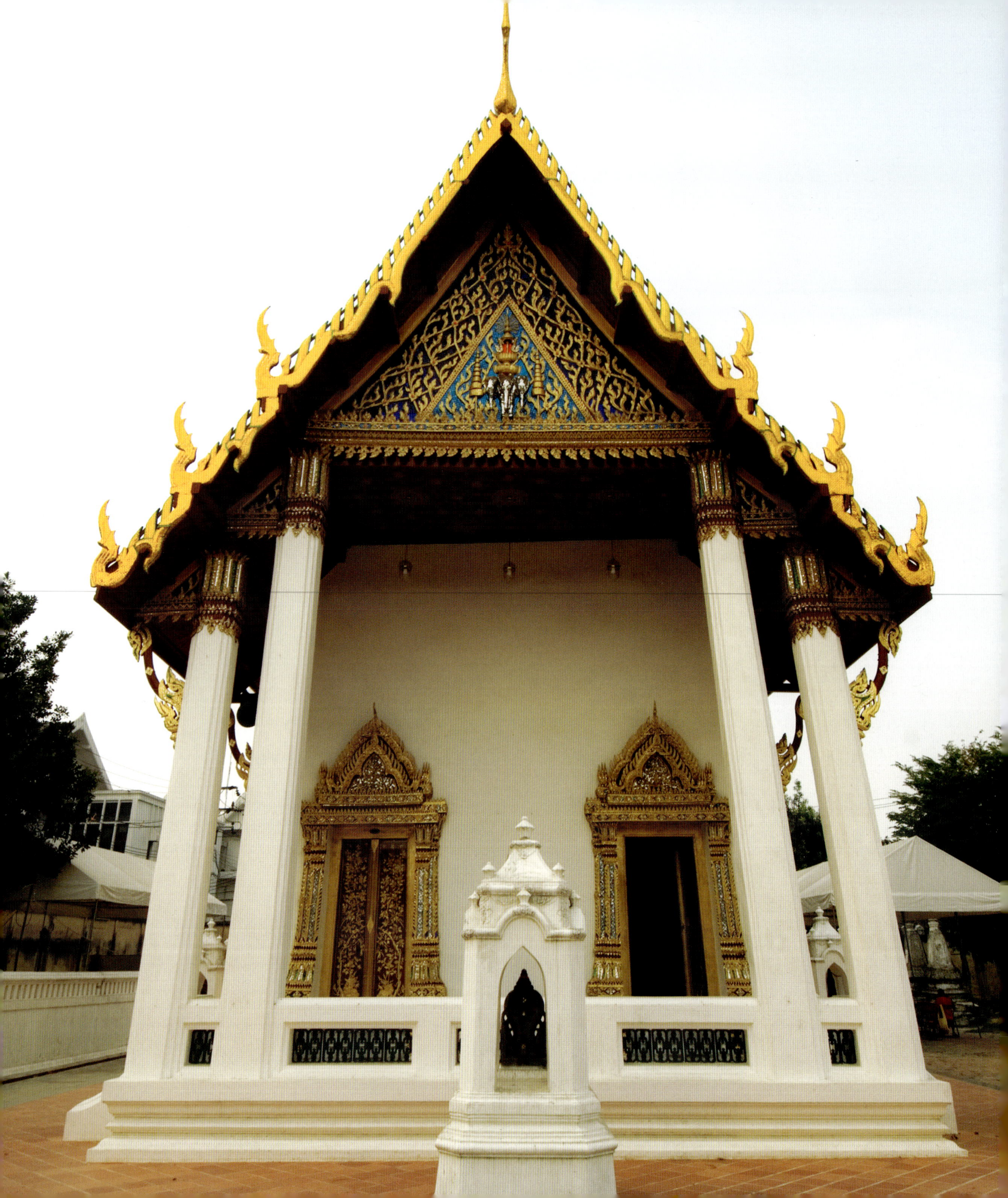

Wat Molilokkayaram

Bangkok

Often cited as the oldest *wat* in Bangkok, Wat Molilokkayaram sits near Khlong Bangkok Yai between Wat Arun to the north and Wat Kalayanimit to the south. The monastery was first built in the mid-18th century, when it was known as Wat Tai Talat, 'Monastery South of the Market.' King Taksin incorporated the grounds and structures as part of his Thonburi Palace in 1767, and resident monks were dispersed.

When Rama I built a new palace on the eastern bank of the Chao Phraya River, the old site captured the interest of his son, the crown prince. After his son ascended the throne as Rama II, he renovated the *bot*, invited monks from nearby Wat Ratchasittharam to reactivate its monastery status and bestowed a new name, Wat Phutthaisawan.

Under Rama III all of the existing buildings were renovated, adding stucco reliefs to pediments, doorsills and windowsills of the *wihan*, characteristics more common to Lanna-style temples in northern Thailand than at Bangkok temples. The monastery underwent yet another name change, to Wat Molilokkayaram, at this time. Rama IV renovated the *bot* yet again, and added wooden monk's residences and a new chanting pavilion.

Rama V renovated the teakwood *ho trai* and initiated a tradition of performing a royal *kathin*, the annual ceremony where new robes are offered to monks at the end of the Rains Retreat, here. His son, Rama VI, continued to celebrate *kathin* here and elevated the monastery's status to that of Rajaworawihan (second class royal monastery).

In 1997 the abbot of Wat Molilokkayaram further developed the *wat* by upgrading the Pali school, thereby attracting larger numbers of monks. Today the monastery houses around 124 monks and novices, many of whom are studying Pali levels 1 to 9 or dhamma levels 1 to 3. In 2005 the temple received private funds to renovate the classic Thai-Chinese wooden monastic residences.

Left: The gable-front of the simple yet majestic *bot* carries a semi-sculptured representation of Airavata (Thai: *Erawan*), the three-headed elephant mount of Indra, Hindu king of the gods and protector of Buddhism.

Above: The interior walls of the *bot* are covered in *khanok*, a flame-lotus symbol unique to Thai Buddhist art. Right: A close-up of the head of the principal Buddha image, backed with delicately painted floral motifs.

72 Buddhist Temples of Thailand

Region: Bangkok

WAT ARUN

BANGKOK

German architect Karl Döjring, in his seminal 1920 study of Thai temples noted that Wat Arun, with its lofty and richly decorated stupa, had an effect on Bangkok's cityscape that was not unlike that of monumental church towers in Europe. Nearly a centrury later his comment still rings true. Even though the capital has become packed with skyscrapers, the 82-metre high stupa still dominates the banks of the Chao Phraya River opposite the city's royal district, Ko Ratanakosin.

King Taksin the Great, who had moved Siam's capital to Thonburi after the 500-year reign of Ayuthaya was brought to an end by a Burmese invasion in 1767, chose the spot where Wat Arun now stands for his palace and royal temple. These were built on the ruins of an earlier temple known as Wat Makok (Monastery of the Hog Plums, whence 'Bangkok' also derived its name). Taksin called his new royal temple Wat Jaeng.

After Taksin's own court executed him in 1782 because he had allegedly gone mad, a new dynasty established its capital across the river from Wat Jaeng, abandoning the temple to the elements. Under the second and third Chakri monarchs it was built anew during the first half of the 19th century and was renamed Wat Arun, after Aruna, the Hindu god of the dawn, commemorating the fact that Taksin had originally come upon the site at dawn.

As was once traditional for most Thai temples, a stupa was built first. One of the most emblematic of Buddhist structures anywhere in the country, Wat Arun's stunning stupa was built in the form of a *prang*, a term the Thais use for stupas that feature the Khmer-influenced 'corncob' shape with a smoothly curving, reticulated superstructure. The stupa's brick core was decorated with a multi-hued mosaic of Chinese porcelain shards embedded in plaster, a common technique used in the early Ratanakosin period.

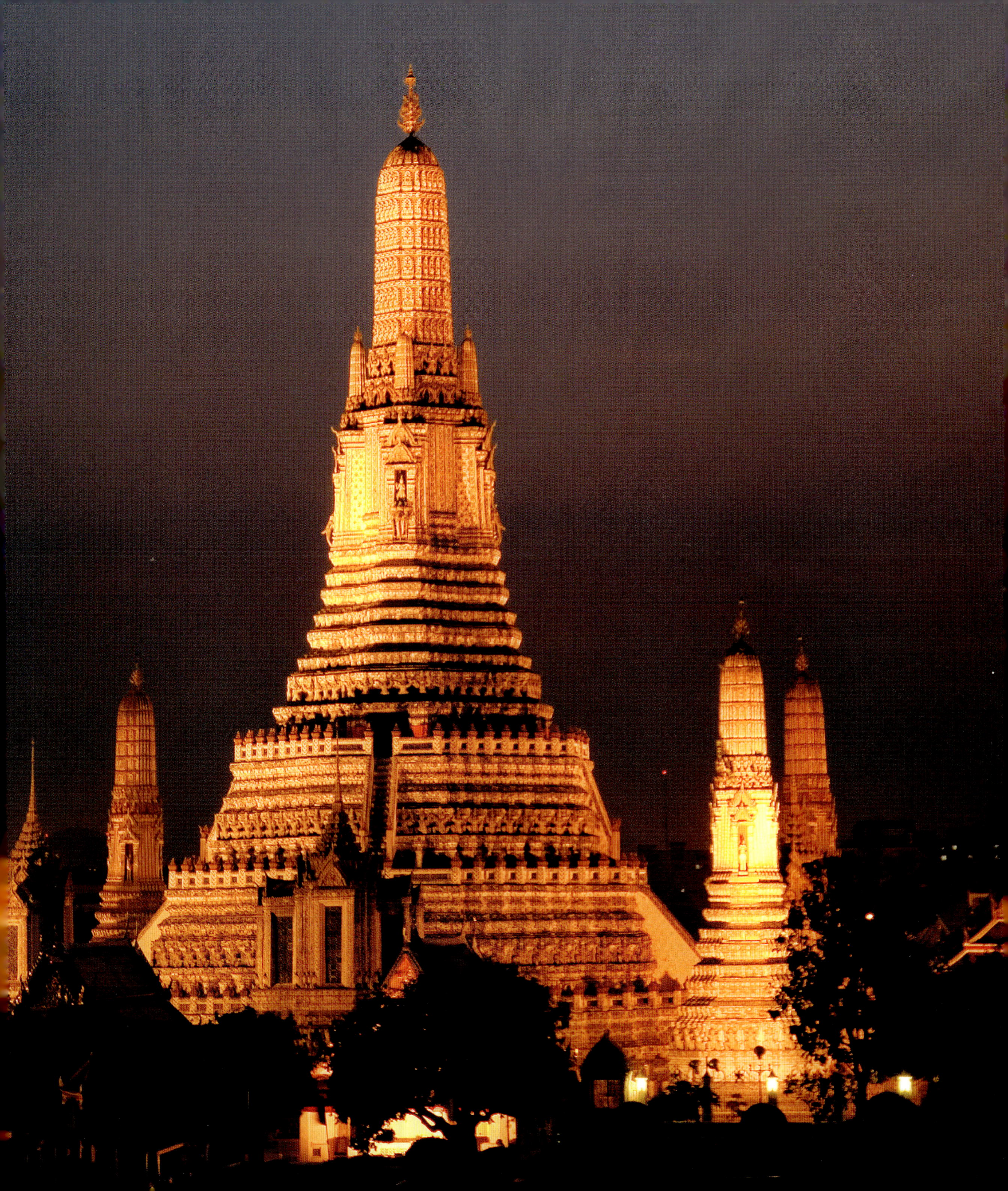

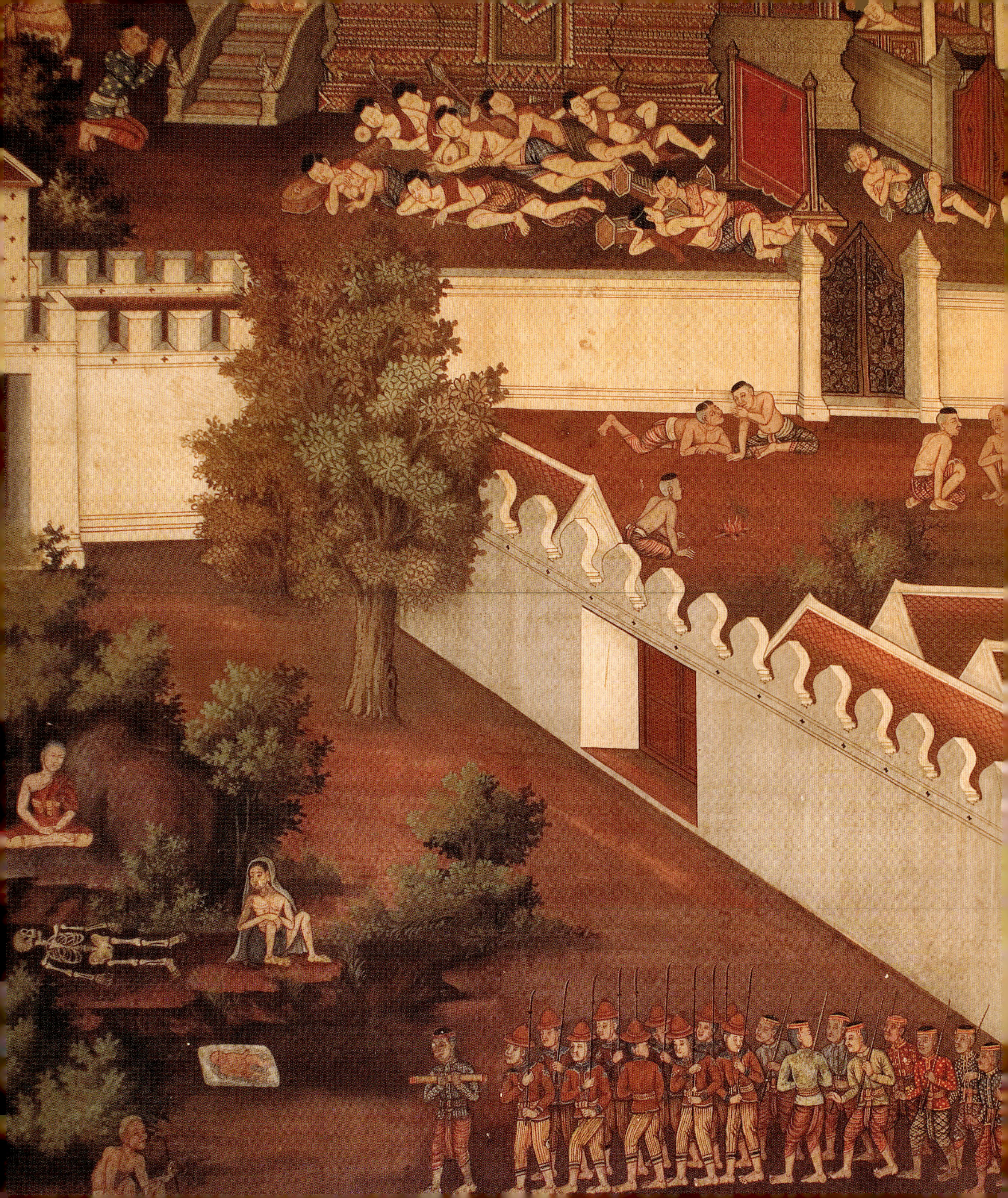

Pages 74-75: The iconic *prang* at Wat Arun, illuminated at night.

Left: These murals in the *bot* at Wat Arun depict court attendants resting inside the walls of Ko Ratanakosin, while a royal procession takes place outside.

A steep, narrow maze of stairways climbs about halfway up the stupa. Projecting skyward from the stupa pinnacle is an iron *vajra* (thunderbolt), a symbolic weapon belonging to Indra, the king of the Hindu pantheon. This is yet another testimony to the monument's Khmer antecedents, most of which were Khmer Hindu temples. The stupa's four main niches hold green-hued images of Indra and his three-headed white elephant Airvata (Erawan to the Thais). Meanwhile sculptures of angels, monkey deities and guardian giants 'support' each of the stupa's three terraces.

At each of four cardinal points around the *prang* stands a richly ornamented *mondop* (open shrine hall), containing Buddha images representing the sage's birth (north *mondop*), enlightenment (east), first sermon (south), and final passing into nirvana (west). Four smaller stupas, holding Buddha images that face the central stupa, stand at the subcardinal points.

Wat Arun's *bot* holds a Buddha image designed by Rama II himself, whose ashes are buried in the base. Murals inside were painted in a typical Ratanakosin format by order of Rama V. Standing to the south of the *bot*, the *wihan* is the largest building in the monastery compound.

Above: Thewada (celestial beings) sculptures 'support' various levels of the *prang* at Wat Arun.

Right: A very steep and narrow stairway leads up the side of the great *prang* to the last terrace before the spire.

78 Buddhist Temples of Thailand

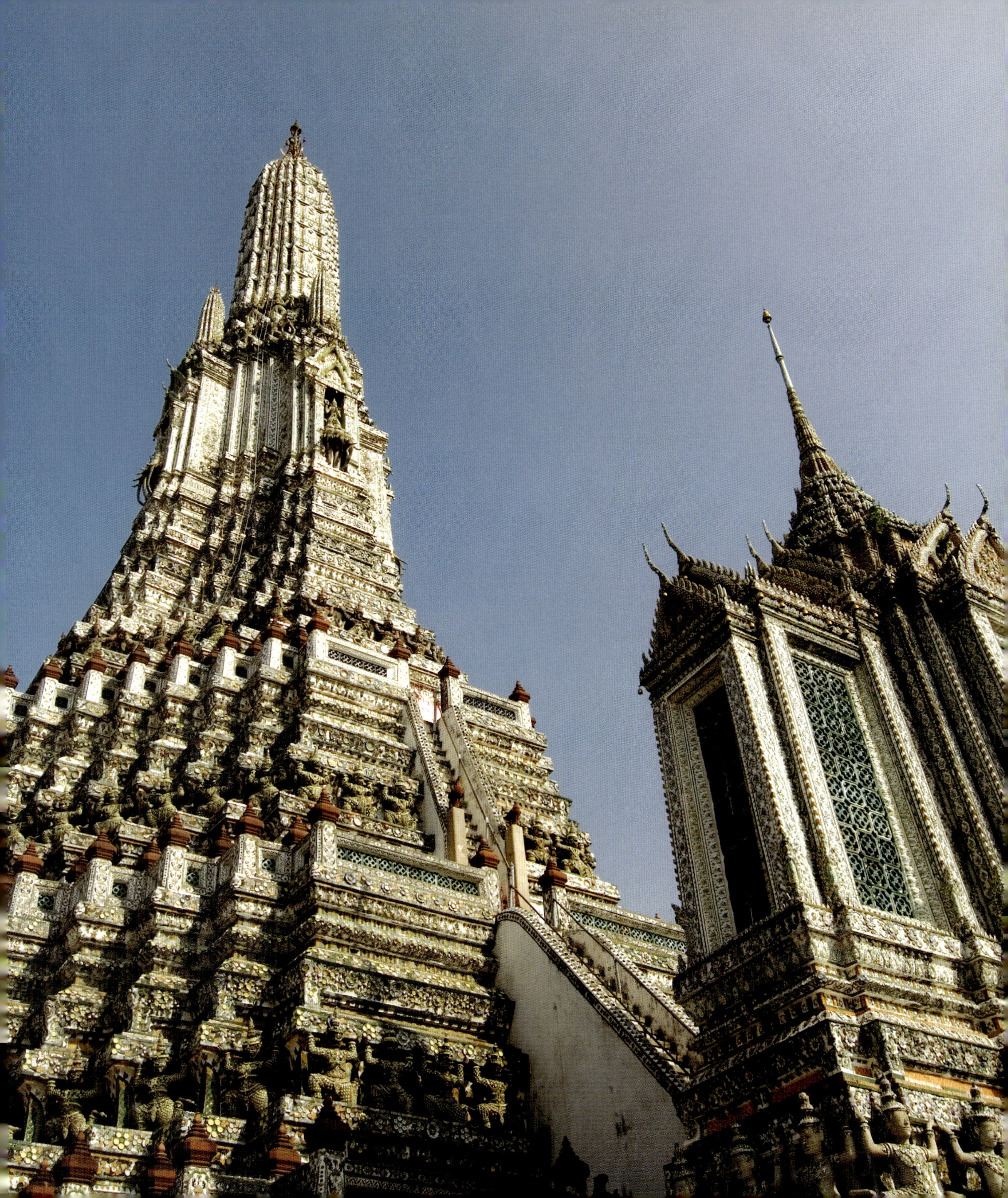

Wat Suan Phlu

Bangkok

Sharing a lane with the Shangri-La Hotel, in the Bang Rak district near the banks of the Chao Phraya River, Wat Suan Phlu is an outstanding example of a late Ratanakosin-era temple that has changed little since its original construction. All of the buildings except the *bot* are built of wood, either teak or *padauk* (Asian rosewood). The two-storey monks quarters represent typical Ratanakosin post-colonial tropical architecture. Painted yellow with maroon window and door frames, they feature lacy 'gingerbread' trim under the eaves and arched ventilator panels carved in delicate floral patterns over the doors. The abbot's quarters, the most prominent of the wooden buildings in the compound, boasts a terrace and reception room projecting out from the rectangular floor plan. In front of the structure is a solitary standing Buddha fashioned in the 'contemplating the Bodhi tree' pose, in which the hands are crossed in front of the body, outer robe flaring in a style more common in Laos than in Thailand.

The *bot* makes ample use of blue-tinted glass mosaics, with a minimum of gold trim. Besides providing a glittering appearance, such mosaics are intended to drive away evil spirits, in the belief that when spirits approach closely they will be frightened away by their own reflection.

The roof of the *bot* is also relatively unique in the proliferation of *kinaree* decorating its gables. A cloister wall surrounding the *bot* features a series of ceramic panels painted in the style of Chinese watercolours. Donated by Chinese lay supporters, the panels display a variety of mythical and natural animals. One panel, for example, depicts a pair of phoenixes, while another shows a lion, a tortoise and a hare.

Although the monastery grounds were long ago cemented over, Wat Suan Phlu still has a number of old, attractive trees.

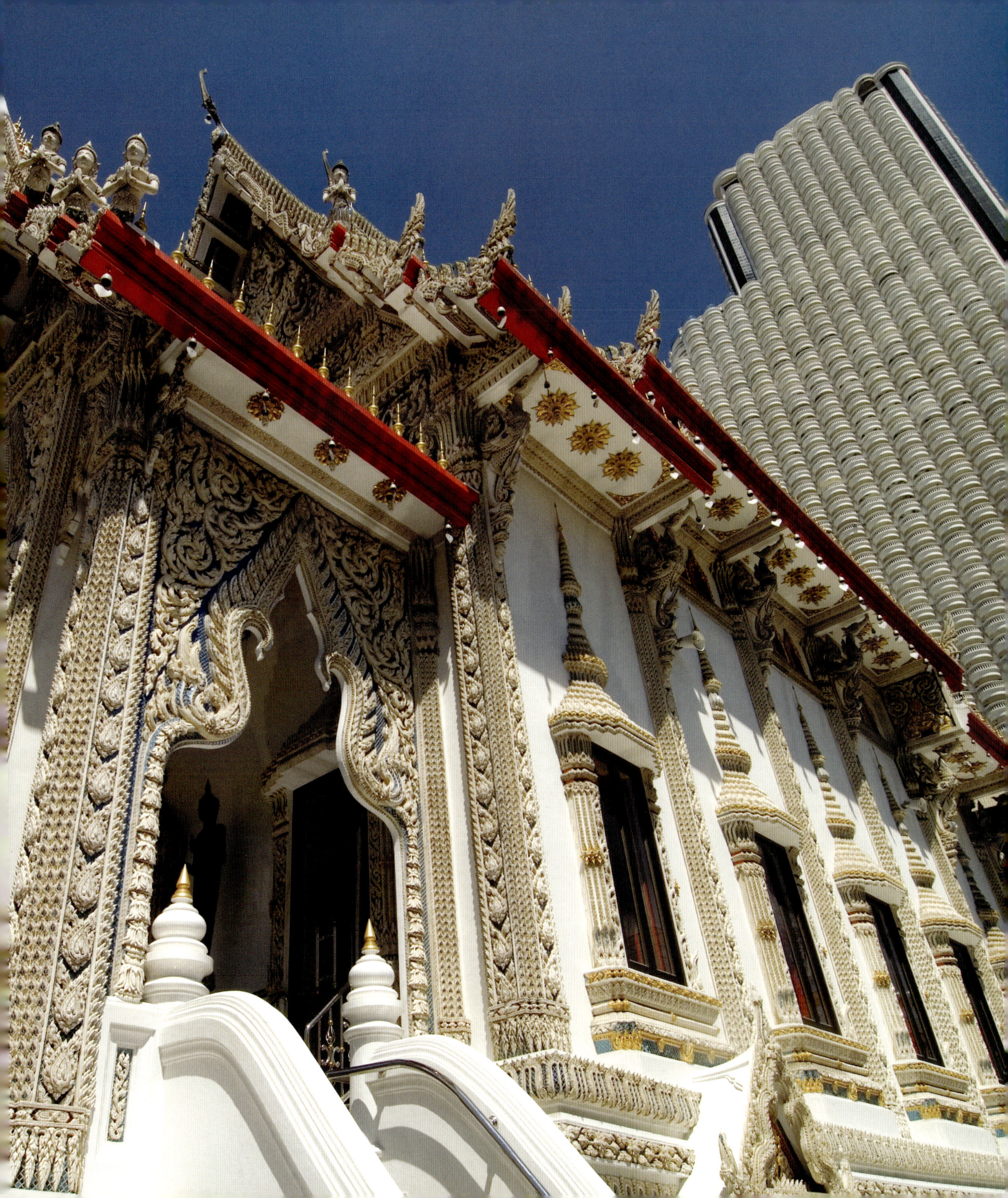

82   Buddhist Temples of Thailand

Pages 80-81: The unusual *bot* at Wat Suan Phlu uses a minimum of gold trim.

Left: The minimally furnished interior of the *bot*.

Above: A teak *ho trai* (scripture library), the oldest structure in the compound, has been converted into a highly revered shrine devoted to Kwan Yin, the Chinese Buddhist goddess of compassion.

Below: Instead of the more common *naga* (water serpent) or *cho fa* ('celestial bunches' representing Garuda), the *bot* eaves are adorned with *kinnaree* (half-human, half-bird figures).

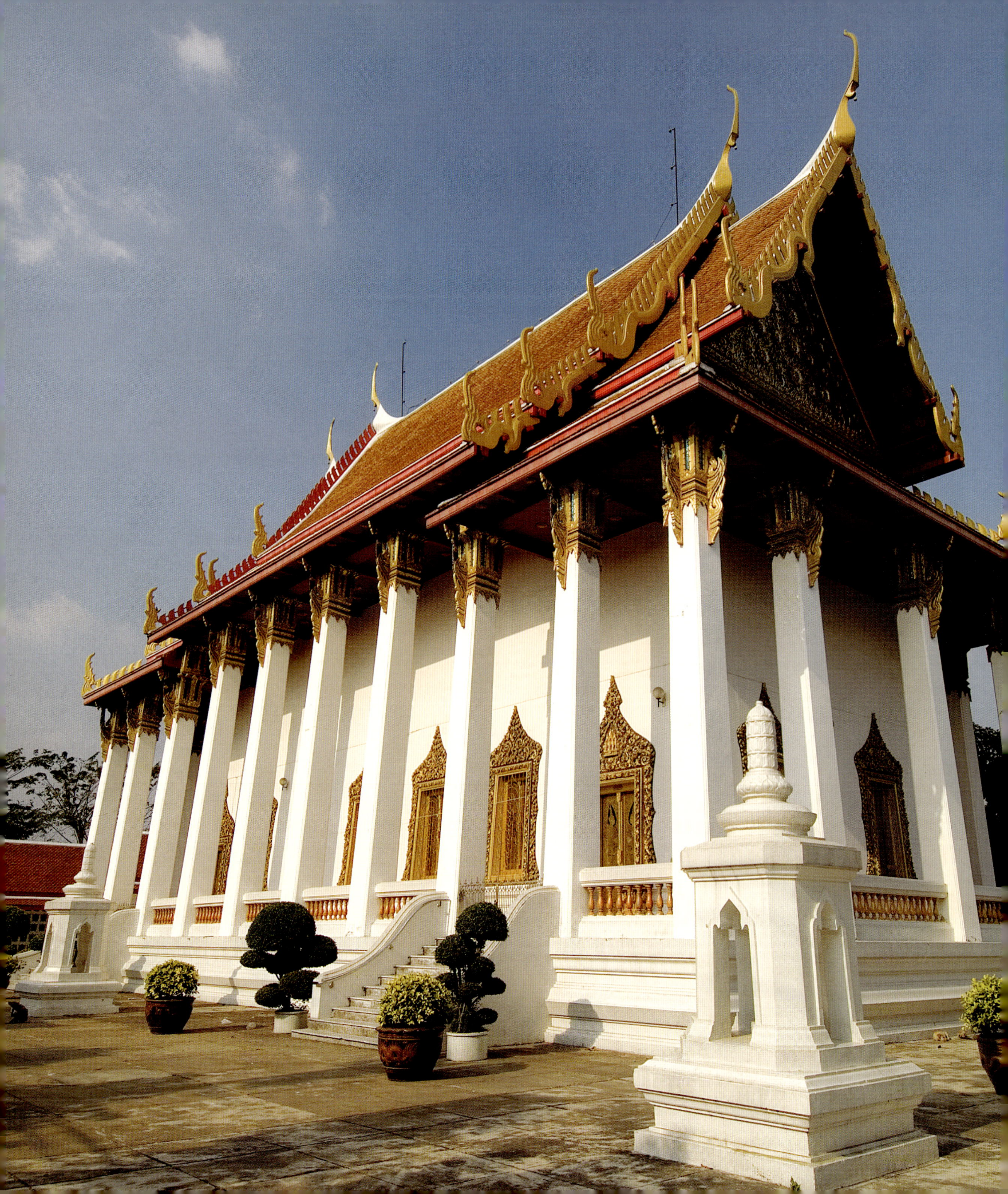

Wat Daowadeungsaram

Bangkok

Set in the midst of a working class neighbourhood near Phra Pinklao Bridge in Thonburi, busy Wat Daowadeung began life during the reign of Rama I when one of the king's favourite consorts, who happened to be Lao, sponsored the construction of the monastery. She invited the *wat's* first abbot, Khruba In, from Laos and although the *wat* presumably had a formal Pali-Sanskrit name, it became known as Wat Khruba In. Some histories of the temple claim the design of the *bot* was inspired by Wat Saket in Vientiane, Laos. However given its great height and the encircling veranda it is more likely to have been inspired by Vientiane's Wat Phra Kaew.

Rama II renovated the monastery and changed its name to Wat Daowadeung Sawan – the Monastery of Tavatimsa Heaven. The buildings were renovated a second time under Rama III, who revised the name to Wat Daowadeungsaram – Monastery of Tavatimsa Hermitage. The king commissioned Luang Seni Borirak (also known as Kong Pae), a major Chinese-Thai artist of the time, to paint murals inside the *bot*. The main subject of the paintings was the *Mahosot Jataka*, which chronicles the legend of Buddha's earlier birth as Prince Mahosot (Pali: Mahosadha), who served his kingdom as a wise sage dispensing advice to all who sought his counsel. Still visible today, these vibrant murals are considered a masterwork of Ratanakosin temple art.

Other than the *bot*, the only buildings of historic interest are two surviving two-storey teakwood monks residences constructed in the multi-panelled Ayuthaya style. A large *pariyat tham* (dhamma study) school on the premises trains novices and monks in the study of Pali Buddhist scriptures.

Pages 84-85: The stately *bot*, with tapered columns to accentuate its height.

Right: Coloured glass mosaics add reptile-like textures to a *naga* bargeboard.

Below: A brightly painted mural scene shows what appears to be a Chinese merchant's residence in the foreground.

Far right: Novice monks studying basic *dhamma*.

Region: Bangkok

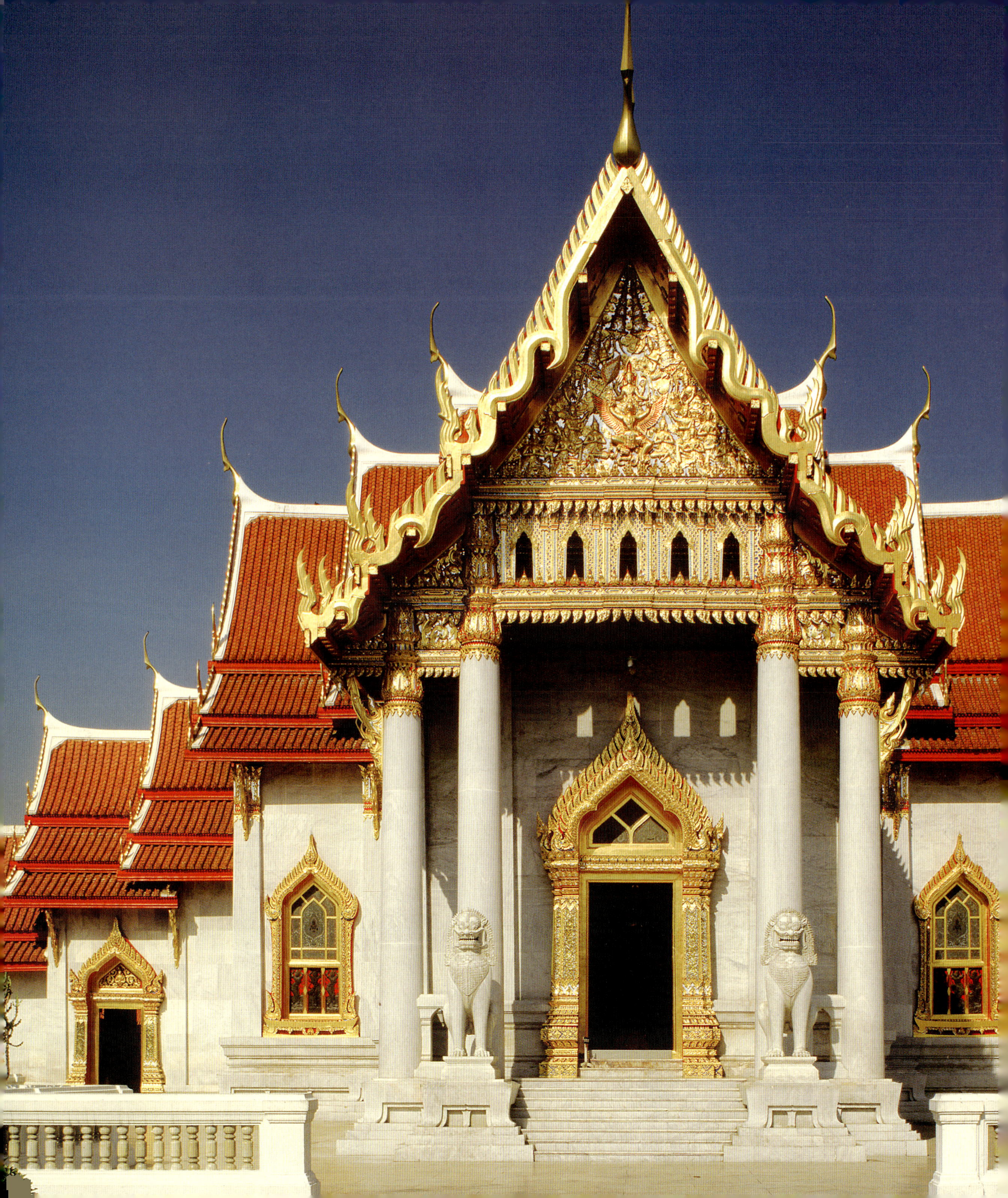

Wat Benchamabophit

Bangkok

An earlier monastery on this site, called Wat Laem or Wat Saithong and dating to the Ayuthaya era (1350–1767), was replaced in 1826 after a prince and his four siblings established a line of defence at the old temple against an invading army from Laos. The army never reached Bangkok, having been halted in Nakhon Ratchasima, and in gratitude, Rama III ordered the reconstruction of the temple as Wat Benchabophit, 'Five Princes Monastery.'

Rama V, while building a new royal palace nearby at the end of the 19th century, restored the temple further in 1899. His half-brother Prince Naris designed a new *bot* with an unusual cruciform floor plan, possibly inspired by European church architecture, covering the walls and floors with imported white Carrerra marble at considerable expense. The *wat* was re-christened Wat Benchamabophit, meaning 'Monastery of the Fifth King,' in deference to Rama V. The king ordained as monk here for 15 days in 1873 after having already served as king for five years. It was his second time in Buddhist robes, having earlier taken novice ordination at Wat Bowonniwet in 1866.

The principal Buddha image inside the *bot* was forged in Phitsanulok in 1920 and is an exact copy of the famous flame-haloed Phra Jinnarat from the same city. After Rama V passed away, his ashes were interred in the base of the image. Backed by an unorthodox, illuminated blue wall, the image altar is considered one of the most beautiful in Thailand. Stained glass windows with Buddhist designs offer another architectural innovation.

The cloistered courtyard behind the *bot* contains 53 Buddha images representing famous styles from all over Thailand and other Buddhist countries. There is also a large banyan tree grown from a cutting taken from a tree in Bodh Gaya, India, beneath which the Buddha is said to have attained enlightenment.

To the east of the *bot* stands a dhamma lecture hall built in 1902 by Queen Sawang Vadhana, the paternal grandmother of King Bhumibol Adulyadej. It commemorates her son, Crown Prince Maha Vajirunhis, who had succumbed to typhoid in 1895 at the age of 17. The two-storey brick building, with its elaborately carved gables, was used on Buddhist holy days by Rama V when he wanted to hear dhamma sermons. A canal crossed by three arched bridges made from red-painted steel separates the main temple area from the monastic living quarters.

Pages 88-89: The late-19th century *bot* at Wat Benchamabophit has one of the most immediately recognisable profiles of any temple in the capital.

Above: A curved bridge over a canal in the vast temple compound.

Right: The principal Buddha image at Wat Benchamabophit, inspired by Phitsanulok's Phra Chinnarat, is displayed against a striking blue background.

90 Buddhist Temples of Thailand

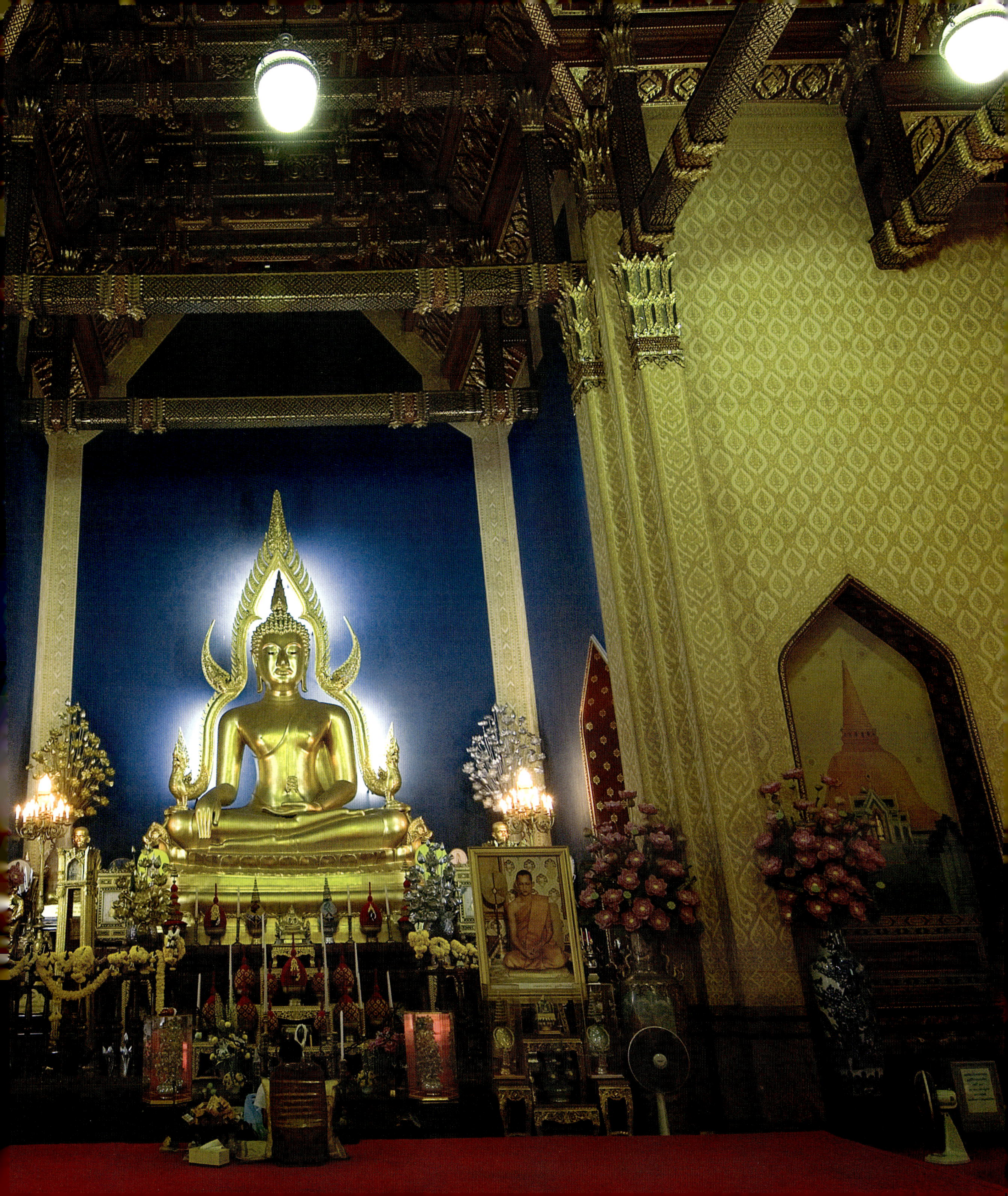

Wat Dusitaram

Bangkok

Just south of Phra Pin Klao Bridge in Bangkok Noi district on Bangkok's Thonburi side of the Chao Phraya River, stands Wat Dusitaram. Little is known about the origins of this monastery except that it was built in the Ayuthaya era and was originally called Wat Sao Prakhon.

Later Kromluang Srisunthornthep, one of Rama I's 42 sons, took an interest in the site, ordered a renovation in 1913, changed the name to Wat Dusitaram and upgraded the *wat's* ranking to that of a *Worawihan* (royal temple). An adjacent abandoned temple known as Wat Phumarin Ratchapaksi was incorporated into the new compound as well.

Between the two temple sites, two original ordination chapels and one *wihan* survive, all of them built with gently curving wall lines intended to resemble sailing ships. There is a dual significance to such designs here. The first relates to the temple's position near a large shed and pier where the Chakri monarchy's royal barges are stored and where they are launched on ceremonial occasions. The second evokes Buddhadhamma as a vehicle transporting the believer from *samsara* (the worldly cycle of rebirth) to nirvana. A surrounding cloister intended for walking meditation contains 64 standing Buddha images.

The walls of Wat Dusitaram's main *bot* are painted with impressive gold-on-red murals dating to the reign of Rama I. A scene representing the Triphum — Three Worlds of Buddhist cosmology — on the west wall behind the principal Buddha image is particularly treasured for its vivid depiction of hell and for its Giotto-like lack of perspective. Concentrating on telling the story rather than applying realism, for example, the artists painted relatively less significant characters in remote corners of the mural larger than those at eye-level locations out of concern that viewers would be unable to see them.

On the opposite wall of the *bot* is a mural of comparable quality rendering the Buddha's valiant battle for enlightenment, in which Torani, the earth goddess, wrings out her wet hair to create a flood to wash away Mara the Tempter. Another well-known panel at Wat Dusitaram shows eight Buddhist kings dividing the remains of the Buddha's ashes and bones at Kusinara, India, with the intent to build stupas throughout their kingdoms.

The murals at Wat Dusitaram have faded considerably and are in danger of disappearing altogether if further extensive restoration is not undertaken soon. Images along the lower portions of the walls have already disappeared due to dampness rising through the structure from the ground.

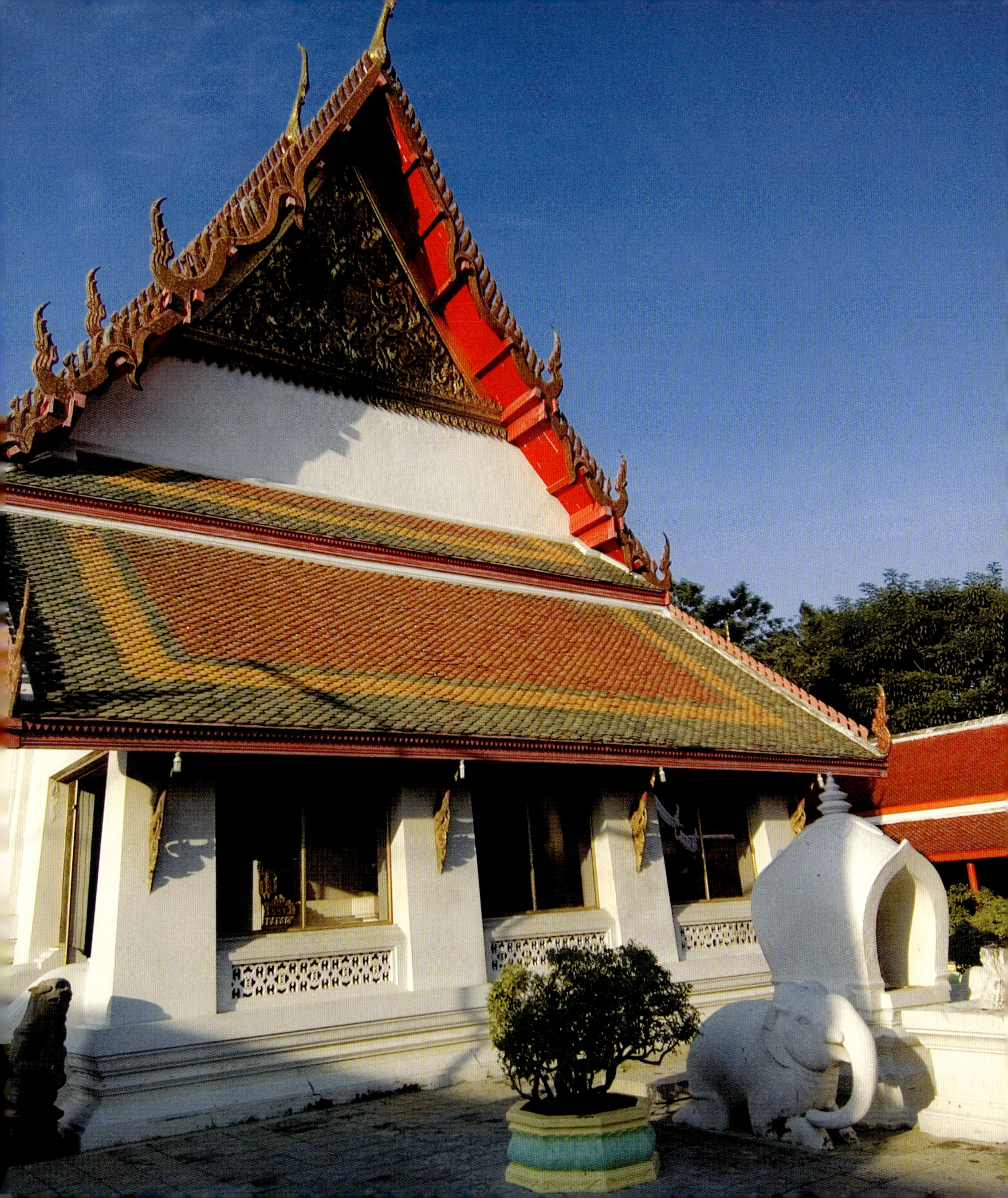

94 Buddhist Temples of Thailand

Pages 92-93: The *bot* at Wat Dusitaram, surrounded by ordination boundary markers and displaying an unusual lateral veranda.

Far left: Faded murals afford glimpses of Ko Ratanakosin in an earlier era.

Left: A *wihan* designed with inward-curving walls.

Below: Inside the thick-walled *wihan*.

Region: Bangkok 95

Central Thailand & Ayuthaya

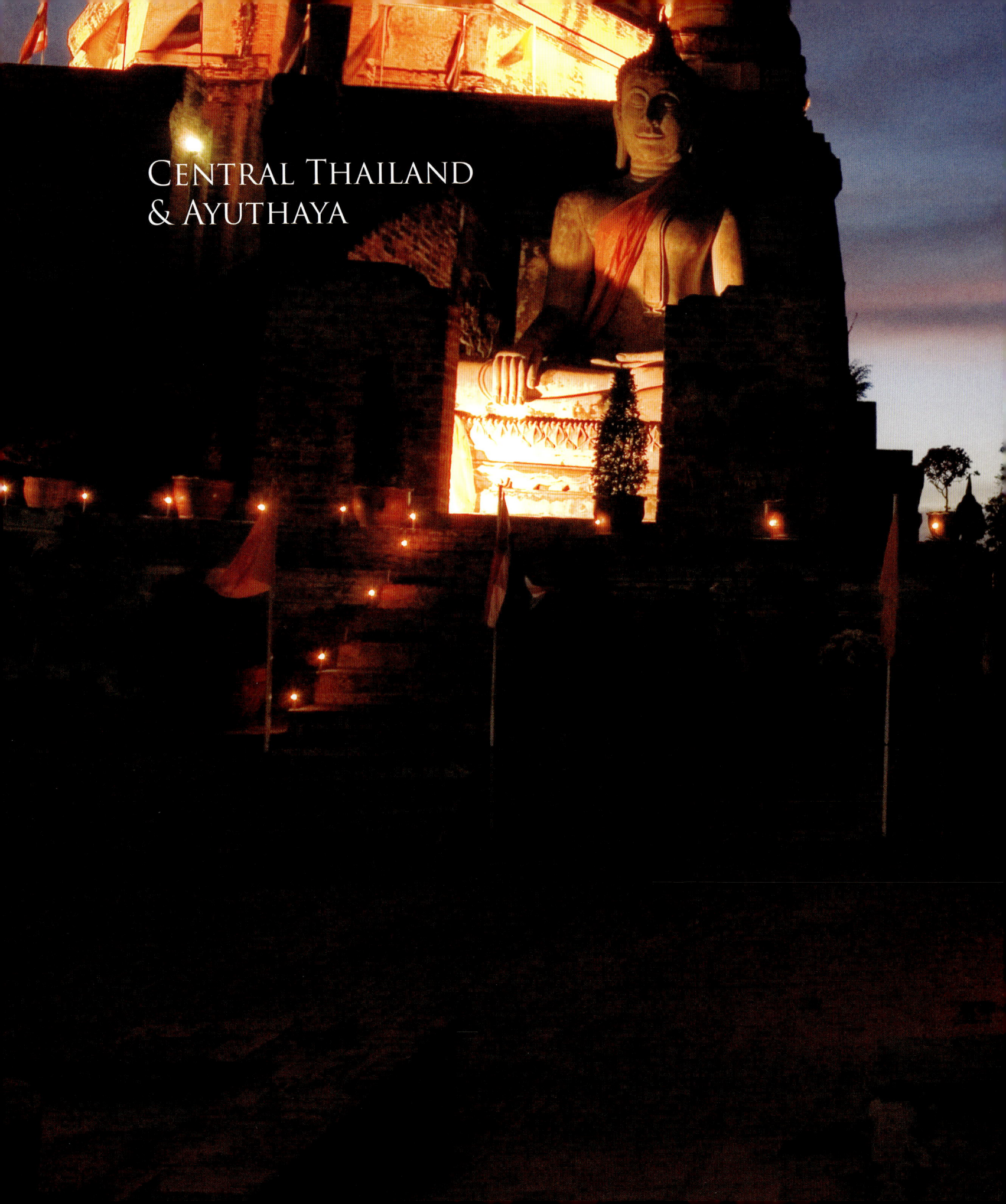

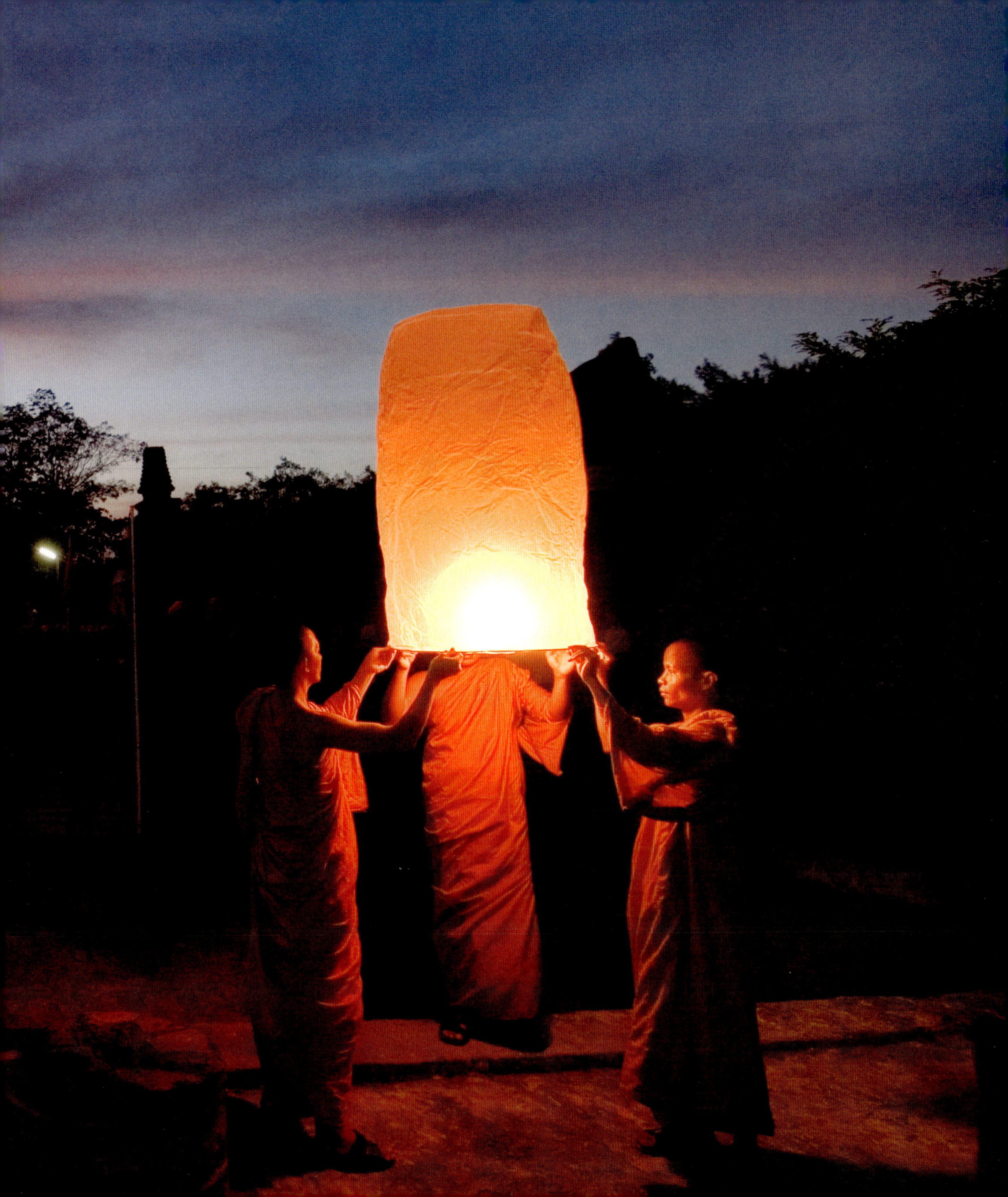

WAT YAI CHAIMONGKHON

AYUTHAYA

King U-Thong founded Ayuthaya in 1350 after fleeing a smallpox outbreak in Lopburi. As the centre of Siam, it became the longest-running Thai kingdom in Thailand's history, and its 1700 population of one million made it one of the largest cities in the world at the time. Burmese armies sacked the city in 1767, after which the Thais moved their capital to Thonburi.

The king built Wat Yai Chaimongkhon – originally called Wat Pa Kaew – southeast of the main island city to serve as a quiet centre of meditation and dhamma study. Its original monastic residents were ordained by Phra Wanratana Mahathera in Ceylon. Somdej Phrawanarat, the supreme patriarch of Siam's Buddhist sangha, was also centred here, a fact that inspires some locals today to refer to the temple as Wat Chao Phraya Thai (roughly 'lord of the Thais monastery'). A substantial community of Buddhist monks and nuns still reside here today.

Pages 96-97: Novice monks launch a *khom lawy* (floating lantern) from the historic grounds of Wat Yai Chaimongkhon

Right: Wat Yai Chaimongkhon's Ayuthaya-era stupa was built to celebrate a 16th century victory over Burma.

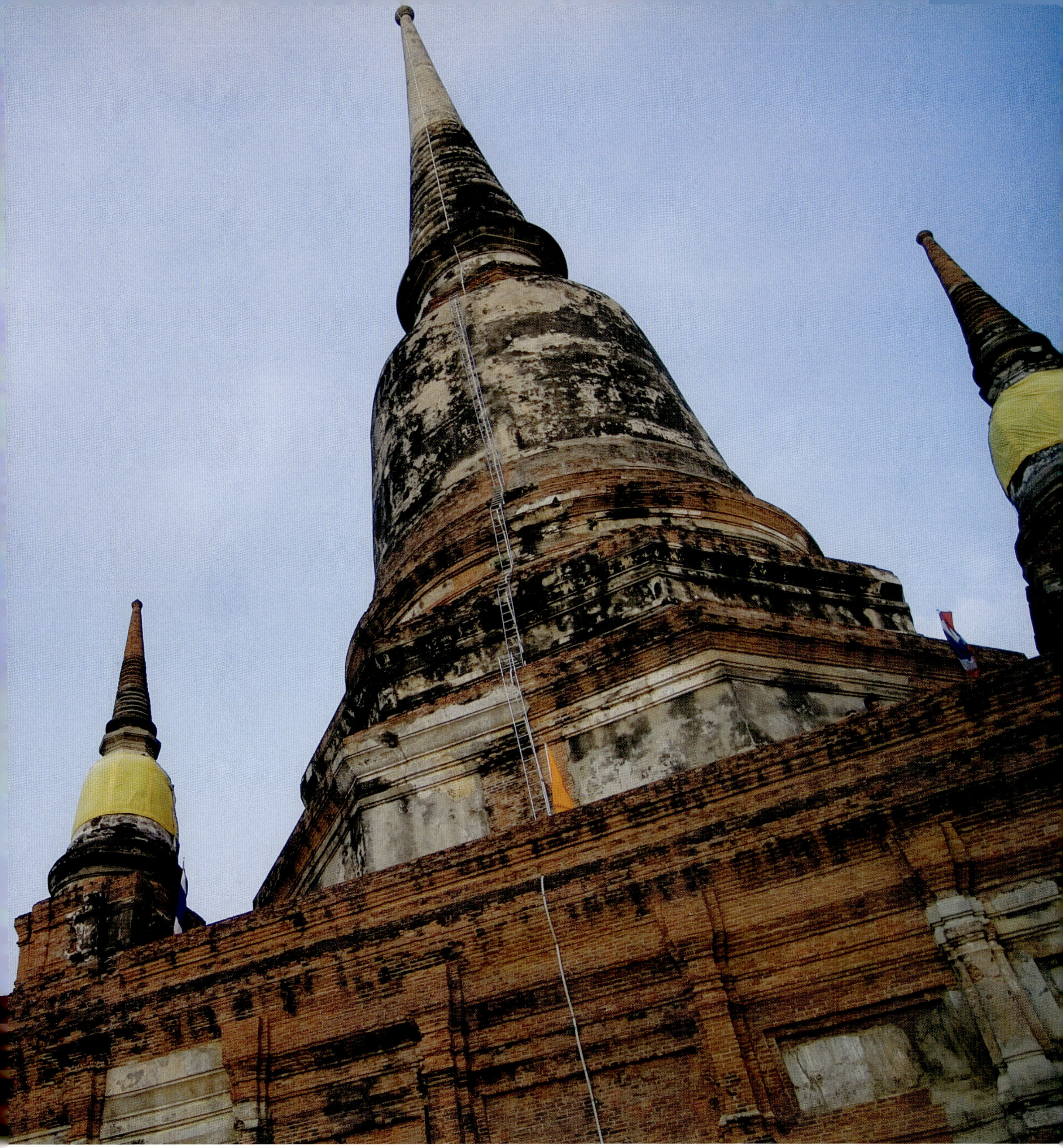

Above: A smaller stupa stands in partial ruins, exposing hand-made bricks that would have once been covered in stucco. The Buddha figures in the foreground have been restored.

Right: The side niches in the 72-metre high main stupa can be accessed by steep stairways on each side.

Pages 102-103: The stupa at night, illuminated by floodlights.

The monastery's lofty stupa was added to the temple by King Naresuan to commemorate a triumphant elephant-back battle fought against the Crown Prince of Burma in 1592. At that point the temple's name was changed to Wat Yai Chaimongkhon (Big Monastery of Blessed Victory). The 72-metre, bell-shaped stupa, designed in Sinhalese-inspired early Ayuthaya style, sits on a very large square base and is surrounded by four satellite stupas. Nowadays the stupa displays a noticeable tilt but can still be mounted by a steep, long stairway. Just after sunset, as the sky turns purple, floodlights add dramatic illumination to the great stupa. A few other ruined stupas stand nearby, fronted by a row of semi-ruined sitting Buddha figures.

A windowless *bot* is ventilated by holes piercing the upper walls, suggesting secondary purpose as a point of defence. The monastery's most well-known and most visited feature is a huge reclining Buddha image made of moulded brick and covered in stucco. The image is whitewashed annually and wrapped in orange satin robes during significant Buddhist festivals. A statue of highly revered King Naresuan also adorns the grounds.

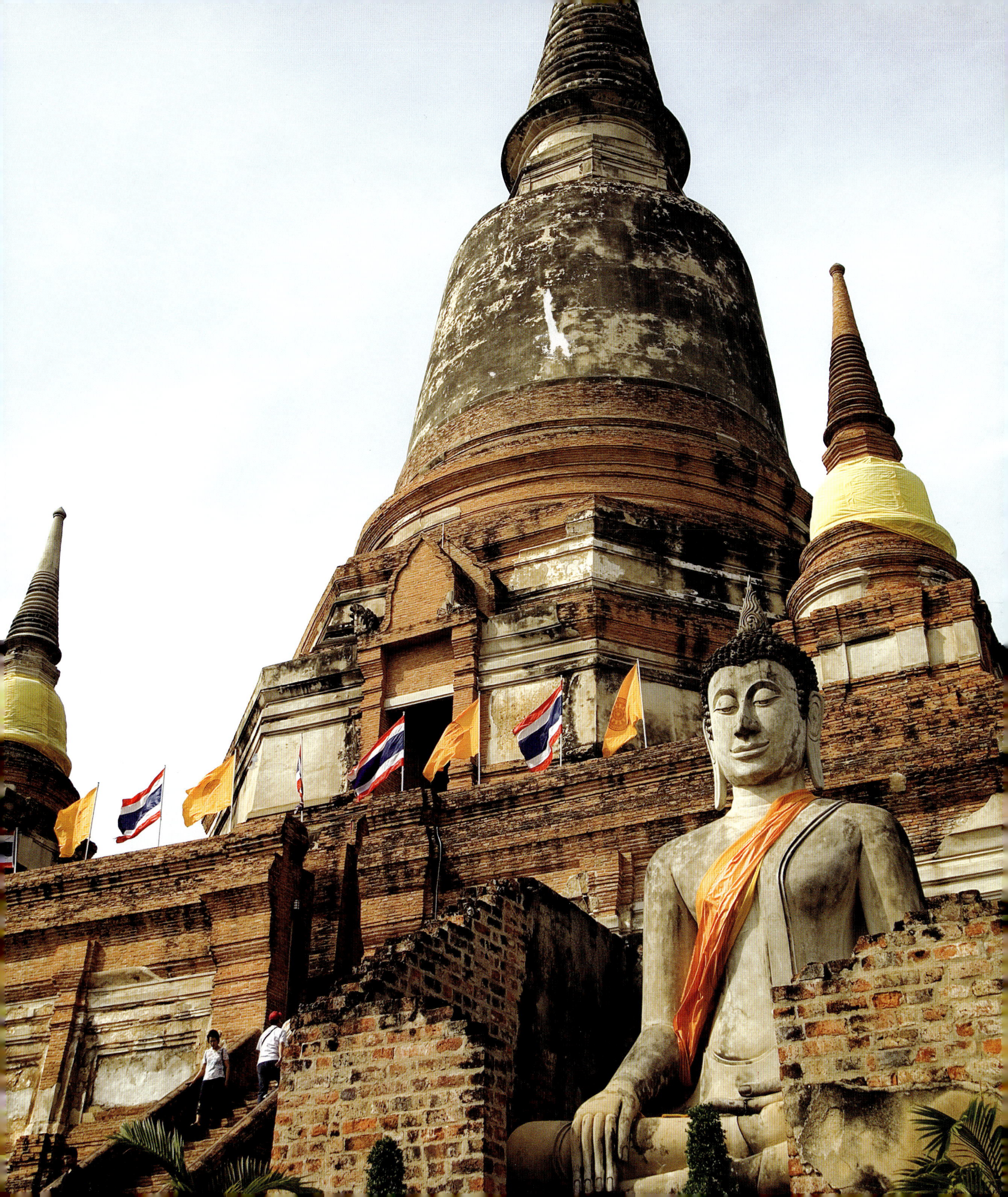

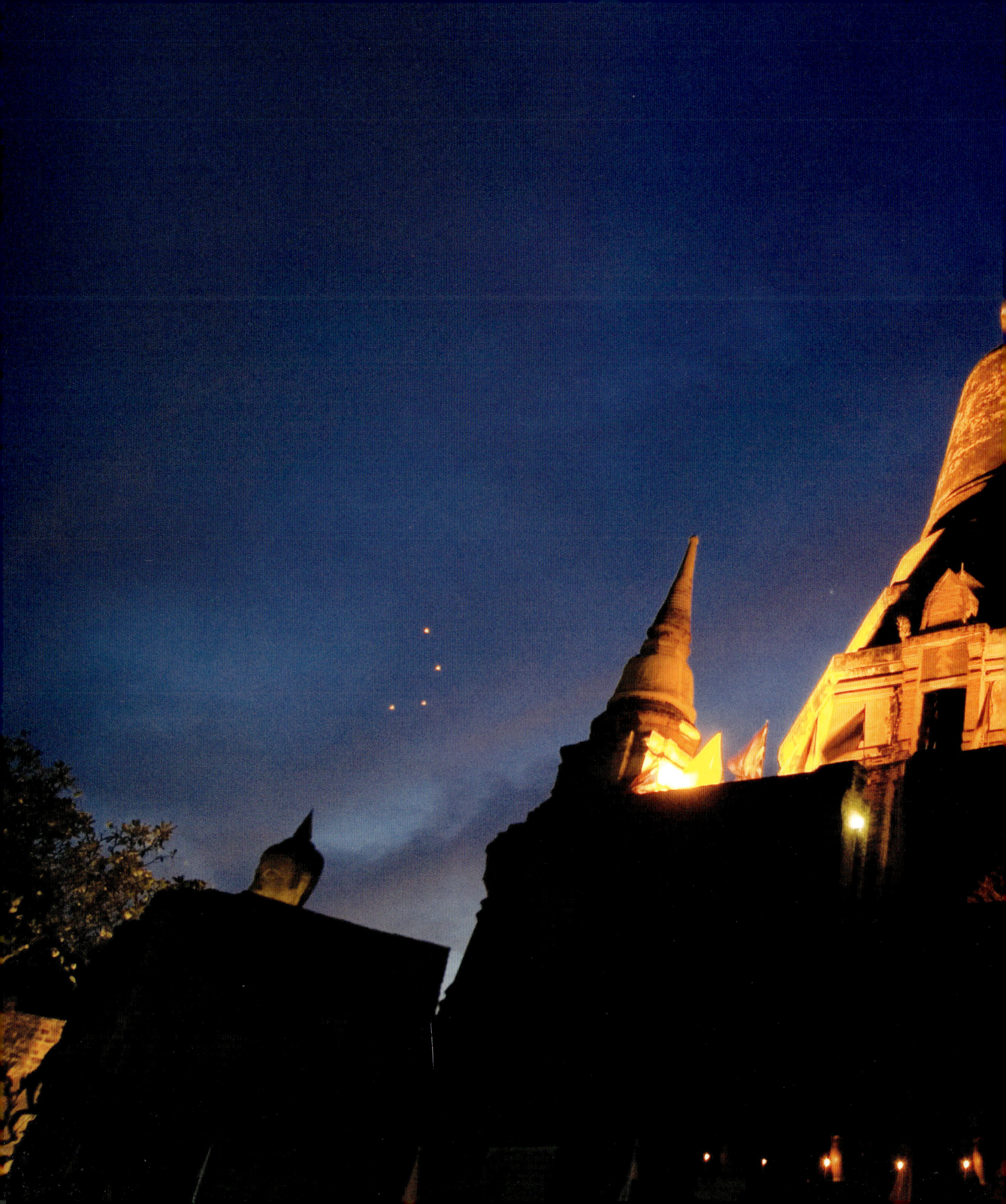

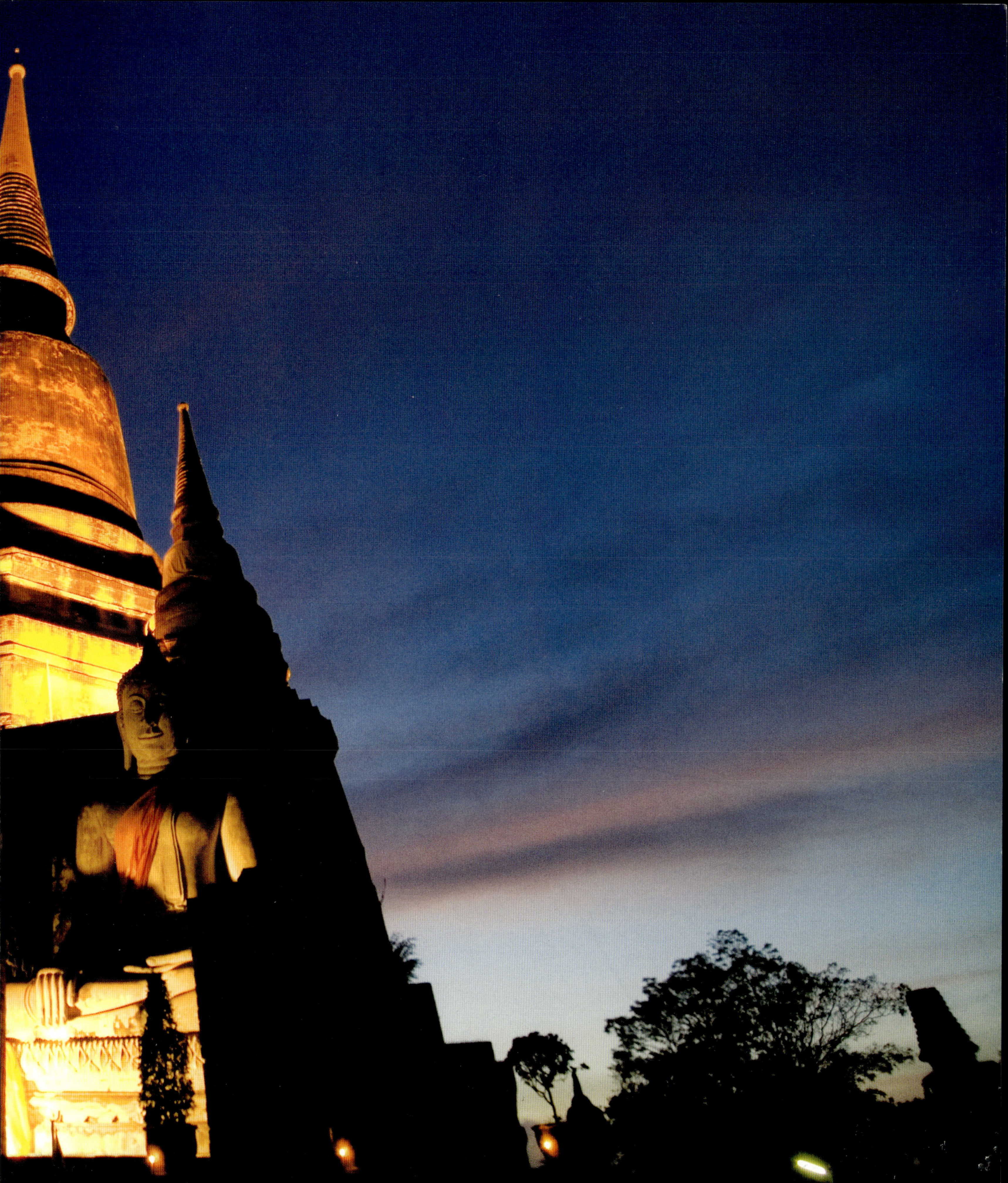

Wat Na Phra Men

Ayuthaya

While most of Ayuthaya's besieged monasteries were abandoned as roofless ruins after the Burmese invasion, Wat Na Phra Men was spared in the protracted battles and left more or less intact. Thai chronicles record that the Burmese used the temple — which stands across a river from a large island formed by the encirclement of three rivers and a canal, where the main portion of the city was located — as a launching point for cannon attacks on the city centre. The Burmese king in charge of the attacks allegedly was fatally injured when a cannon misfired at Wat Na Phra Men, adding spiritual power to the temple's survival.

Built in 1546 in classic early Ayuthaya style, Wat Na Phra Men was restored under King Boromakot (1732-58). The name means 'Monastery in Front of Cremation Grounds,' suggesting that it originally faced an area dedicated to Buddhist funeral pyres. A large, stately *bot* boasts richly carved wooden door panels, and, on the gable, a Garuda suspended over Kala, the Brahman god of death and time. The imposing entry veranda is flanked on each side by smaller but equally elegant porticos, a design not often seen elsewhere in Ayuthaya.

Inside, a ceiling studded with carved and gilded rosettes is supported by lofty octagonal columns ending in pineapple-inspired capitals and decorated throughout their entire length with gold-on-red *lai kham*. The principal Buddha image, seated in *bhumisparsa* pose and bearing regalia on arms, chest and head, is considered an exemplar of Ayuthaya bronze casting. The ruins of a large stupa base stand in front of the bot.

A smaller, adjacent *wihan* houses a black stone Buddha in 'European pose,' that is, with the legs dangling as if seated on a throne. The figure, carved in Mon style, is thought to date to the earlier Dvaravati period and may have come from Wat Phra Men in Nakhon Pathom. Some sources claim the image is a copy of a similar quartzite image still present at Nakhon Pathom.

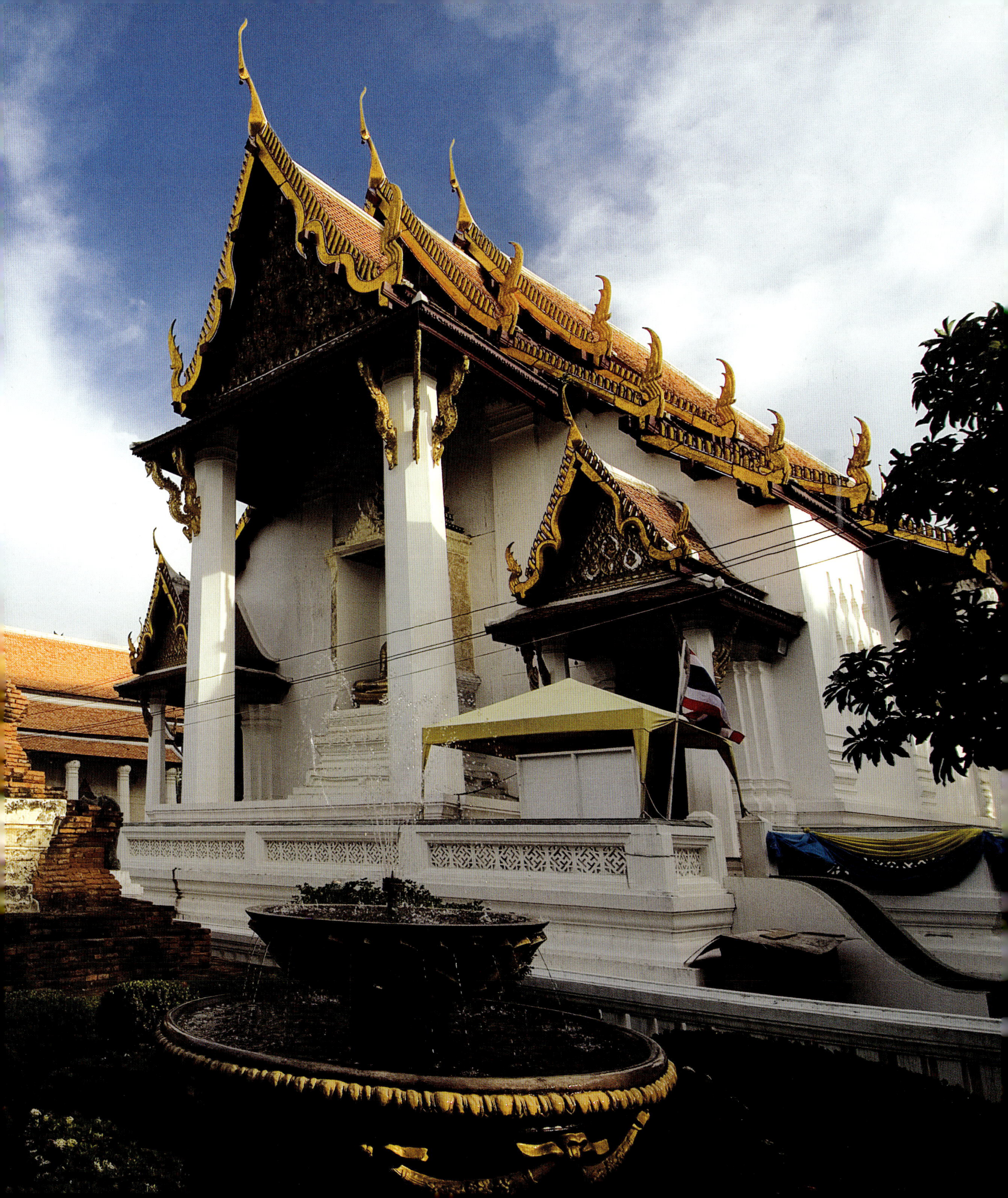

Pages 104-105: The *bot* at Wat Na Phra Men is one of the few roofed structures that survived the Burmese sacking of Ayuthaya.

Above: The principal Buddha image bears royal paraphernalia on the head, chest and arms, a common feature of Ayuthaya bronzes.

Right: This Mon-style Buddha image, cast in 'European pose', dates to the Dvaravati period.

106 Buddhist Temples of Thailand

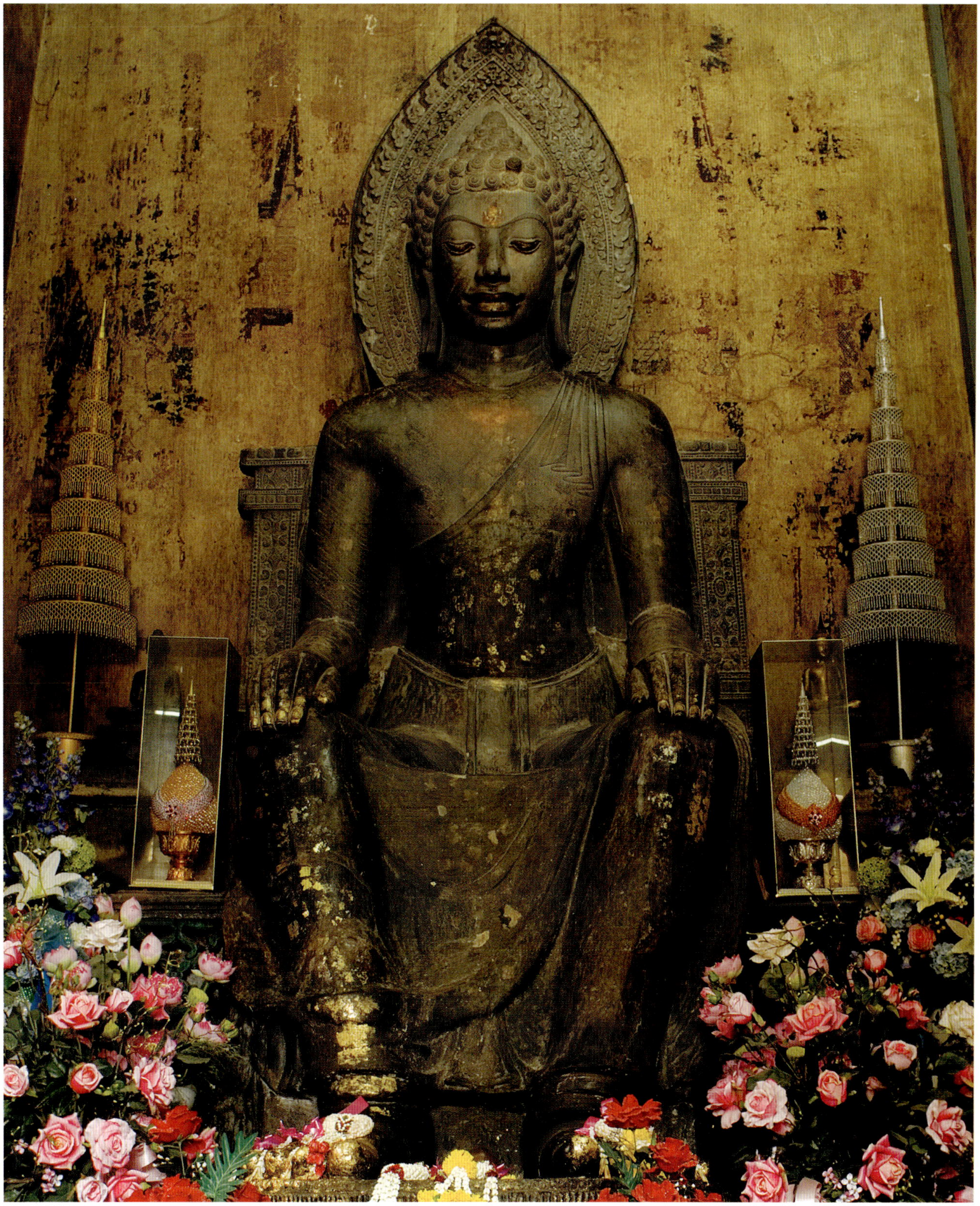

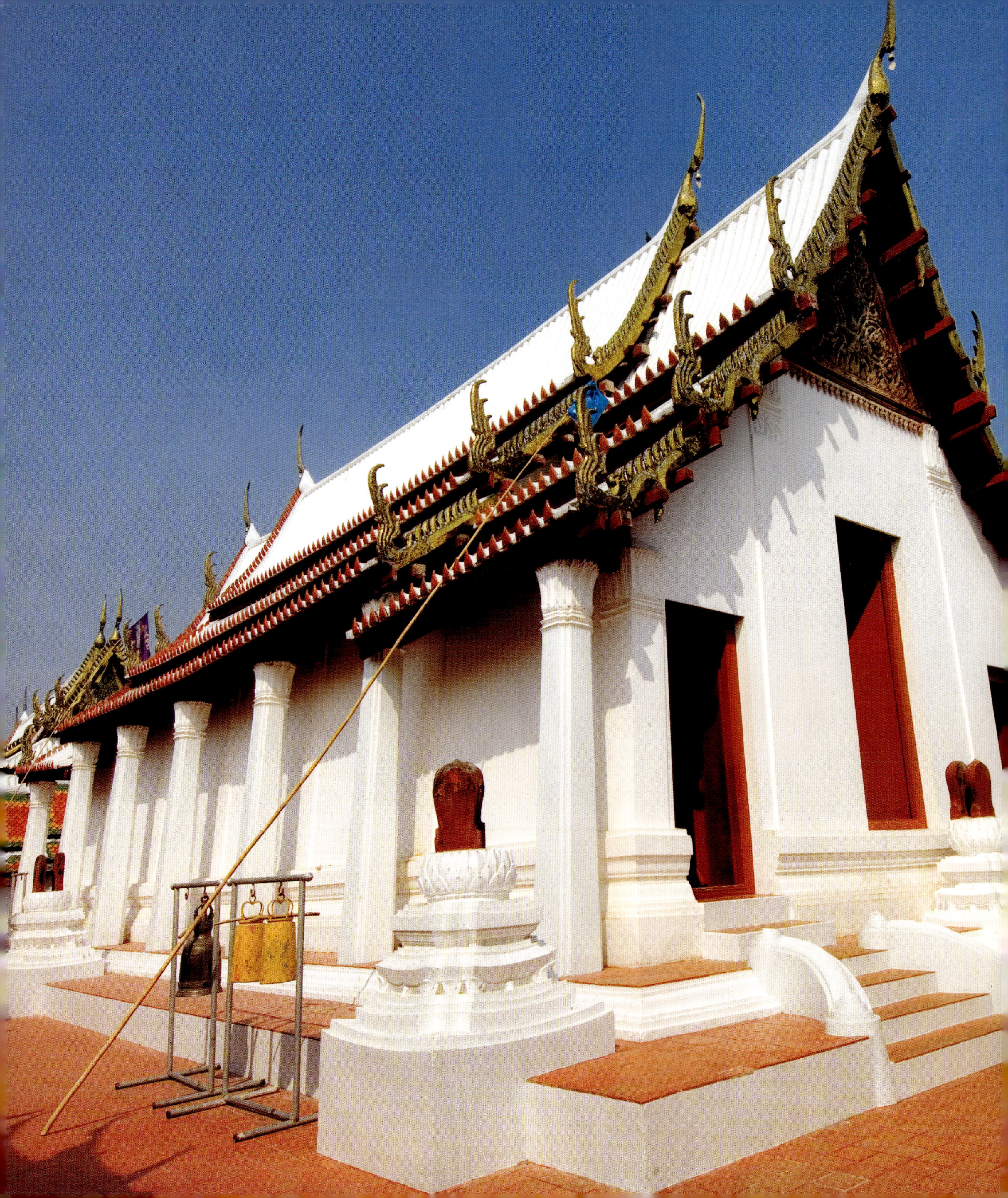

Wat Yai Suwannaram

Phetchaburi

The 'City of Diamonds,' continually inhabited since the Mon kingdom of Dvaravati, came under Khmer rule when the Angkor Empire expanded at its peak and served as an important relay point for trade coming across the Isthmus of Kra from the Andaman coast. It is likely that Wat Yai Suwannaram, built during the Ayuthaya era as a royal temple, occupies a site that was once sacred to both the Mon and the Khmer. When Burmese armies laid siege to Siam in 1767, most of the city was burned to the ground but fortunately Wat Yai was spared.

The majestic ordination hall, built in Ayuthaya style, has no windows whatsoever, only doors. The lack of light may explain why the interior walls bear one of the only surviving examples of Ayuthaya-era painting and the oldest known murals anywhere in Thailand, dating to the late 17th century. Forgoing the usual *Jataka* tales, the paintings here represent celestial deities arranged in three levels. The upper level displays Brahmas (creator gods), hermits, giants and minor deities, while the lower two represent guardian deities, Garuda and assorted birds. *Kinnaree* paintings on the inside of the doors are still visible. The artistry shows a high level of skill.

The ordination hall also houses an intricately carved and gilded wooden preaching throne, said to have been used by Sangharaja Taengmo, head of the Buddhist order in Ayuthaya. The presiding Buddha image is a beautiful Sukhothai sitting bronze which is famously unusual for having six toes. Roof pillars are square with reticulated corners, and feature red and gold *lai kham*. Original stucco

110 Buddhist Temples of Thailand

ornamentation on the main gable shows Garuda, Vishnu's mount, surrounded by vine motifs.

A cloister surrounding the *bot* is lined with sitting images of the Buddha, while its eastern gable bears a stucco relief of Airvata, the three-headed elephant mount of Indra. Small stupas from both the Ayuthaya and Sukhothai eras — the latter distinguished by its Khmer-style spire — are also on the grounds, as is a bell tower with quasi-colonial-style pillared arches.

A 17th century *sala kan parian*, built entirely of teak and enclosed rather than open-sided, displays multi-tiered roofs and elaborately carved and gilded wooden doors. One door panel bears a jagged hole, allegedly made by invading Burmese armies who tried to enter the building. Octagonal pillars in four rows of 11 support the *sala*. Faded paintings are barely visible on teak panels inside.

A third building of note is the small two-room, tile-roofed wooden *ho trai* standing on three pillars in a huge pond. The three pillars, which probably symbolise the three 'baskets' of the Tipitaka, were once made of teak but have been replaced by concrete. The library was restored in 1975 by the Siam Society.

Pages 108-109: The Ayuthaya-style *bot* at Wat Yai was designed without windows, possibly as a defence measure.

Left: A 17th century *sala kan parian* (scripture study pavilion), whose teak walls bear faded murals.

Above: Paintings of celestial deities inside the *bot* are the oldest surviving Ayuthaya murals in Thailand. The principal Buddha image hails from Sukhothai.

Wat Ko Kaew Sutharam
Phetchaburi

Wat Ko Kaew Sutharam, like Wat Yai Suwannaram, was one of the few monasteries that Burmese armies spared during their violent conquest of the Ayuthaya kingdom in 1767. The most historically and artistically significant structure in the compound is the *bot*, which, like the *bot* at Wat Yai, was built without windows. While no doubt enhancing the monastery's dual purpose as a line of defence, it has had the unintended effect of helping to preserve the magnificent interior paintings, among the only known surviving examples of 18th century, Ayuthaya-style murals. Boldly painted, lively scenes from the *Jatakas* were composed and framed as inverted triangles, leaving spaces between them that form upward-pointing triangles, perhaps to echo stupa design.

The murals, which epigraphs state were painted in 1734, are also significant as they appear to document the visit of a French mission which passed through Phetchaburi en route to Ayuthaya during the reign of King Narai, at the height of western contact with Siam. One panel depicts a Jesuit priest wearing the robes of a Buddhist monk, while another shows other foreigners receiving Buddhist teachings.

Behind the principal Buddha altar, paintings depict Buddha's victory over the temptations of Mara. The main Buddha image itself, a 180-cm tall gilded bronze in meditation pose cast in the Ayuthaya style, is flanked by standing bronzes of Sariputta and Mogallana, close disciples of the Buddha. The front wall of the *bot* is adorned with a scene representing Tribhumi, the three-tier Buddhist cosmology.

North of the *bot* stands a simple *wihan* of brick and stucco which also dates to the early-18th century. A wooden pulpit inside, with an elaborately carved wooden seat, is one of the only surviving Ayuthaya-era *thammat* in Thailand.

Between the *wihan* and *bot*, a large round stupa built in 1925 features a dome decorated with stucco reliefs in the shape of draped floral garlands and 13-ring spire topped by a small *chatree*. Local historians claim this stupa was built on top of an older Ayuthaya-period stupa. Also on the grounds is a wooden *sala kan parian*, built in 1888 in typical central Thai style, a well-preserved, large wooden monastic hall on stilts dating to around the same time.

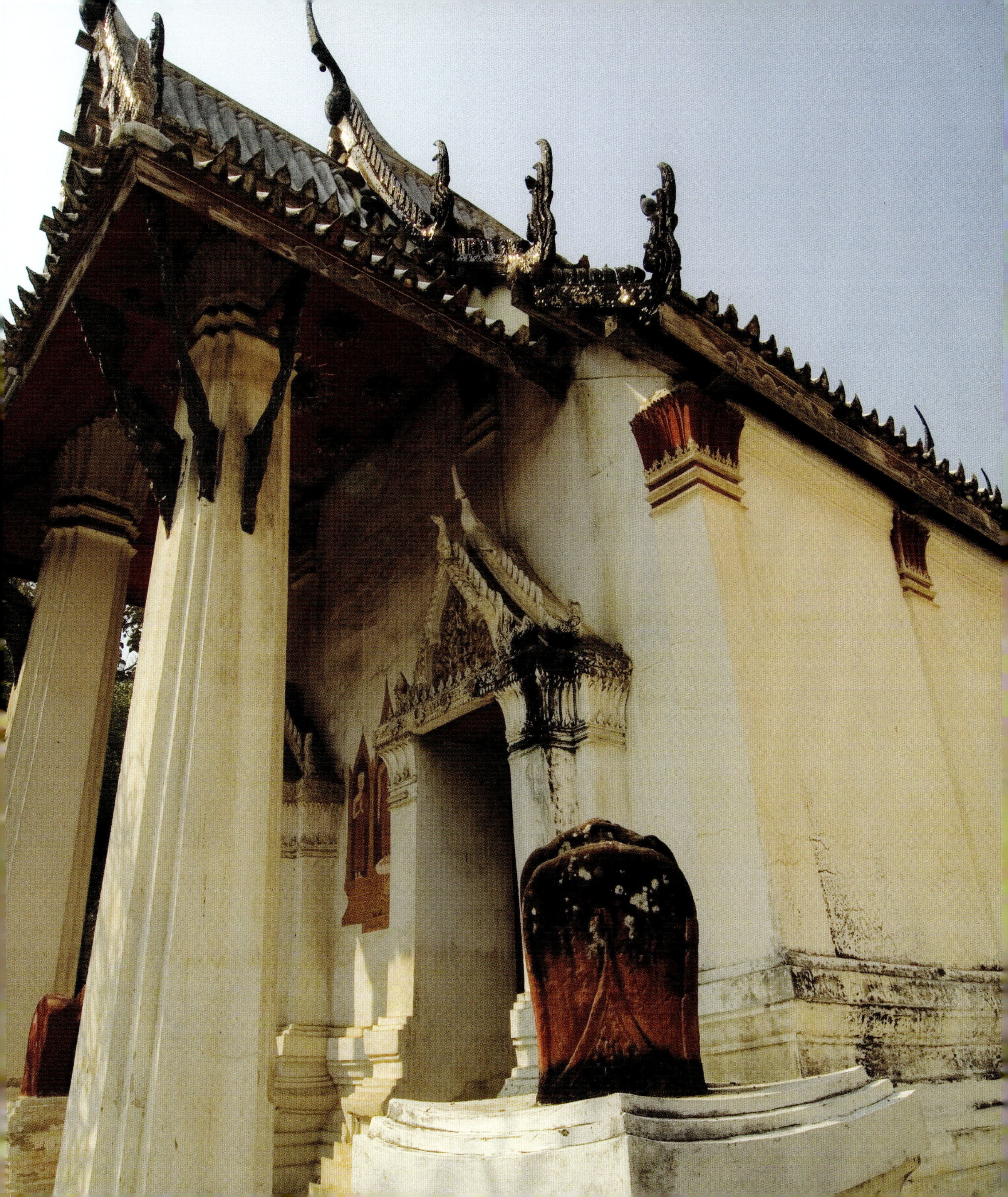

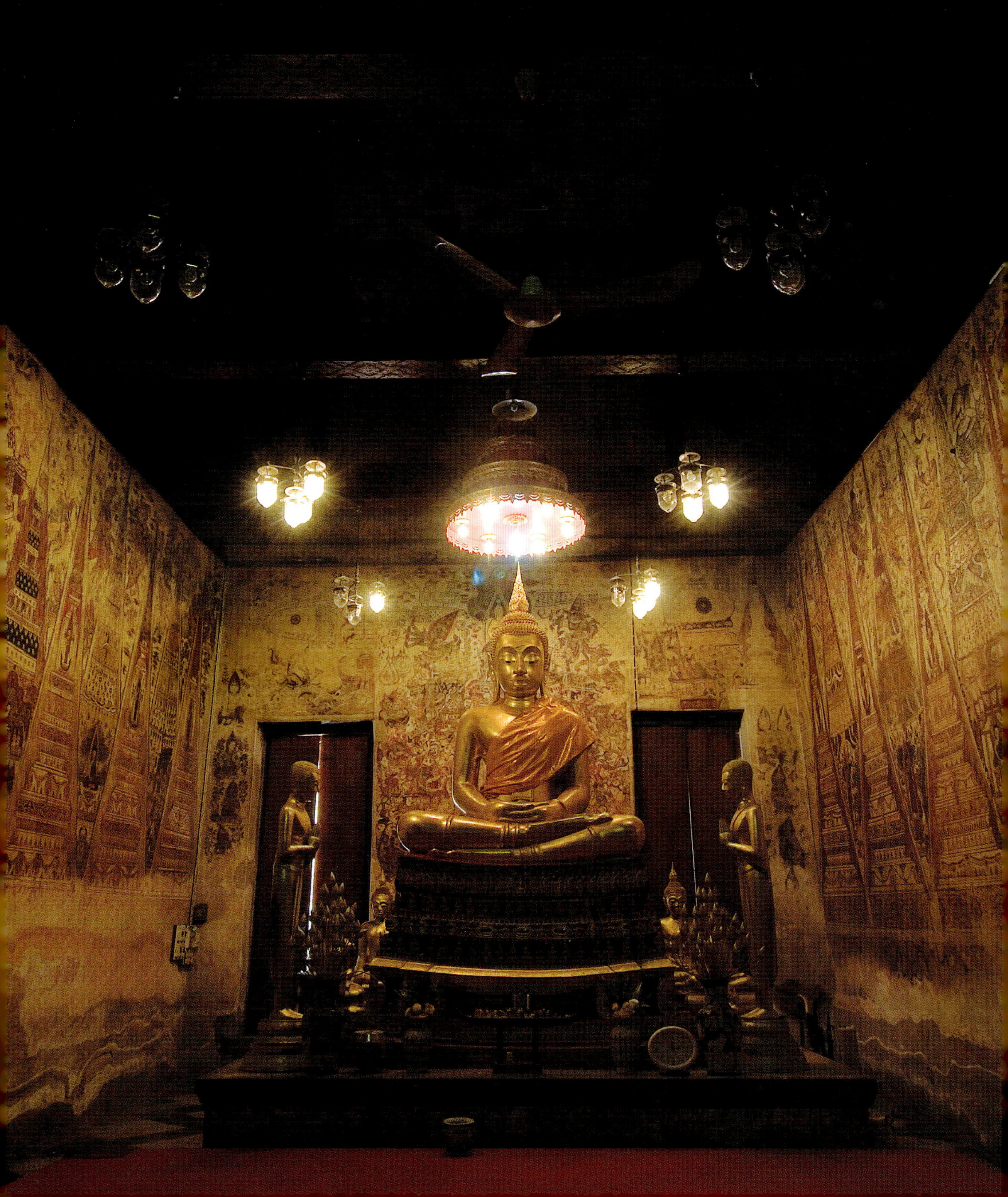

Pages 112-113: The windowless, Ayuthaya-style *bot* at Wat Ko Kaew Sutharam.

Far left: The principal Buddha image is cast in early Ayuthaya style and flanked by standing bronzes of Sariputta and Mogallana, close disciples of the Buddha. The still-vibrant murals are the only known surviving examples of early-18th century Ayuthaya-era Buddhist painting.

Left and below: Murals inside the *bot* date back to 1734. The long-nosed Westerner among the depicted figures is thought to have been inspired by the visit of a French mission which passed through Phetchaburi during the reign of King Narai, at the height of western contact with Siam.

Wat Phra Dhammakaya
Pathum Thani

Founded in 1978 on 80 acres of land in Khlong Luang District, Pathum Thani Province, Wat Phra Dhammakaya represents Thai Buddhist architecture at its most modernist. The concrete-and-steel *bot*, completed in 1982 and consecrated three years later, gives a nod to typical Thai temple design with its traditional rectangular floor plan and steeply curving rooflines but for the most part it is devoid of architectural ornamentation. In 1998 the structure was honoured with an Association of Siamese Architects (ASA) Architectural Design Award.

The monastery soon acquired adjacent lands from donors and expanded to encompass four square kilometres. The Dhammakaya Cetiya, a huge stupa covering a square kilometre itself, represents the single strongest image to monastery visitors. It was completed and consecrated in 1999 when the last of 300,000 Buddha images were installed on its hemispherical middle level and domed top. The images, each in meditation posture and measuring 15cm tall, were forged of silicon bronze, a material normally used for submarine propellers due to its strength and resistance to chemical erosion, and then plated with a titanium-gold ion coating. The underlying stupa was made with a special concrete formulated to last at least a thousand years. The stupa's interior is being installed with another 700,000 Buddha images, to bring the overall total to an eventual one million.

Opposite the main entrance to Wat Phra Dhammakaya, the dome-shaped Phramongkolthepmuni Memorial Hall contains a central chapel with a capacity of

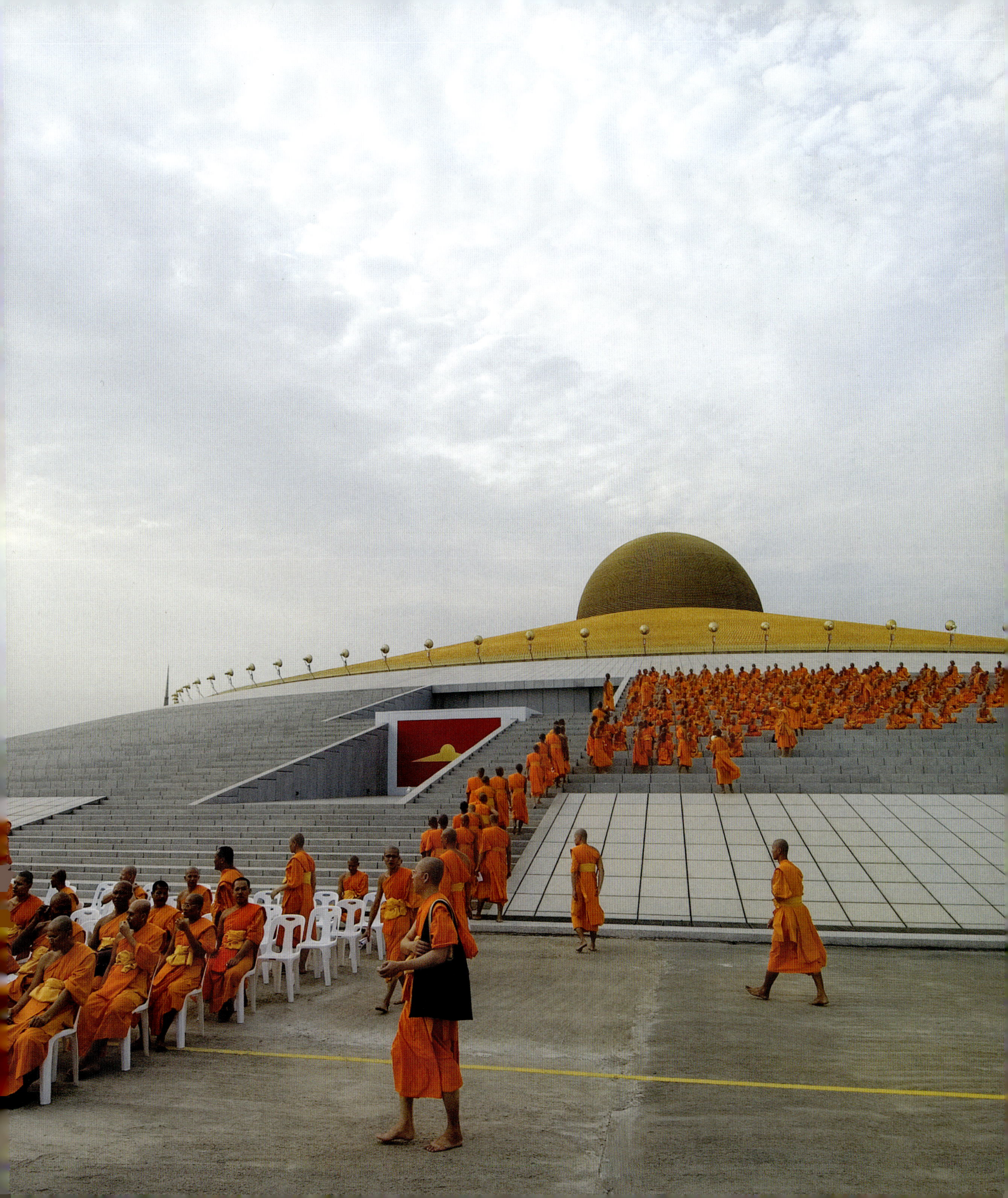

118   Buddhist Temples of Thailand

Pages 116-117: Novice monks gather at the stupa for a public event.

Far left top & left: Laypeople belonging to the Dhammakaya movement celebrate a Buddhist festival.

Far left bottom: Newly ordained novice monks in procession.

Above & right: A huge crowd of white-garbed laypeople seated in meditation around the stupa.

1,500 people, along with seven meditation rooms with a capacity of 350 people. At the centre of the shrine stands a stone altar topped by a solid gold statue of the late Phra Phramongkolthepmuni, a famous meditation master from Wat Pak Nam.

A hexagonal, pyramid-shaped Khun Yay Archaraya Chandra Khonnokyoong Memorial Hall, built to commemorate the founder of the monastery, sits in the middle of a tranquil pond and contains a museum displaying Khun Yay's memorabilia.

The Wat Phra Dhammakaya community today numbers 3,000 monks, novices and laypeople, making it the most populous monastery in Thailand. During Buddhist festivals as many as 100,000 devotees congregate on the grounds, an impressive sight especially during candlelit nighttime ceremonies.

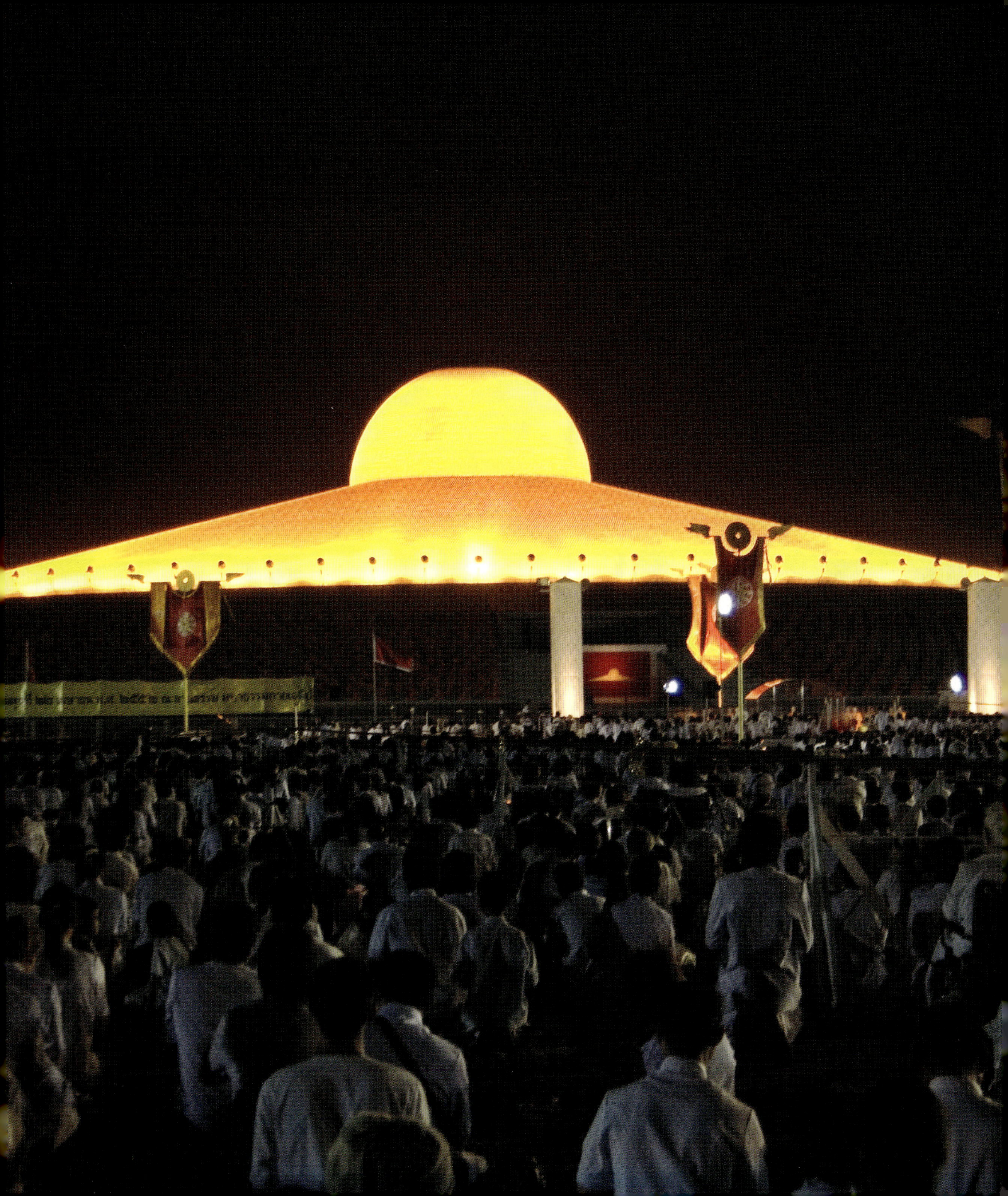

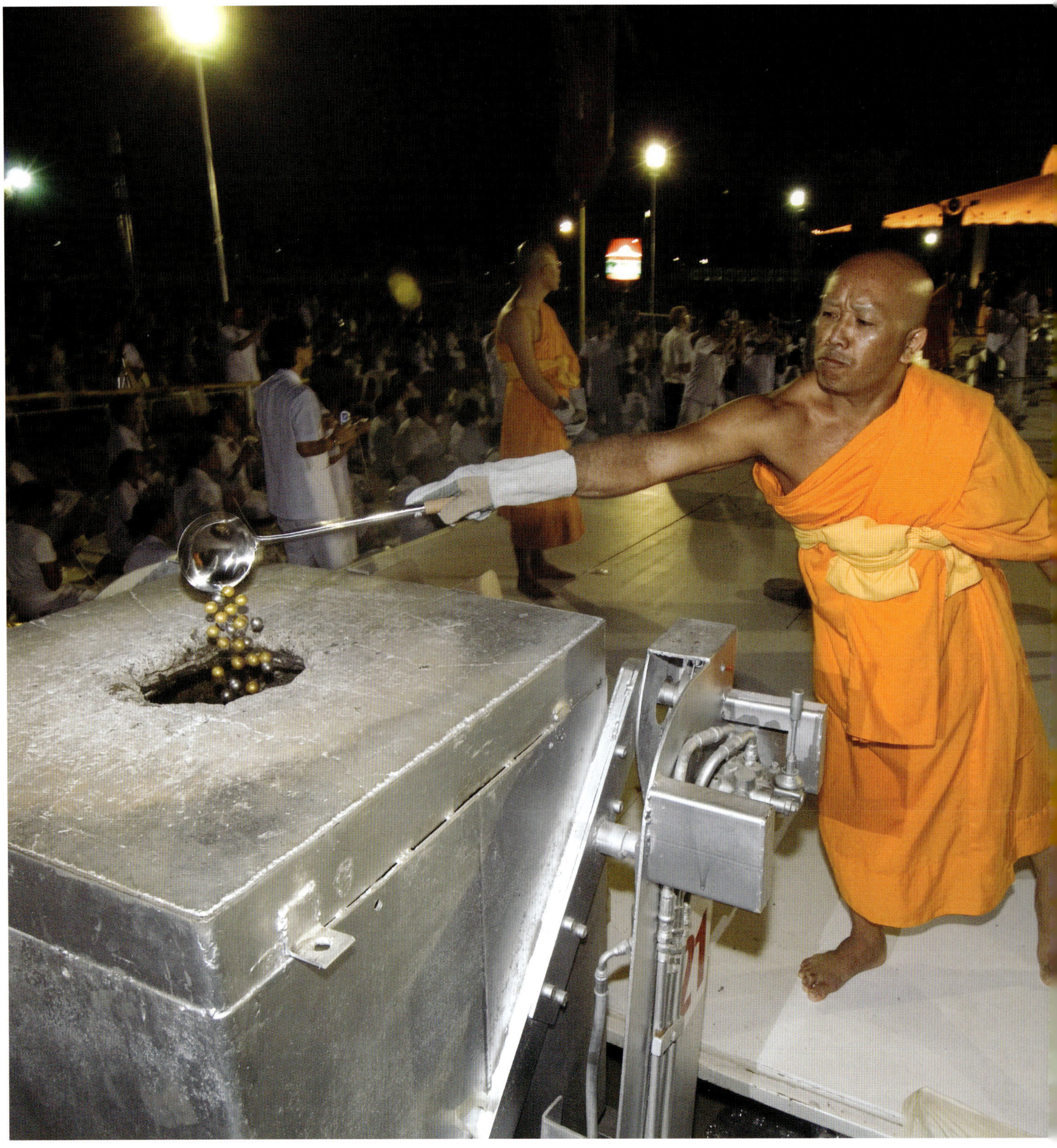

Far left & below: Monks melt pallets to be forged into bronze votive Buddha images. When ready, these images will be placed inside the great stupa.

Left: A monk says a blessing during the forging process.

Region: Central Thailand & Ayuthaya

Northern Thailand

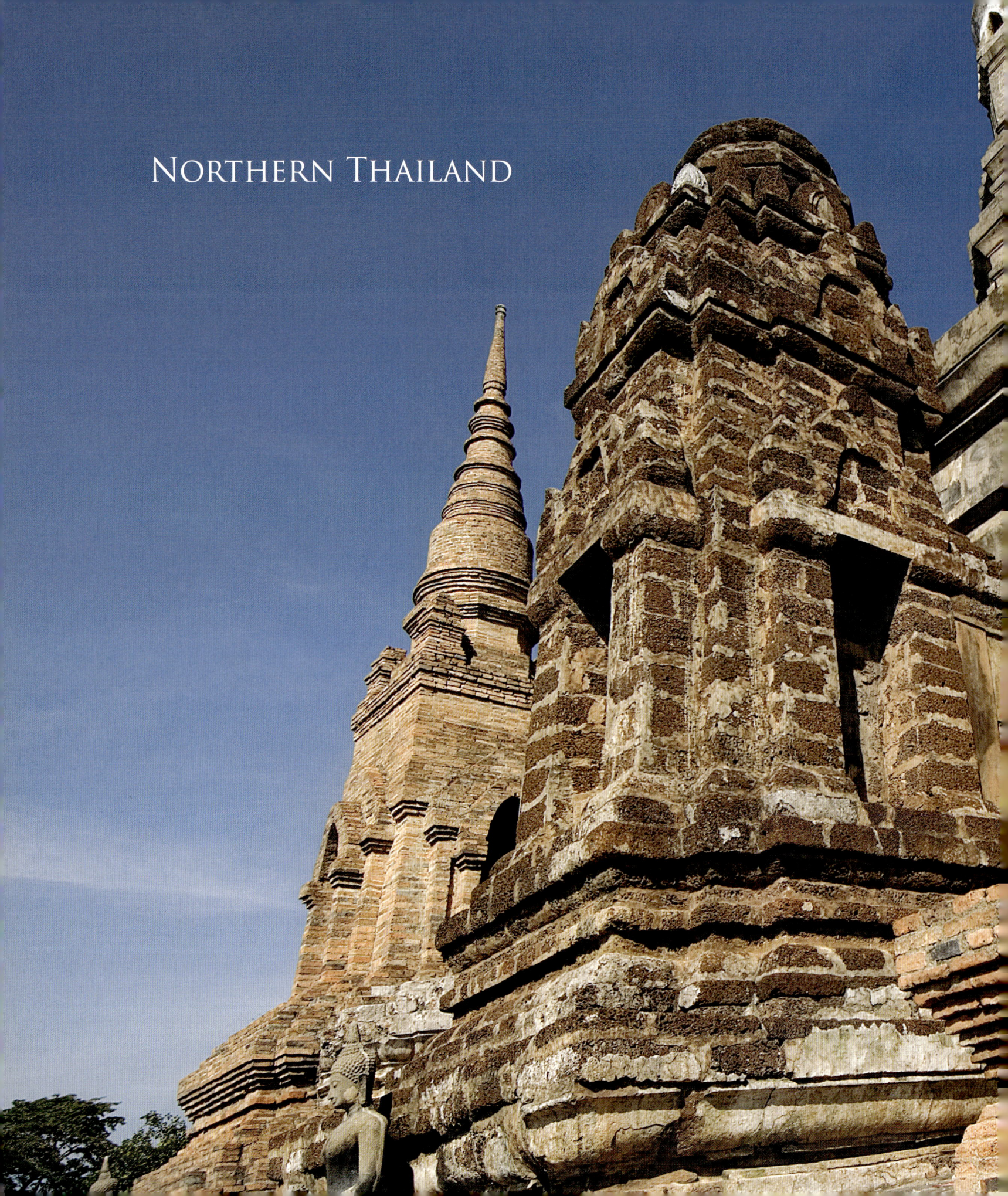

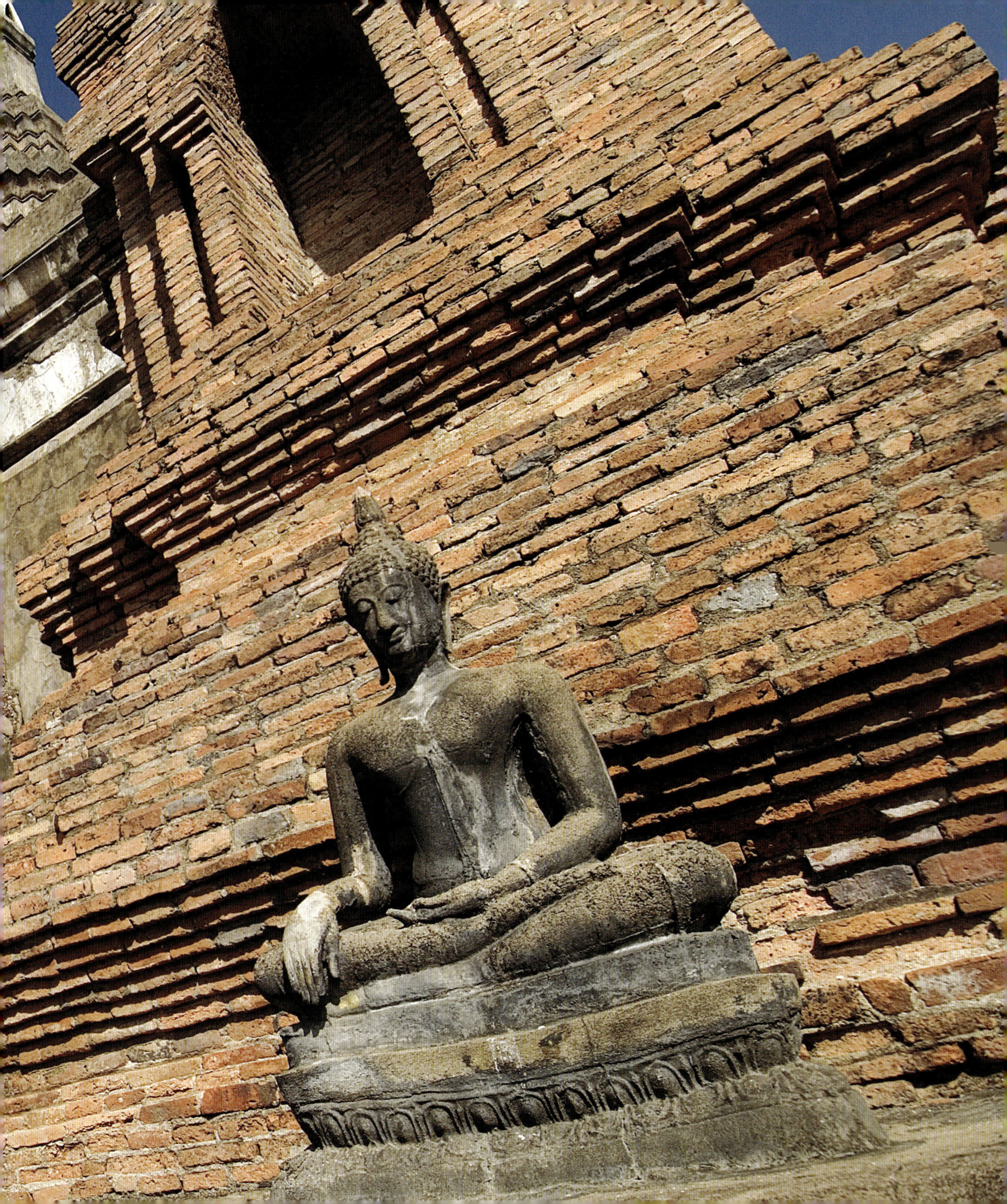

Wat Phra Sing
Chiang Mai

The most venerated monastery in Chiang Mai is home to more than 700 monks and novices and is a principal site for the celebration of Songkran, the joyous Thai new year festival held in mid-April. Wat Phra Sing also represents a prime example of Lanna temple architecture.

King Pha Yu built the main stupa here to enshrine the ashes of his father, King Kam Fu in 1345. In typical classic Lanna style, it is fashioned in a round shape sitting on a square base, and features a gilded *chatree* (ceremonial 'umbrella').

Adjacent to the stupa stands Wihan Lai Kham, thought to have been built between 1385 and 1400 to house the highly revered Phra Sing Buddha image, which was brought to the site by King Muang Ma in 1400. Although Thai folklore says the Phra Sing Buddha originally hails from Sri Lanka, it is sculpted in classic Lanna style, or what Carol Stratton, in her book *Buddhist Sculpture of Northern Thailand*, refers to as 'classic Phra Sing,' found in a wide swathe from Chiang Mai to Luang Prabang during this period. Behind the Phra Sing Buddha, extensive, elegant *lai kham* (goldleaf patterns on red lacquer) in flame and serpent-scale shapes cover the wall.

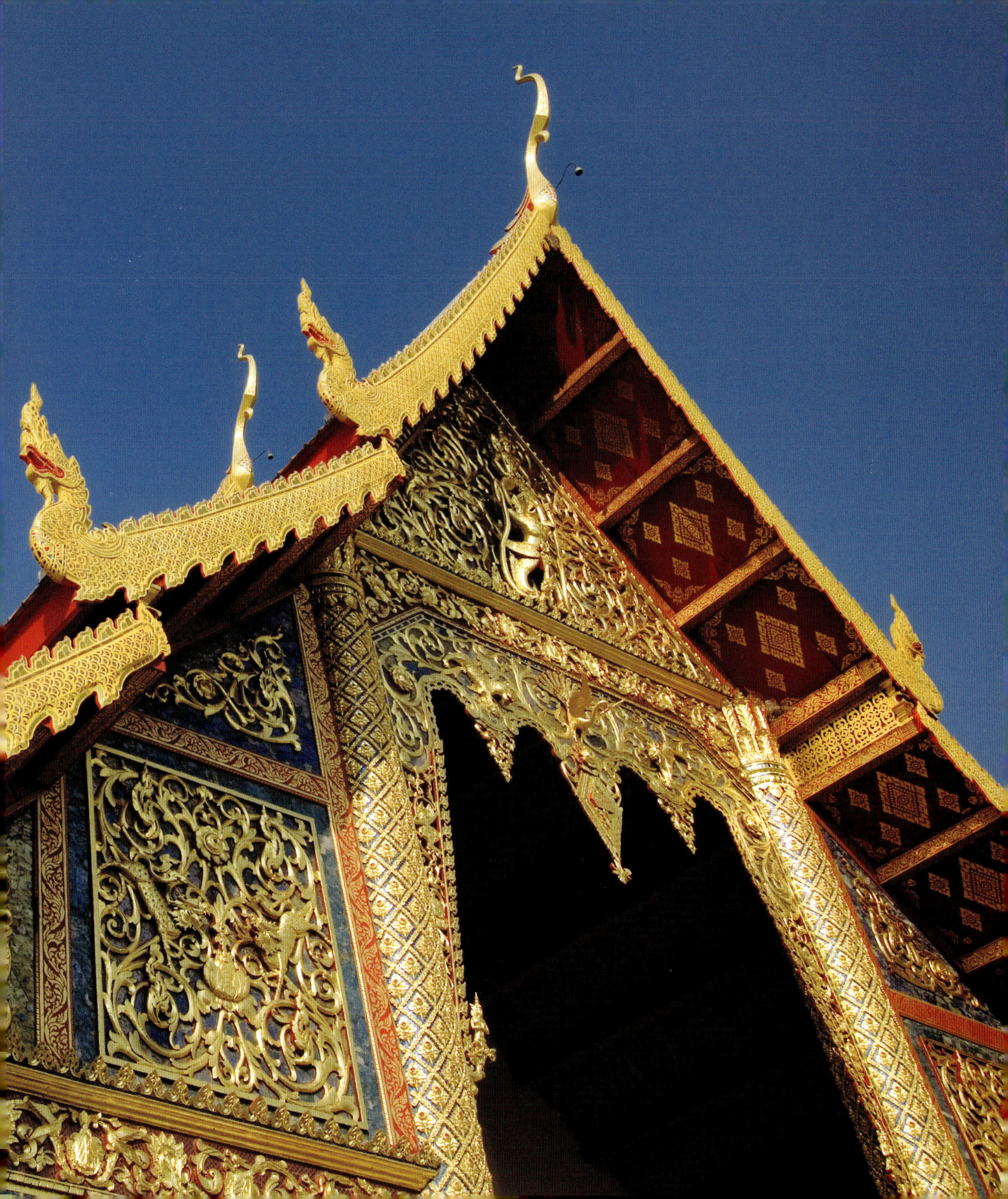

Pages 124-125: The main stupa at Wat Phra Si Ratana Mahathat, Sukhothai.

Pages 126-127: The elaborately carved eyebrow-shaped screen over the *bot* veranda.

Above: Intricate gold-on-lacquer patterns inside Wihan Lai Kham.

Right: The *bot* at Wat Phra Sing, larger than average for a northern Thai structure of this kind, maintains the hallmarks of Lanna architecture.

Similar designs cover the heavy teak pillars which support the roof of the *wihan*.

The other three interior walls feature fine narrative murals dating back to around 1870. The mural on the south wall, depicting the popular northern Thai story of a divine golden swan, *Phra Suwannahong*, is believed to have been painted by a local Chiang Mai artist. Paintings on the north wall, executed by an ethnic Chinese artist thought to have trained in Bangkok, display a much higher level of skill. A small figure crouching in a Chinese sampan above the northwest window may be a self portrait of the artist. The mural here narrates *Sang Thong* (Golden Conch), a non-canonical *Jataka* tale popular in the north about a princess who refuses the courtship of the princes of all the neighbouring kingdoms. Much to her father's regret, she falls madly in love with a terribly ugly, common fellow from a nearby village who, in the end, turns out to be a prince in disguise.

Scattered among the narrative are authentic scenes of northern life, including farmer children cavorting with water buffalo and bare-breasted women wearing Chiang Mai pattern skirts. The range of muted colours, especially ochre and powder blue, are typically Lanna. A carved wooden gable façade extends down from the roof to form a curtain-like screen in floral motifs.

A larger *bot* nearby dates to 1600 and contains a highly ornate *ku* (enclosed shrine for Buddha images) and roof pillars festooned with *lai kham* in diamond patterns. Another building of artistic interest is the *ho trai*, featuring red-lacquered teak walls with gilded rosettes on the top floor, and a bottom floor with thick brick walls decorated with stucco reliefs of *thewada* (Buddhist angels).

Renovations to the *bot*, *wihan*, stupa and *ho trai* were carried out in the 1920s by famous northern monk Khruba Srivichai.

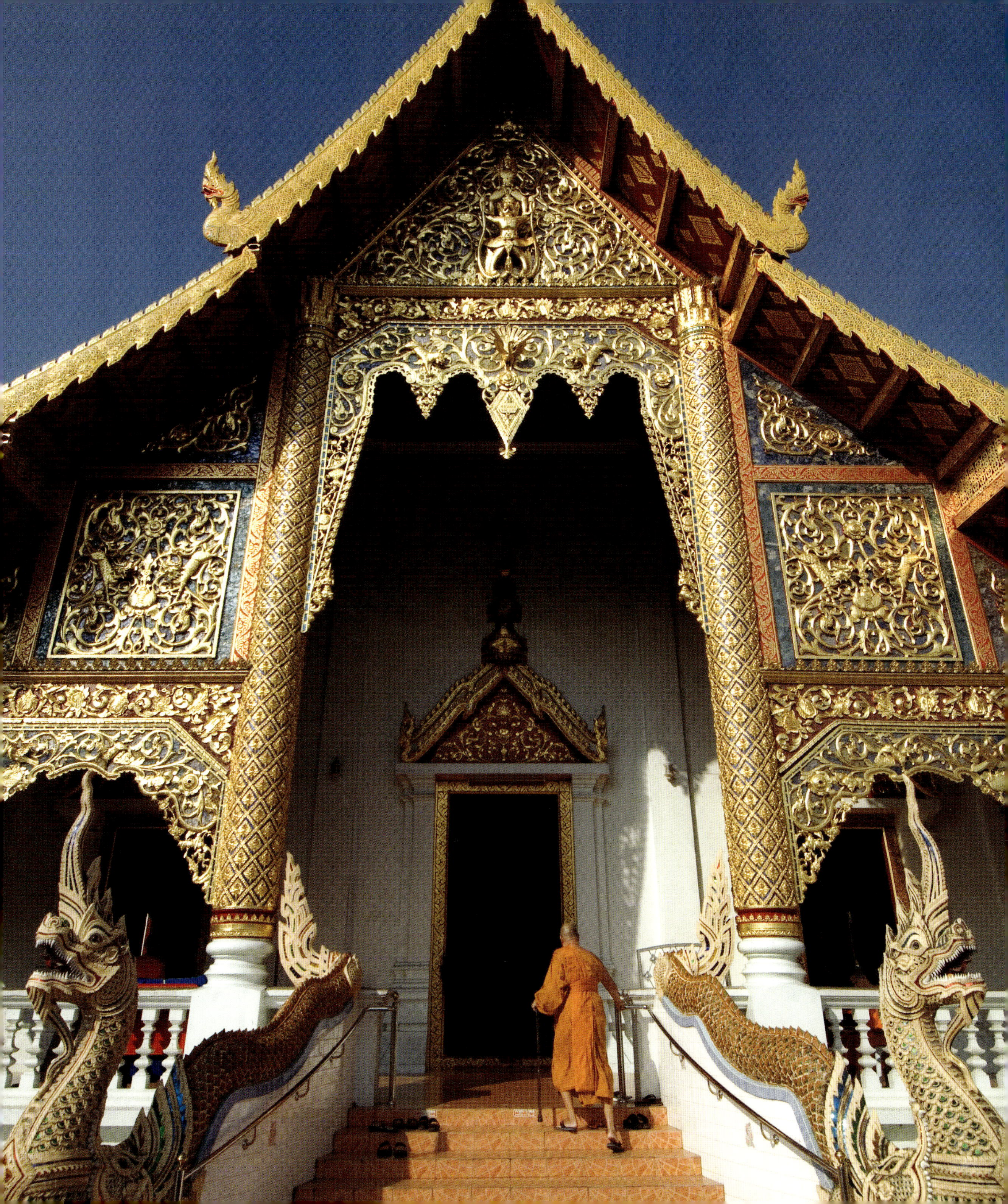

Right & below: Scenes of Lanna court life, folded into *Jataka* murals, tell us much about the costumes of the era.

Far right: Wihan Lai Kham, illuminated after sunset.

130 Buddhist Temples of Thailand

Region: Northern Thailand 131

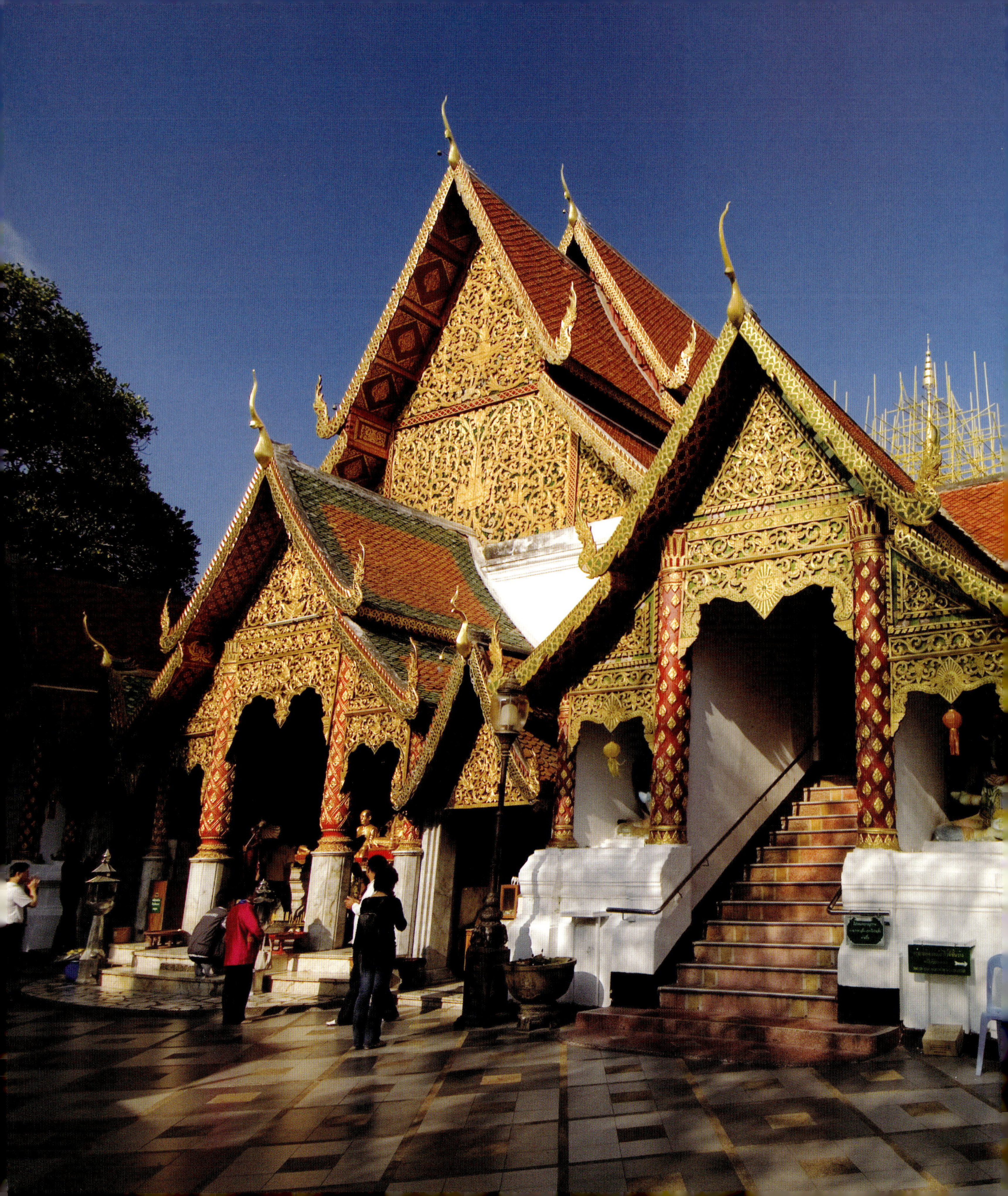

Wat Phra That Doi Suthep

Chiang Mai

Sixteen kilometres northwest of Chiang Mai, Doi Suthep looms over the city like a doting mother. Often shrouded in clouds during the rainy season, and obscured by haze in the dry season, the 1,676-metre high peak is named for the legendary hermit Sudeva, who is said to have lived on the mountain slopes for many years in the 13th century. Believed by Chiang Mai residents to be a guardian entity in itself, the mountain serves as the city's most potent geographical symbol.

Wat Phra That Doi Suthep stands near the summit and is northern Thailand's most important Buddhist pilgrimage point as well as an extremely popular tourist attraction. A *naga* staircase of 309 steps leads up the mountain slope from a parking lot to the *wat*. A steep tram line also ferries visitors up to the monastery grounds.

Established in 1383 by King Keu Na, the centrepiece of the monastery is an exquisite Lanna-style, copper-plated stupa topped by a five-tiered gold umbrella.

According to local legend, the stupa contains a collarbone relic of the Buddha. In fact the relic was originally meant to be enshrined at Wat Suan Dok on the plains below, but just before the interment, the bone replicated itself.

Unable to decide on a site for the new magic relic, King Keu Na mounted it in a shrine *howdah* on the back of a white elephant and waited to see where the animal might take it. The tusker eventually found its way to the summit of Doi Suthep, trumpeted three times, turned three times, knelt down, and died. A stupa was immediately built on the auspiciously selected site. As workers had to carry

134 Buddhist Temples of Thailand

building supplies through thick forest up the mountain, construction took several years. A road leading to Wat Phra That Doi Suthep was only completed in 1935.

The temple was expanded and renovated over the centuries and today is part of Doi Suthep National Park, a richly forested area supporting some 330 species of birds. Fine views over the city of Chiang Mai can be had from a large terrace at the rear of the complex.

On Magha Puja, observed on the full moon day of the third lunar month (usually in February), Thais celebrate the anniversary of a sermon the Buddha gave to a spontaneous gathering of 1,250 monks with inspiring candlelit processions up the mountain to the temple.

Pages 132-133: The main entry portico through the cloister surrounding Phra That Doi Suthep.

Left, top: A reclining bronze Buddha beside the main stupa.

Left, bottom: Oil lamps lit in homage to the stupa.

Above: Phra That Doi Suthep, the octagonal Lanna stupa around which the monastery was built.

Region: Northern Thailand 135

Wat Umong Suan Phutthatham

Chiang Mai

Phaya Mangrai, born near present-day Chiang Saen to a Lao father and Tai Lü mother, founded Chiang Mai as the capital of the Lanna kingdom in 1296. Mangrai is said to have frequently consulted a clairvoyant monk named Thera Chan on issues of state as well as personal problems while the monk was resident at a temple known as Wat Umong Maha Thera Chan – Monastery of the Tunnel of the Great Elder Chan, so named because the *wat* boasted an underground tunnel which the monk used for solitary meditation.

As the walled city grew and flourished, Thera Chan, as the story goes, could no longer meditate in peace. So Mangrai ordered several tunnels dug through a large, flat-topped hill about 4km outside the city. The tunnels were then lined with brick, plastered and painted with Buddhist art, to serve as a refuge for the clairvoyant monk.

Later a Lanna stupa was built atop the hill, and a forest monastery oriented towards solitary meditation grew up at the base of the hill, possibly founded by monks visiting from Sri Lanka after the 8th World Buddhist Synod was held in Chiang Mai in 1477. The monastery was abandoned during subsequent Burmese invasions on Chiang Mai, although Japanese troops were said to have used the tunnels as a stronghold during World War II.

In 1948 a Thai prince named Jao Chun Sirorot began rebuilding the monastery, and in 1949 he invited celebrated Buddhist reformer Buddhadasa Bhikkhu (founder of Wat Suanmok in southern Thailand) to take over the re-establishment of the monastic community here. Buddhadasa Bhikkhu instead sent Ajahn Paññananda, famed meditation master from Bangkok's Wat Cholaprathan, along with other monks to help set up and run Wat Umong

Region: Northern Thailand 137

Pages 136-137: A Buddha shrine at the interior end of a 15th century tunnel.

Above: A monk practices meditation next to his *kuti* (monastic cottage).

Right: Resident monks chanting.

Suan Phutthatham (Monastery of the Tunnels and Buddhadhamma Garden). The revived Wat Umong community thrived and in the 1960s and 1970s was joined by several Western monks who established a "spiritual theatre" containing various works of art explicating Buddhadhamma.

Today the grounds for Wat Umong extend all the way to Doi Suthep, connecting with a natural wildlife corridor that sees deer, birds and other animal life from Doi Suthep National Park. Locals make use of an artificial lake for quiet evening walks. The meditation tunnels and stupa have been restored and are open to the public. A smattering of old murals is still visible in portions of the tunnels. Near the stupa stands a black image of a fasting Buddha, complete with protruding veins and ribs. Although nowadays the resident foreign monk population is relatively low, a Sunday tradition of English dhamma talks still takes place every Sunday afternoon by the lake. A small library with English-language books on Buddhism is also on the premises.

138 Buddhist Temples of Thailand

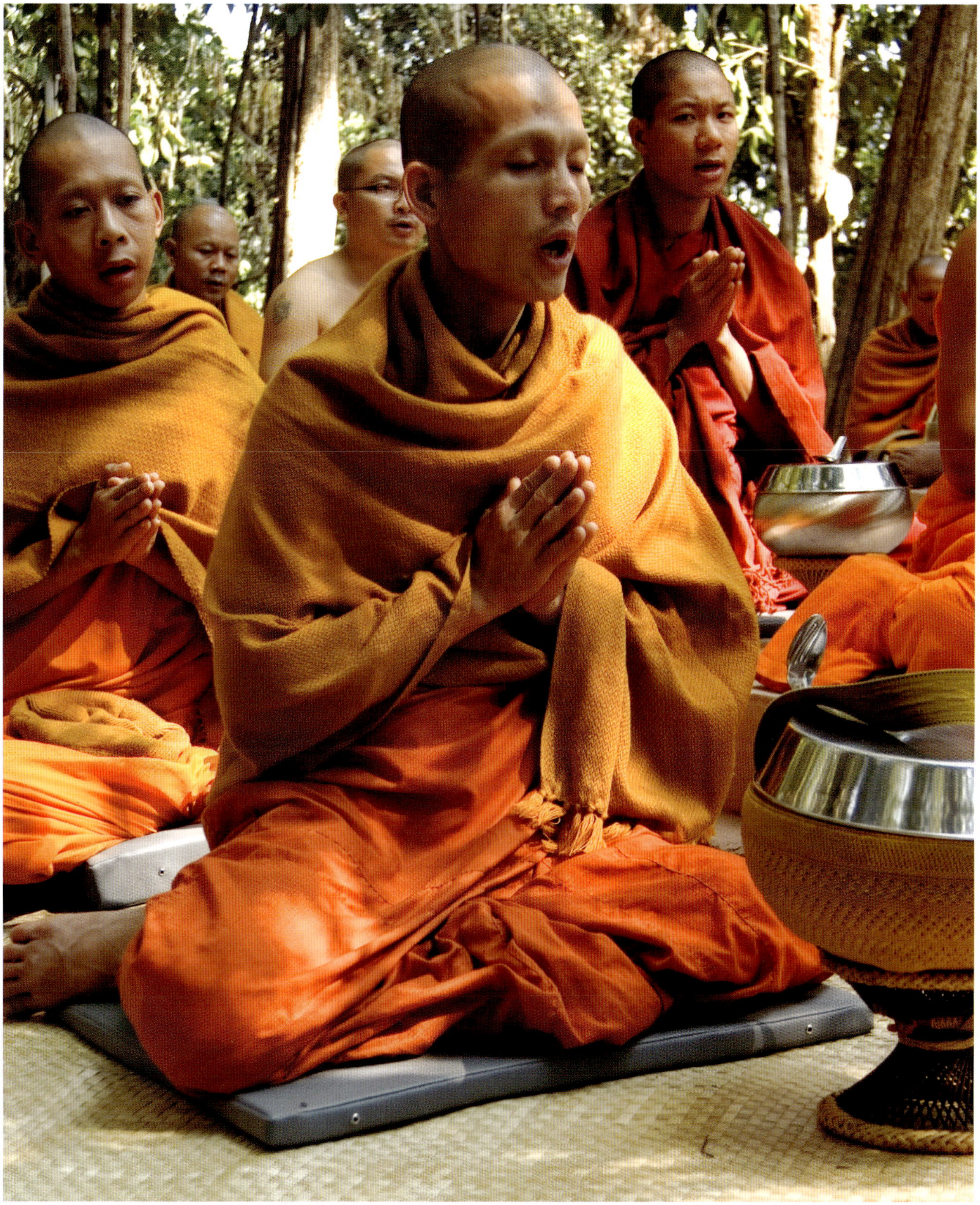

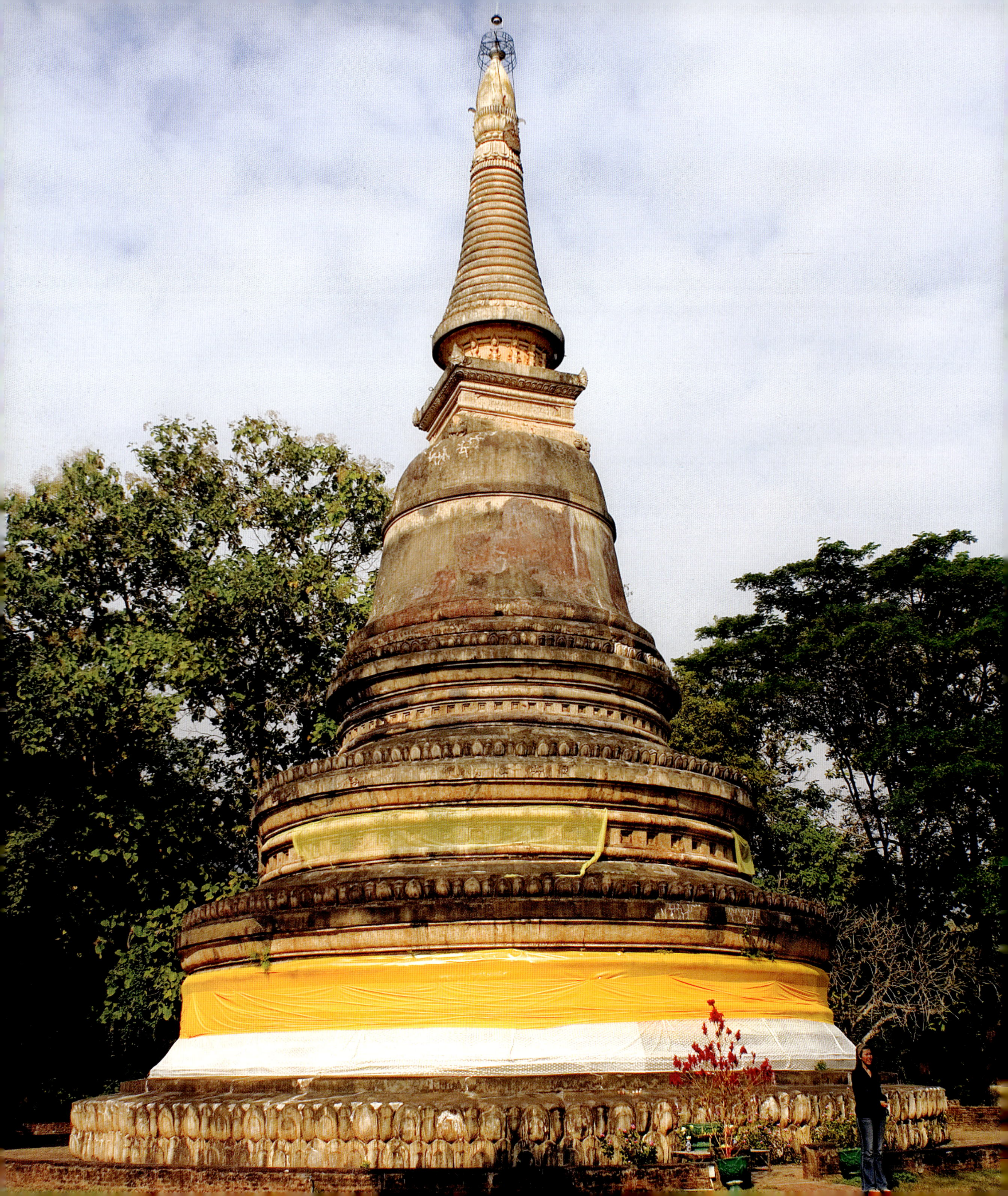

Left: Lanna-style stupa at Wat Umong.

Above: Restored *naga* heads.

Region: Northern Thailand

Wat Ton Kwen
Chiang Mai

Ten kilometres south of Chiang Mai, in the village of Ban Ton Kwen, Hang Dong District, sits one of the least visited yet most valuable Lanna temples in Thailand. In Chiang Mai Province it is perhaps the only surviving monastery where no modern buildings have been added to the compound, and thus the basic layout has not changed since its inception. The Fine Arts Department moved the monks' residences out of the main grounds and into a separate compound in the 1980s. The temple is thought to have been built in the middle of the 19th century – allegedly the first abbot, Khruba In, built the *wihan* in 1858 – and it is remarkably well preserved for its age.

The *wihan* at Wat Ton Kwen, like most classic Lanna temple buildings, features a steeply pitched, three-tiered roof. The influence of Tai Lü architecture is evident in the relatively small windows and doors. Two explanations for their diminutive dimensions exist; first, that they help the building better maintain its warmth, as befits a people who originally migrated from relatively colder climate in southwest China (specifically Sipsongpanna, the Tai Lü homeland), and second, that it made temples more difficult to break into, thus protecting valuable

Region: Northern Thailand 143

Pages 142-143: Sunlight spills through the small Tai Lü-influenced interior of the simple *wihan*.

Right: The wooden roofs and pillars of the *wihan* rest on a solid-looking brick-and-stucco pediment, partly surrounded by an open-air cloister.

Buddhist art and allowing the temple to serve as a fortress when the community was under attack.

The *wat's* official name is Wat Intharawat, but the northern Thai name takes note of the very tall sugar palms (*ton kwen* in northern Thai dialect) that stand just outside and inside the eastern walls. An entrance flanked with lion sculptures is very much in the old Lanna style, while the *naga* balustrade leading up to the portal of the *wihan* also shows Tai Lü influence. Roof ridges, gables and brackets are decorated with fine wood carvings and gilded stucco with coloured glass mosaics. The interior walls are decorated with gilded red lacquer and mural paintings.

The façade and veranda of the *wihan* features beautifully carved wooden panels fitted together. Floral motifs abound in the inside framing and cornices, and the ceiling is adorned with masterfully carved rosettes called *dao phehdan* (ceiling stars).

A long L-shaped, open-sided pavilion, called *sala bat* (almsbowl pavilion), was where Lanna monks would gather to receive almsfood on holy days. The gables are decorated with stuccos reliefs, including a magnificent *makara* (a crocodile-like creature identified by its toothy jaws from which issue either a *naga* or floral matter), and roof tiles are made from local terracotta. All the components are joined with teak dowels and fastened with handmade nails using local construction techniques.

Region: Northern Thailand

Wat Phra Kaew Don Tao
Lampang

Said to have originally been founded by Prince Anantayot, son of Queen Chama Devi of the Mon kingdom of Hariphunchai (today's Lamphun), in the 7th century, Lampang is one of the oldest continually inhabited towns in northern Thailand. With its succession of Mon, northern Thai, Shan and Burmese influences, it is no surprise that the town today claims a few of the north's most interesting historic experiments in monastic architecture. There is no better example of this attractive fusion of cultures than Wat Phra Kaew Don Tao, standing on the north banks of the Wang River.

The dating of the current *wat*, which was most likely built atop an earlier Mon monastery, is problematic but stylistically since it blends Lanna, Shan and Burmese elements its earliest elements date no earlier than the 14th century. The oldest component of the striking complex is the Chedi Phra Boromathat, a beautiful 50-metre Lanna stupa which is of round shape on a square base and said to contain a hair of the Buddha.

An adjacent *mondop* (square, spire-topped shrine room), built in 1909 and decorated with glass mosaic in typical Burmese style, contains a Mandalay-style Buddha image. Standing in front of the gilded stupa is a pillar mounted by a sculpture of a *hamsa* (the Sanskrit word for the Brahminy duck, also known as the sheldrake), a bird important to the Mon cultures of Burma and Thailand as a symbol of royalty and to India as the sacred mount of Brahma, the creator god. The pillar was probably added at about the same time as the Burmese mondop.

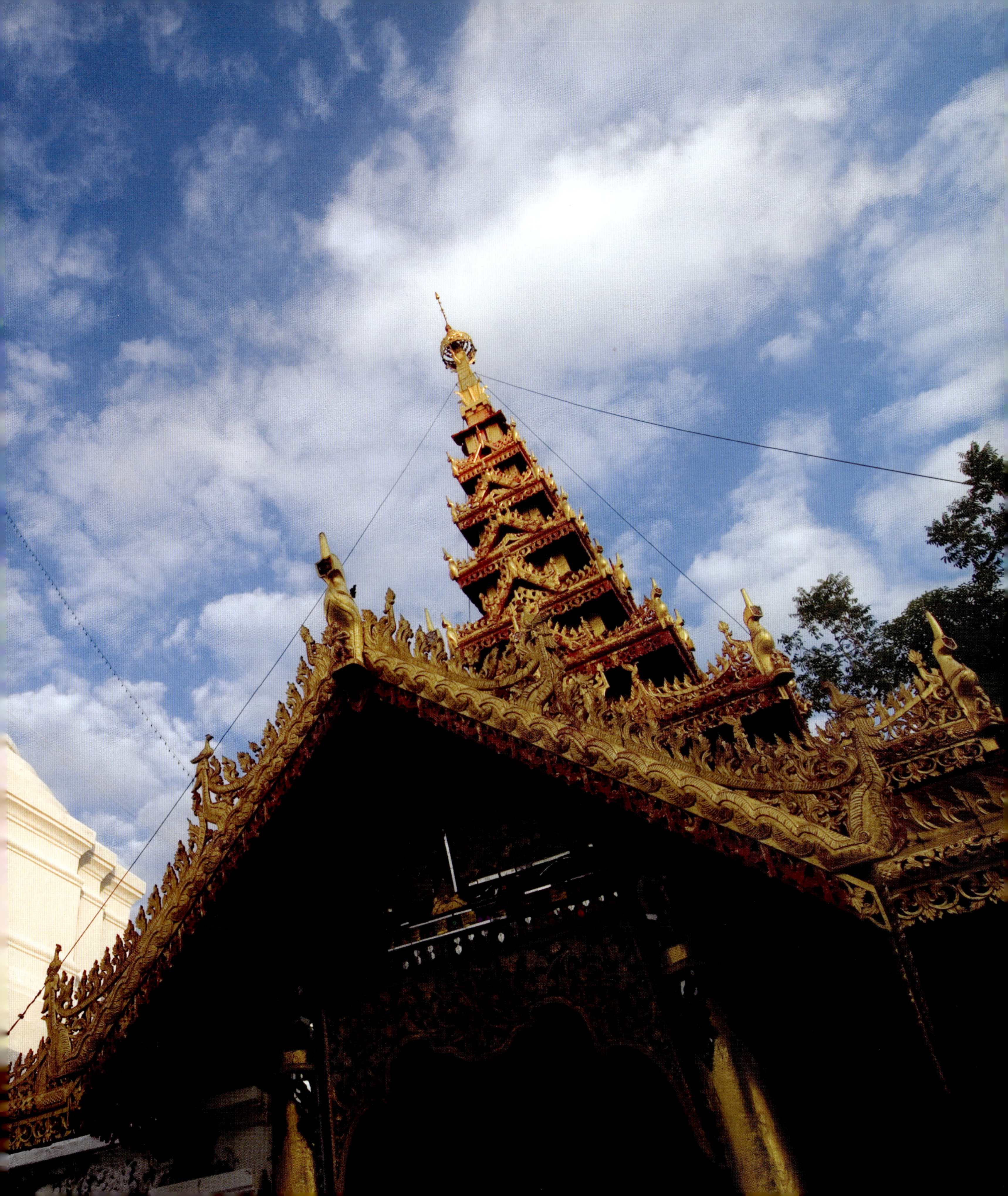

According to northern Thai chronicles, from 1436 to 1468 the temple housed the Phra Kaew, the so-called Emerald Buddha (actually made of jasper) today found in Bangkok's Wat Phra Kaew. If so, it would have been installed in a *wihan* built in the classic Lanna style, of which there is none standing in the complex today. The main sanctuary instead is an exquisitely designed teakwood building showing Shan and Burmese influences, suggesting construction in the 19th century, during the height of the teak industry in Lampang, when many wealthy Shan and Burmese timber merchants sponsored temple construction.

Pages 146-147: The main stupa and *wihan*.

Above: Intricate glass mosaics decorate a roof pillar. In the background sits a Shan-style Buddha image.

Right: A wood carving of a Mandalay-style standing Buddha, surrounded by floral motifs.

148 Buddhist Temples of Thailand

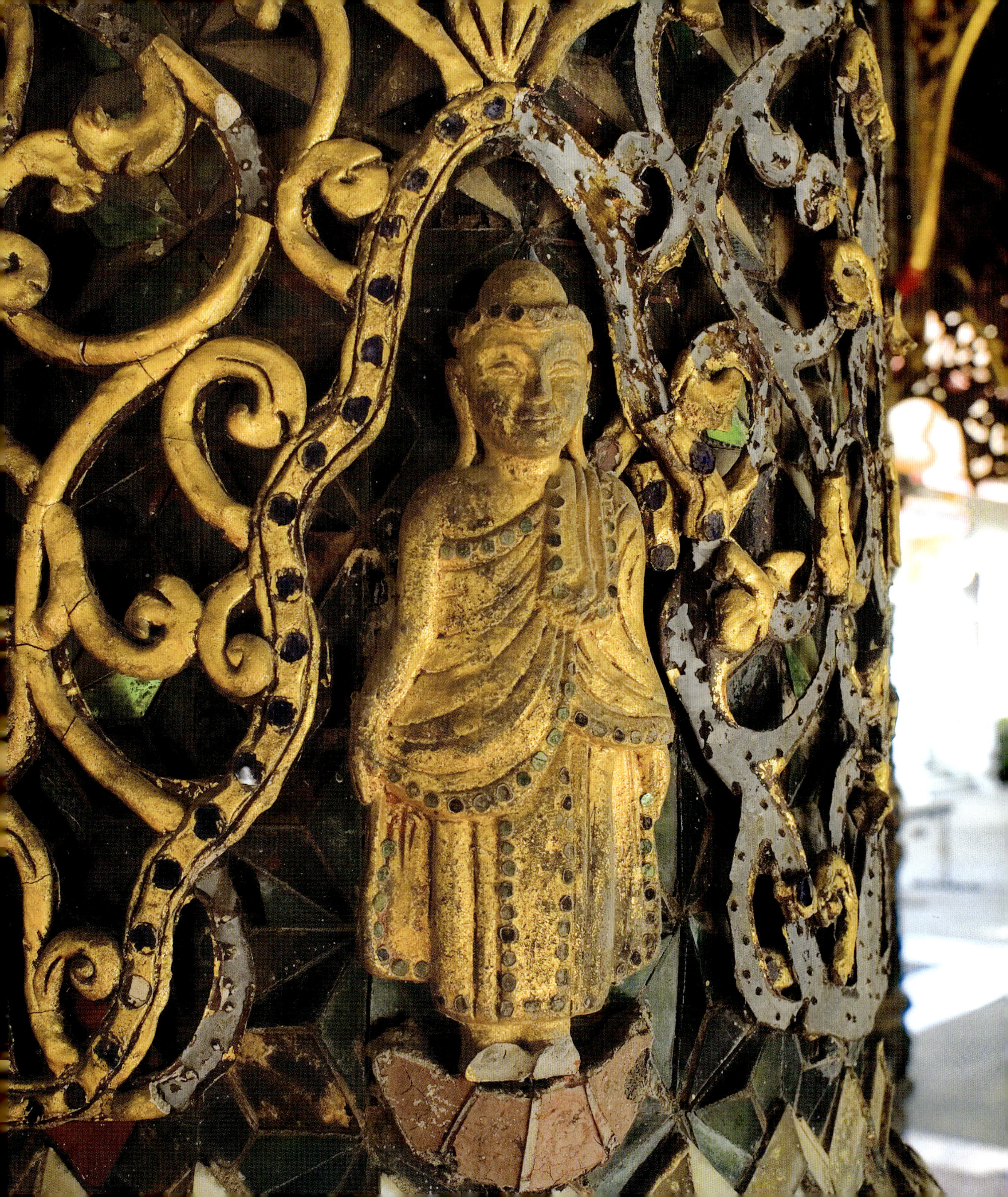

2008 UNESCO Asia-Pacific Heritage Award
Winners
Wat Pongsanuk, Lampang, Thailand
Award of Merit

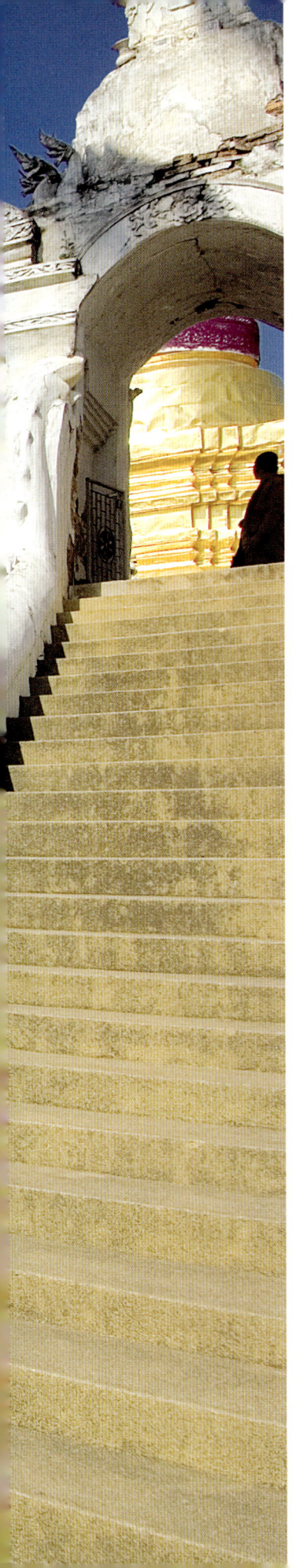

Wat Pongsanuk

Lampang

Also known as Wat Pongsanuk Lampang (Monastery of the Lampang Happy Swamp) this monastery was built on the banks of the Wang River, like Wat Phra Kaew Don Tao. As at the latter, a fusion of artistic traditions traces Lampang's rich ethnographic history. Excavations beneath the *wihan* have revealed at least three layers of ancient foundations which may date back as far as 500 years ago. Successive empires inscribed different names for the temple, including Wat Si Jomkhlai, Wat Si Chiang Phum, Wat Don Kaew and Wat Phayao.

One of the earliest references to Wat Pongsanuk in local chronicles recounts a time when two princes, Prince Kaew and Prince Lin Kan, competed in a river diving competition in 1759 to see who would rule the Lampang. New members migrated to the community when the city of Chiang Saen was defeated by Lampang in 1821, and again when the Burmese invaded Phayao. So important did the temple become that Lampang's city pillar was first erected here in 1857, only to be moved to its current location later.

Today the temple has two adjacent branches, Wat Pongsanuk Nua to the north and Wat Pongsanuk Tai to the south. Standing atop a flat rise, the southern branch is approached by steps threading through a large brick-and-stucco gate that shows Tai Lü influence in its *naga* reliefs. Atop the temple mound, inside the cloister, stands a Lanna-style stupa clad in gleaming copper sheets.

Immediately adjacent to the stupa is the monastery's main claim to fame, Wihan Phra Chao Phan Ong, a unique and impressive structure that follows a general late Lanna layout, with a cruciform floor plan, open walls and triple curving roofs, but with a number of Shan and Burmese details. The *wihan* houses four Buddha images, sitting with their backs facing an iron representation of the Bodhi tree. The images were forged in Chiang Saen workshops in the Thai Yuan style, dating to the mid-16th century. Rows of votive Buddha tablets lining the upper walls of the interior give the *wihan* its name (Sanctuary of 1,000 Buddhas).

Following general decay the local community planned to rebuild the temple in modern style in 2004, but under pressure from Thai art historians they agreed to restore the historic structure instead. The work was carried out using original construction and decorative techniques, with funds raised from religious ceremonies organised by local villagers and businesses. In 2008 the community received a Heritage Award of Merit from the United Nations Educational, Scientific and Cultural Organization (UNESCO) for its efforts.

Pages 150-151: The stepped entry to Wat Pongsanuk shows Tai Lü design.

Right: Reclining Buddha.

Below: The principal structures at Wat Pongsanuk blend Lanna and Shan architectural elements.

Far right: Four Thai Yuan-style Buddha images, sitting back to back.

152 Buddhist Temples of Thailand

Region: Northern Thailand 153

WAT SI RONG MEUANG

LAMPANG

As Lampang, along with Chiang Mai and Phrae, became an important centre for Thailand's late-19th century and early-20th century timber trade, British companies such as the Borneo Company, the Siam Forest Company and especially the Bombay Burmah Trading Corporation received Thai royal concessions for logging operations in the Lampang area (then known to the British as 'Lakon'). They typically brought experienced company employees from Burma, many of them Shan and Pa-O from the Shan States.

Among the more well-paid company officers from Burma, it was customary to donate funds for temple construction to make religious merit. Wat Si Rong Meuang, a product of Pa-O and Shan magnanimity, was initiated on the west side of the town around 1905 and remained under construction till 1912. Originally named Wat Tha Kha Noi Phama, after the village where the Shan craftsmen who constructed the temple lived, it features an impressive teakwood *wihan* laid out so that instead of proceeding from front to back, as in the typical Lanna *wihan*, one takes in a panorama of the richly decorated interior on a horizontal axis, following Shan Buddhist tradition.

The *wihan's* multi-tiered roofs are decorated with filigreed, zinc-coated, iron sheets affixed to the gables, and clustered into nine roof groups or spires said to honour the nine families who sponsored the construction. Carved wooden screens shade the broad veranda. Inside the *wihan* are gleaming polished teak floors and teak roof pillars thickly encrusted with multi-hued glass mosaics. A column in front of the principal Buddha image is carved with images of guardian angels, demons and monkeys, while the ceiling bears elaborate rosettes of gilded carved wood and lesser mosaics. Several Mandalay-style bronze and marble Buddha images adorn the interior altars, along with an impressive Lanna Buddha encased in a *mondop*, plus a number of smaller images of northern Thai provenance.

Region: Northern Thailand 155

156   Buddhist Temples of Thailand

Instead of facing the Wang River, as would be traditional for a Lanna *wihan*, the building faces away from the river. On the grounds stands a typically slender gilded and whitewashed Shan-style stupa, built a few years earlier with donations from an elderly and respected Pa-O lady from the community.

Pages 154-155: The *wihan* was built in the first decade of the 20th century by Shan and Pa-O artisans.

Left: The horizontal layout of the *wihan* is typically Shan/Pa-O, as are the heavily decorated pillars and carved ceiling panels.

Above: The principal stupa, designed and built in the Shan style.

Wat Phra That Lampang Luang

Ko Kha, Lampang

Widely considered to be an exemplar of Lanna religious architecture, and one of the most famous temples in Thailand regardless, Wat Phra That Lampang Luang is located 18km southwest of the provincial capital of Lampang in the district of Ko Kha. The complex was built on a flat-topped hill and enclosed by a high wall, giving the appearance of a fortress as well as a monastery. In fact the *wat* was besieged by Burmese troops in the early-18th century, then retaken by 300 locals under the command of a Lampang warrior known as Thippachak. Legend says the defenders stealthily entered the compound via an underground drainpipe. Today a crude statue of Thippachak stands atop a pillar in the courtyard.

The centrepiece of the complex, Wihan Luang, is believed to have been built in 1476, making it the oldest existing wooden building in Thailand. Entering the open-sided structure, one immediately notices the heavy, round pillars supporting the triple-tiered roof. Originally fashioned from solid teak logs (later replaced with concrete), the pillars are decorated with *lai kham*, gold patterns stencilled onto black lacquer, as is typical of most Lanna *wihan*. Early-19th century *Jataka* murals are painted on wooden panels around the inside upper perimeter of the structure.

Towards the opposite end of the chapel stands a gilded *ku* ('cave' altar) containing a highly revered sitting Buddha image, the Phra Kaew Don Tao, cast in 1563 and once resident at Wat Phra Kaew Don Tao. The local custom is for temple-goers to leave small gold-coloured votive Buddha

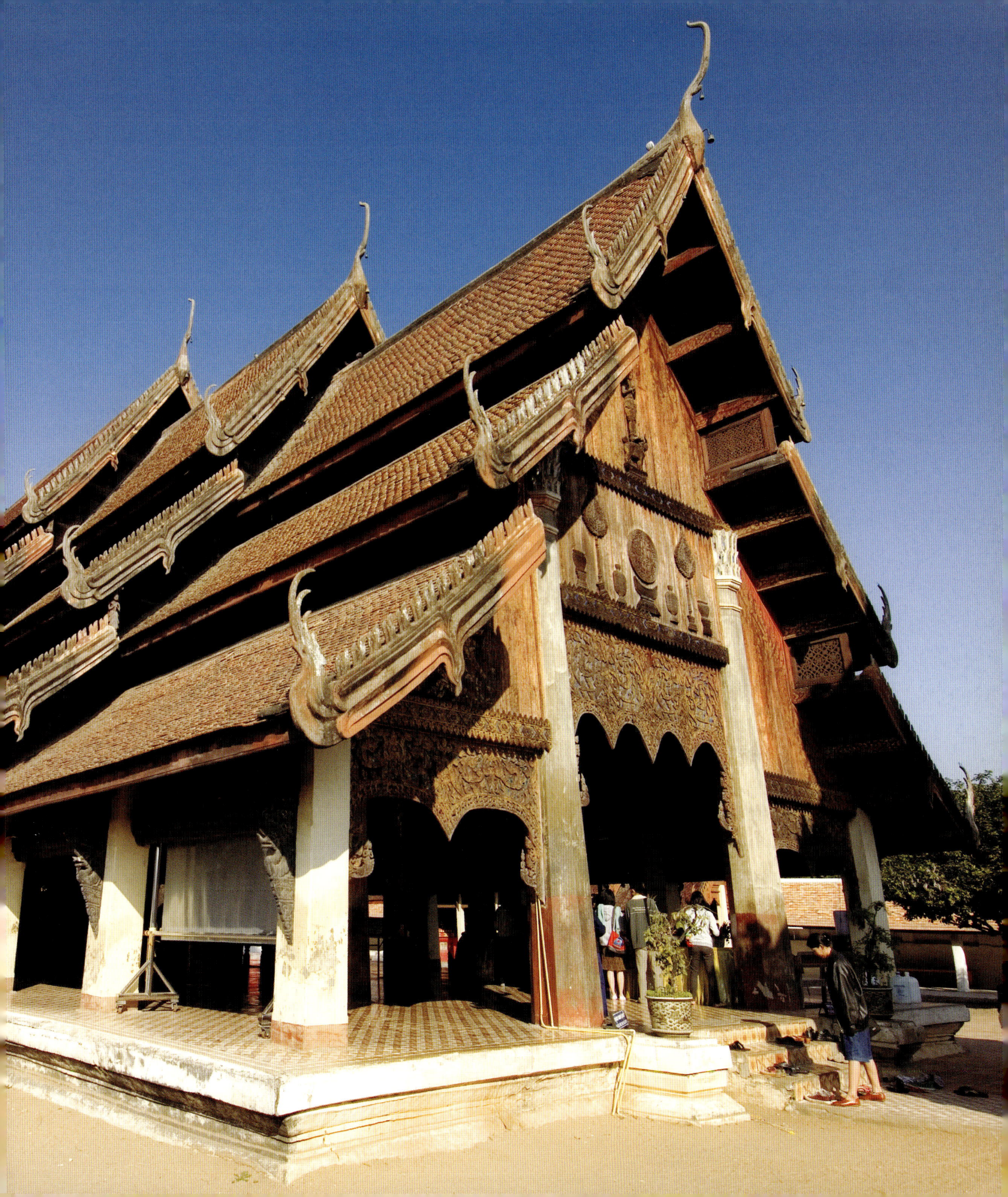

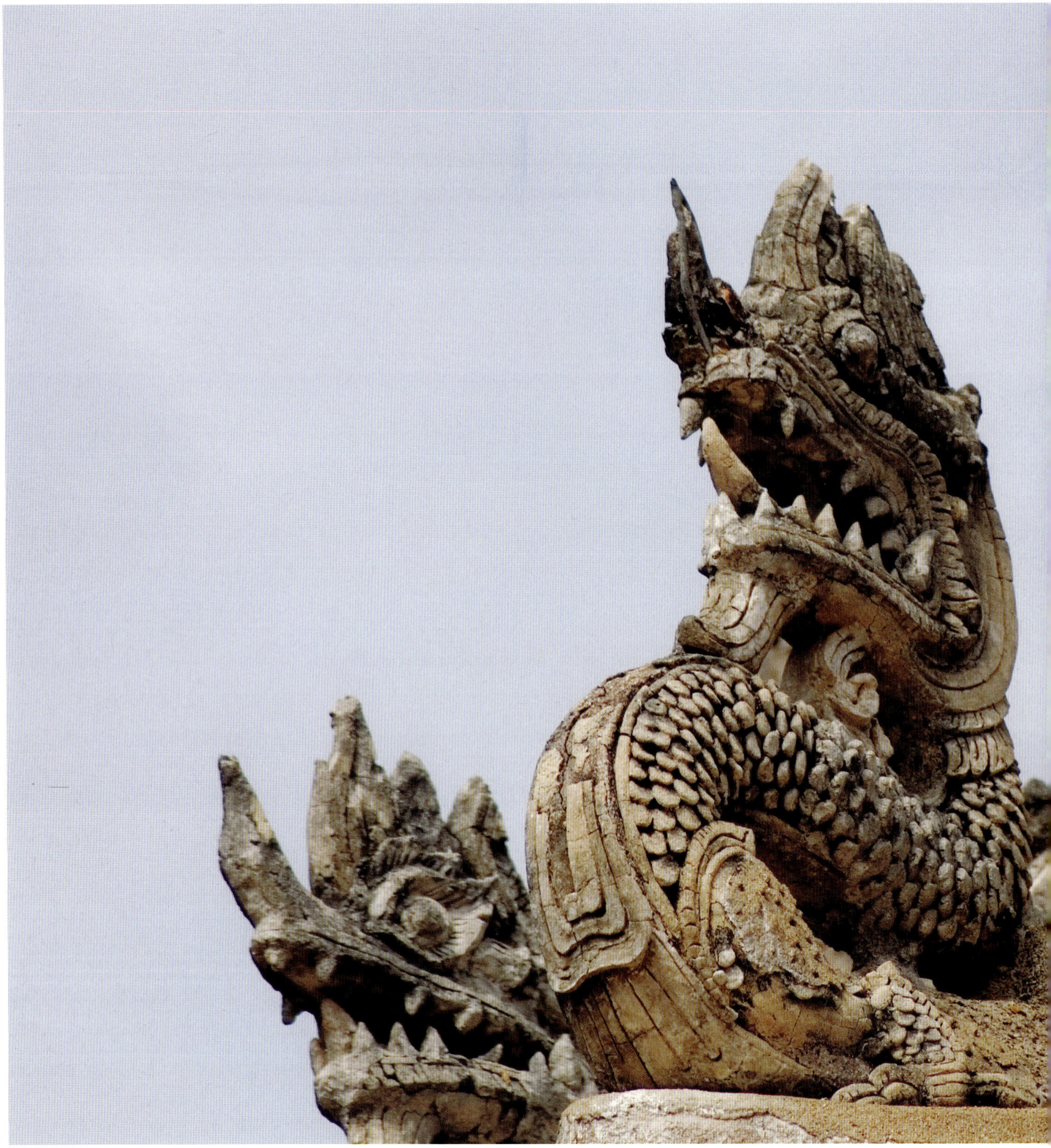

Pages 158-159: The open-sided Wihan Luang is believed to be the oldest surviving wooden building in Thailand.

Left: Ferocious-looking *naga* balustrades.

162 Buddhist Temples of Thailand

figures at the base of the *ku* and to hang *tong* (vertical banners woven of cotton and bamboo, to aid the faithful as 'ladders' to liberation) behind it. A 45-metre high Lanna-style stupa behind the *wihan* was built in 1449 and restored in 1496.

The oldest structure in the compound, the smaller 13th century Wihan Phra Phut, stands to the left of the main stupa and is notable for its original teak pillars and for the striking coloured glass mosaics on its front façade. Wihan Nam Taem, to the right of the stupa, was built in the early-16th century and still contains traces of the original murals, which happen to be the oldest surviving religious paintings in Thailand. Carved wooden eyebrow-shaped screens typical of Lanna temples protect the *wihan* veranda against the late afternoon sun.

Left: The venerable Phra That Luang stupa dates to 1476.

Above: A gilded 'cave altar' in the main wihan contains the Phra Kaew Don Tao Buddha image.

WAT LAI HIN
KO KHA, LAMPANG

Not far from Wat Phra That Lampang Luang in the same district is Wat Lai Hin, a smaller Lanna-era compound offering much charm and few tourists. Its full name is Wat Lai Hin Kaew Chang Yeun (Monastery of the Standing Elephant with a Jewelled Shoulder), a reference to the common apocryphal story that an elephant bearing a Buddha relic clairvoyantly discovered the site. Formally it is known as Wat Sela Ratana Papphataram, which carries the same meaning in Pali.

Wat Lai Hin was founded in 1683 by Phra Kesarapañño, a monk from the Tai Khün principality of Chiang Tung (also known as Kengtung) in what is today Myanmar's Shan state. The learned abbot assiduously collected Pali Buddhist manuscripts from the late-15th to the early-17th centuries, and today the monastery boasts the second largest palmleaf manuscript collection in northern Thailand, as well as the nation's earliest known edition of the *Pathama Sambodhi*, a text about the Buddha's enlightenment which is read aloud annually during Visakha Puja throughout Thailand.

A brick-and-stucco entry gate, so low many visitors must stoop to pass through, is profusely decorated with relief representations of *naga* (dragon-serpent), *kinnaree* (half-bird, half-human), *hong* (Brahminy duck) and other mythical creatures. The interior walls of the gate's arch also boasts ceramic mosaics, made from shards collected from Lampang kilns.

The small *wihan* in the centre of the compound is all original save for the columns and floor, both once teak, but now cement. The bargeboards along the front gable finish in *naga* shapes, a Tai

Left: Wooden gable panels have been decorated with elaborate stucco reliefs, a difficult art.

Above & below: Decorations at Wat Lai Hin include a variety of whimsically carved animal figures.

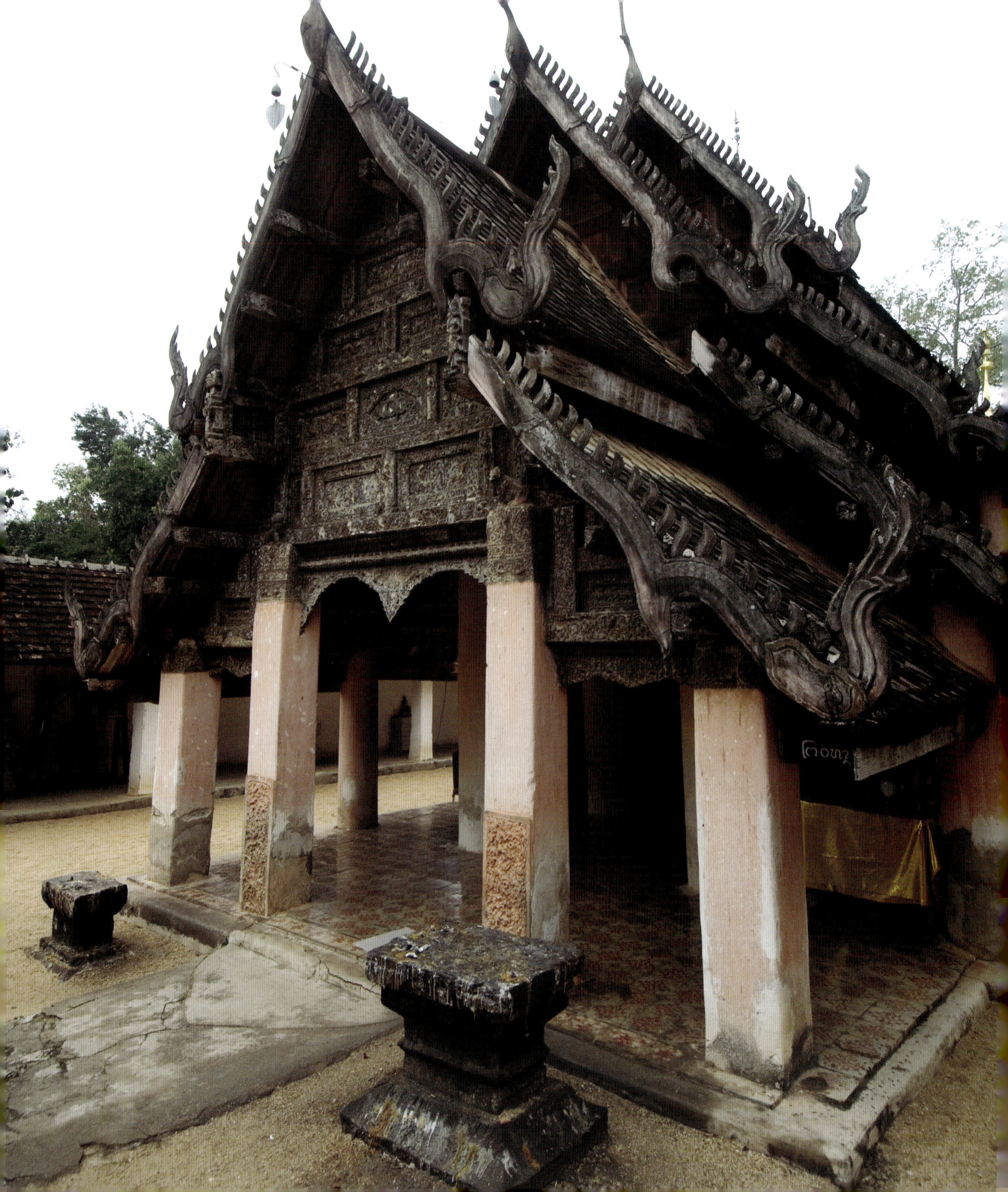

Lü influence found at many older Lanna *wihan*. Inside, the principal Buddha image also appears to be of Tai Lü influence or origin. The wall immediately behind the image is adorned with *lai kham* forming a stylised Bodhi tree into a body halo. The low walls of the structure have been whitewashed, concealing any murals that may once have been painted there.

A small octagonal Lanna stupa stands immediately to the west of the *wihan*. It is likely that the stupa was built first, and that the *wihan* and *bot* were kept relatively small so as to match the stupa's scale. A *bot* next to the *wihan* faces in the opposite direction, and features a distinctive open-sided design seen only in the earliest Lanna temples. Behind the *bot* stands a *sao hong* (pillar surmounted by a Brahminy duck), a Shan/Burmese touch that was probably added in the 19th century.

Left: The wooden pillars of the *wihan* have been replaced with concrete but the carved wooden bargeboards remain intact.

Above: A novice monk inspects a Thai description in the compound of Wat Lai Hin.

Region: Northern Thailand

Wat Sasanachotikaram (Wat Pa Fang)

Lampang

One of the lesser known gems of northern Thailand, this unique, well-preserved monastery on attractive grassy grounds is found on the eastern outskirts of Lampang's provincial capital. A Mon couple in the teak business sponsored the original *wihan* construction in 1892 and immediately invited monks to reside there. In Mon, Shan and Burmese monasteries, monks often sleep in the *wihan* itself or in back rooms attached to the *wihan*.

The two-storey structure is designed in the Shan style, on a horizontal axis with broad polished teak floors on two levels, suggesting that Shan craftsmen were employed. The upper storey is built of teak, the lower storey is brick covered in stucco. The original teak roof pillars still stand, and are unique in Thailand in that the upper half of the pillars are gilded and the lower half are finished in red lacquer, with a wide border of *lai kham* separating them. Ceiling panels feature coloured-glass mosaic rosettes with *lai kham* borders, very elaborate yet dignified. At the back of the hall sit four large Mandalay sitting Buddhas, one of marble and three in bronze. The carved wood throne behind the left-most image is richly adorned with stucco floral designs imbedded with coloured glass mosaic.

Right: The main stupa is Shan in design, and is one of the few gilded Shan stupas in the country.

Region: Northern Thailand

Above: The *wihan* dates to 1892 and contains Mandalay-style Buddha images.

Right: The very unique ordination chapel at Wat Pa Fang.

A room to the side of the main hall holds cabinets containing antique Shan and Burmese Buddhas, lacquerware and ceramics.

A *bot* added in 1906 appears to be one-of-a-kind in Lampang and indeed throughout Thailand, consisting of brick-and-stucco hall topped with multi-tiered wooden roofs. Stucco reliefs on the rear of the *bot* are fashioned in the shapes of a peacock (a Shan-Burmese solar symbol), and angels. Door and window frames also feature floral reliefs, while tidy *lai kham* designs decorate the window sashes. Uniquely Burmese, the *sema* (ordination marker) are rectangular rather than shaped like Bodhi leaves, and are inscribed in Burmese script. According to the temple history, the *sema* were blessed by the Siamese monarchy in 1906 even though Lampang had not yet been annexed to Siam.

A *sao hong* (pillar topped by a Brahminy duck sculpture) stands next to the *bot* and is the only visibly Mon detail in the compound. It was given to the monastery by donors in the Mon cultural capital of Hamsavadi (today's Bago, Myanmar). The base of the pillar is protected by a lavish brick-and-stucco hall, similar in design to the *bot*. A second, more modern *sao hong* stands nearby.

Also dating to 1906 is a gilded Shan-style stupa with octagonal sides. Eight niches at the base of each side contain Burmese-style sitting Buddha images. Each niche is labelled for one of the eight days in the Myanmar Buddhist week, with reliefs of the animals associated with each Buddha beneath the image.

170 Buddhist Temples of Thailand

Region: Northern Thailand

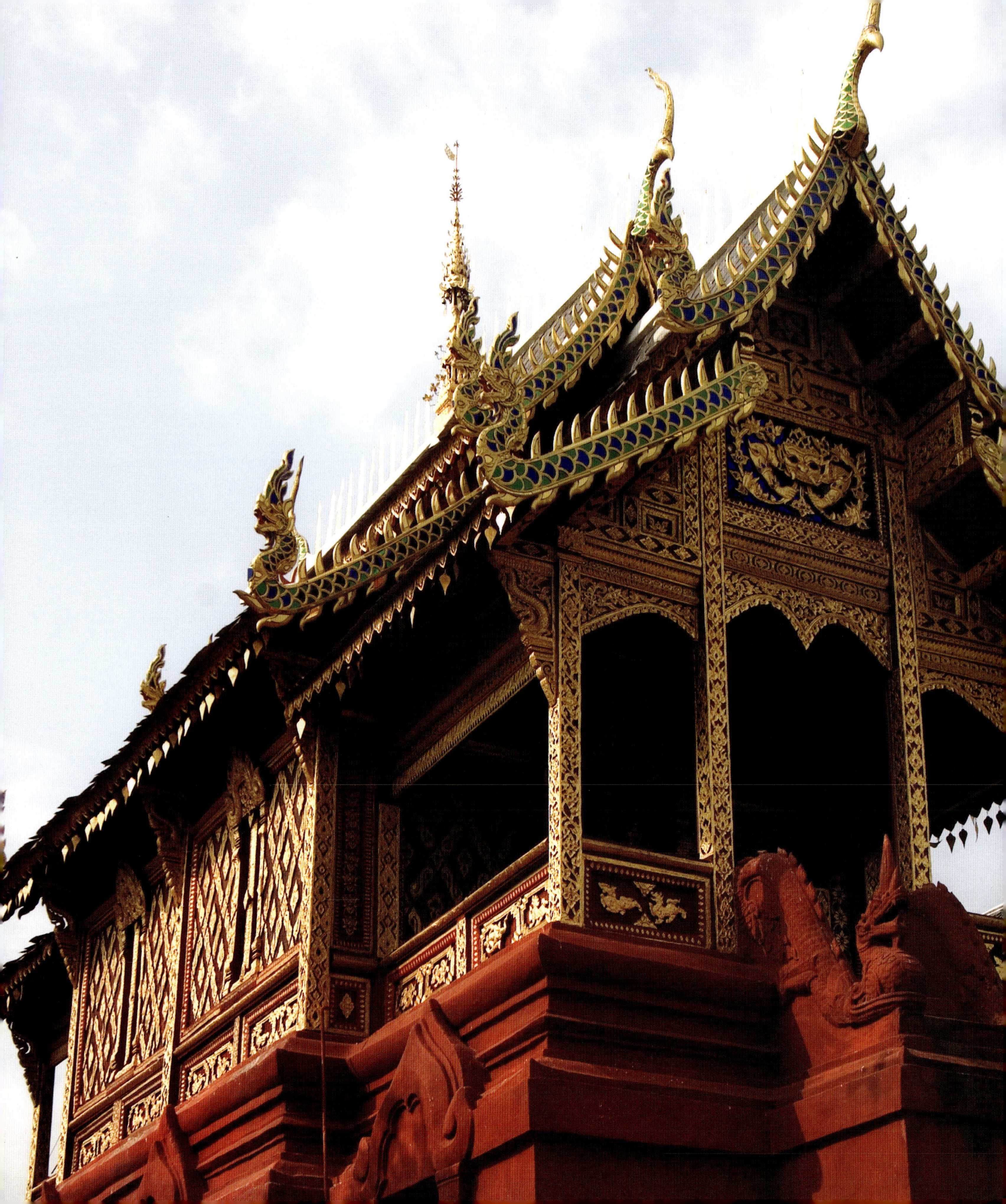

Wat Phra That Hariphunchai

Lamphun

Lamphun, capital of the province of the same name just south of Chiang Mai, often claims to be Thailand's oldest continuously inhabited city, having been founded as 'Hariphunchai' in AD 663 by Mon immigrants from Lopburi farther south. A monastery on the site where Wat Phra That Hariphunchai now stands was built during the reign of Mon King Athittayarat in AD 897.

In the late-12th century, King Mangrai of Chiang Mai invaded Hariphunchai and made it part of the Lanna kingdom, and in 1433 the monastery was renovated and expanded under King Tilokraj, who added five new stupas to enshrine Buddha relics. The most significant Tilokraj-era stupa, monastery namesake Phra That Hariphunchai, mixes Lanna and Sinhalese styles, stands 46 metres high and is topped by a nine-tiered umbrella made of gold weighing 6.5 kg. This stupa later served as a model for Phra That Doi Suthep in Chiang Mai. It was allegedly built on top of a smaller Mon-style stupa in 1477.

Considered to be one of the 10 holiest stupas in Thailand, the monument's most famous features are eight copper plates on its bell bearing life-size repoussé figures of walking and standing Buddha images, which may have been stripped from the earlier Mon stupa. Although a 1980 restoration obscured the Buddhas with lacquering and gilding, the faint outlines of the figures can still be seen when the sun hits the stupa at the right angle.

An older stupa on the monastery grounds, Pathumawadi Chedi, features five, stepped brick terraces with niches for Buddha figures similar to the more

Pages 172-173: The upper storey of the Lanna-style *ho trai*.

Above: A graceful reclining Buddha image.

Right: The dome of the principal stupa, built in Lanna style to encase a smaller Mon stupa inside, is decorated with standing Buddha repoussé panels thought to have been removed from the original stupa.

famous Chedi Kukut at Wat Chama Thewi. Although often considered a Mon architectural style, there is a very similar stupa in Sri Lanka, the Satmahal Prasada in Polonnaruwa. It is possible, however, that the Sri Lankan version was influenced by the Lamphun stupas.

The *wat's* main *wihan* bears all the standard features of a Lanna *wihan*, such as an elaborately carved eyebrow-shaped screen and abundant *lai kham* decorations, but is much larger than is typical. Inside are several antique Buddha images, the most striking of which is the 'Buddha with Sharp Shins,' a Lanna-era Buddha that blends characteristics from the Thai Yuan, Hariphunchai, U Thong and Lopburi schools. Cast in 1489, it is named for the image's sharply delineated shinbones. There is only one other similar example in northern Thailand, found at Wat Si Koet, Chiang Mai. Also on display in the *wihan* is a Thai Yuan-style sitting Buddha dating to 1807.

The monastery grounds also contain a Lanna-style *ho trai* (Tipitaka library), boasting a teak sanctuary resting high on a red-painted pedestal. Another *wat* attraction is a huge bronze gong hanging in an open-sided pavilion, and said to be

Region: Northern Thailand 175

Wat Chom Sawan

Phrae

Surrounded by vast teak forests, Phrae became a vital centre for the teak trade in the late-19th and early-20th century, with many Shan and Burmese migrants participating as skilled workers, accountants and warehouse managers for Siam-licensed British companies. Around 1910–1912 a group of Shan teak workers built Wat Chom Sawan outside the walled city of Phrae to the northwest. Unlike at the more Lanna-influenced, 'hybridised' monasteries inside the city, the design and construction at Wat Chom Sawan followed traditional Shan and Burmese norms.

While most monasteries in northern Thailand consist of several buildings, separated by function, here a single rambling, multi-tiered wooden structure encompasses the functions of *wihan* (for public gatherings), *bot* (for monastic ordination) and *kuti* (monks residences). Roofs on the main body of the building are gabled in double tiers in typical Shan style, while two stepped entry porticoes are topped by tall, elaborate stacked roofs such as those commonly seen in Burmese temples in Yangon and Mandalay from the same era. Bargeboards along the main roof gables are Lanna/Tai Lü in design.

The interior of the *wihan* features pillars and coffered ceilings decorated with goldleaf on red lacquer along with the relatively restrained use of coloured glass mosaics and carved wooden detailing. The *wat's* most notable Buddha image is made of lacquerware. Several layers of lacquer were applied to a bamboo lattice frame woven in the shape of a sitting Buddha, and then carefully covered in goldleaf. Named Luang Pho San, it gives the appearance of a heavy bronze image although in fact it is relatively light and easy to lift. Another Buddha on the main altar is carved from elephant tusk, while a small marble image sits inside a diminutive crystal stupa. One final prized possession on display at Wat Chom Sawan is a set of Pali Buddhist texts inscribed on 16 ivory sheets in Burmese script.

A tall, slender copper-crowned stupa built in Shan style has lost much of its ornate stucco to reveal the artful brickwork beneath.

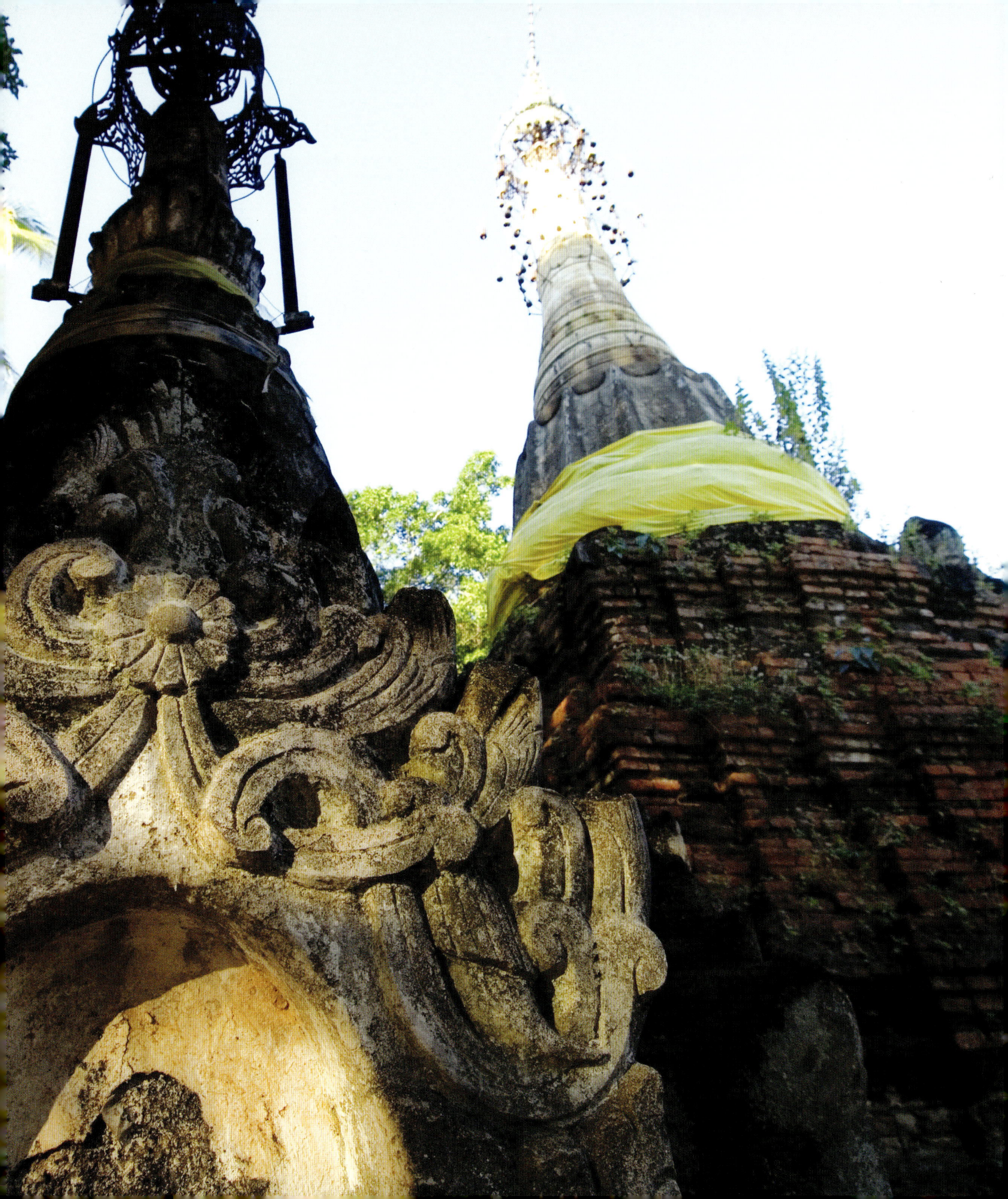

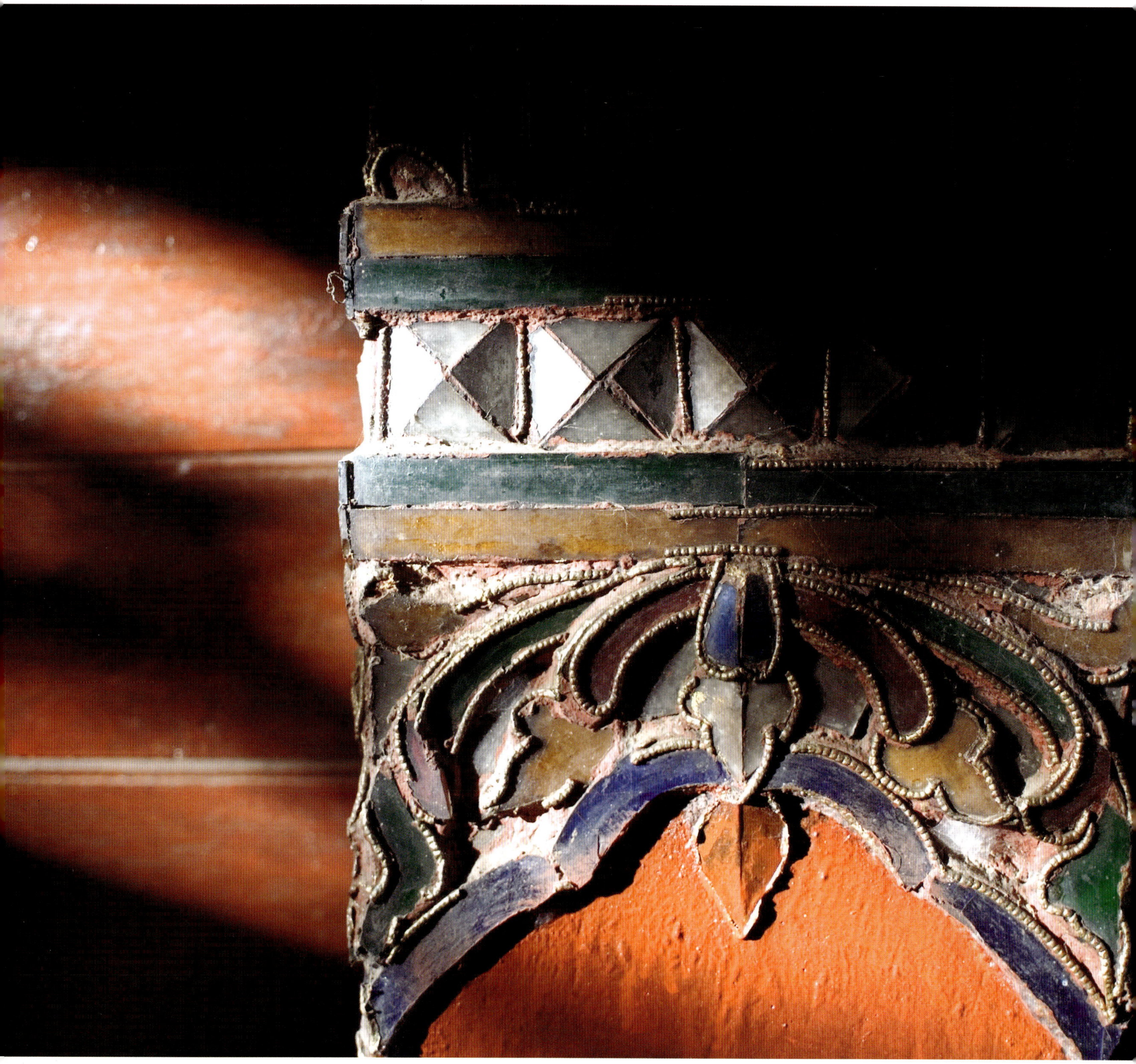

Pages 176-177: Shan-style stupas stand in partial ruin.

Far left: Burmese-style coloured-glass decorations on the interior of the *wihan*.

Left: This seated Buddha image is made of lacquer layered over a bamboo frame, a Shan innovation seldom seen in Thailand.

Below: Porticoes fronting the *wihan* are Burmese in style, and may have been a later addition.

Region: Northern Thailand 179

Wat Phra Si Ratana Mahathat

Phitsanulok

Archaeologists believe Phitsanulok was originally established as a small Angkor satellite state in the 11th century. No reliable written records of that era exist however, and it is not until the Sukhothai era that history stands on firm ground, when King Lithai created a Thai-dominated city here, using the junction of the Nan and Yom rivers as a line of defence against Siam (Ayuthaya) to the south.

King Lithai commissioned Wat Phra Si Ratana Mahathat in 1357. Legend says he sent for well-known artisans from Si Satchanalai, Chiang Saen and Hariphunchai (Lamphun) to cast three high-quality bronze Buddha images for the temple. Five Brahman priests oversaw the work to ensure proper ceremonial protocol. The first two castings came out well, but the third required three attempts before it was decreed the best of all. Legend has it that a white-robed sage appeared from nowhere to assist in the final casting, and then disappeared. This third image was named Phra Chinarat (Victorious King), and it became the centrepiece of the monastery. All three remained at the *wat* for 400 years, at which point the other two, Phra Chinasi and Phra Satsada, were moved to Wat Bowonniwet in Bangkok

Considered by many to be the most beautiful Buddha image in Thailand, Phra Chinarat Buddha was cast in classic late Sukhothai style, but with the major stylistic addition of a flame-like halo circumscribing a dramatic silhouette around the head and body. The flame halo transforms into dragon-serpent heads on either side of the image. In addition the head of the image is proportionately wider than for standard Sukhothai Buddhas, adding an impression of strength and solidity. A local bronze foundry in the city – one of the most successful in Thailand – does a steady trade casting Phra Chinarat copies, small and large.

The *wihan* containing Phra Chinarat is also a masterpiece of Thai temple art.

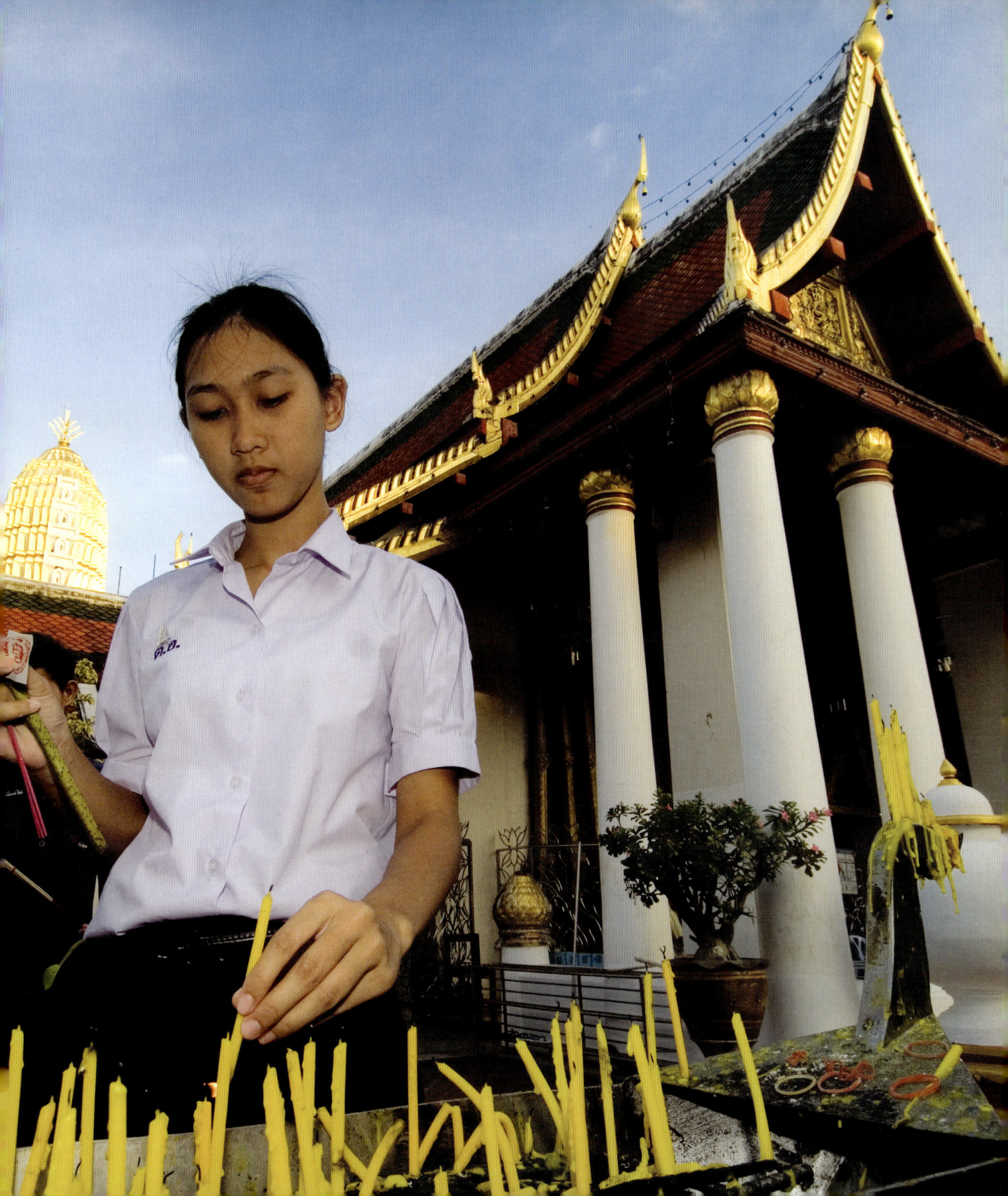

Pages 180-181: A schoolgirl offers candles, incense and flowers at an outdoor altar in front of the *wihan*.

Right: The famous Phra Chinnarat.

182   Buddhist Temples of Thailand

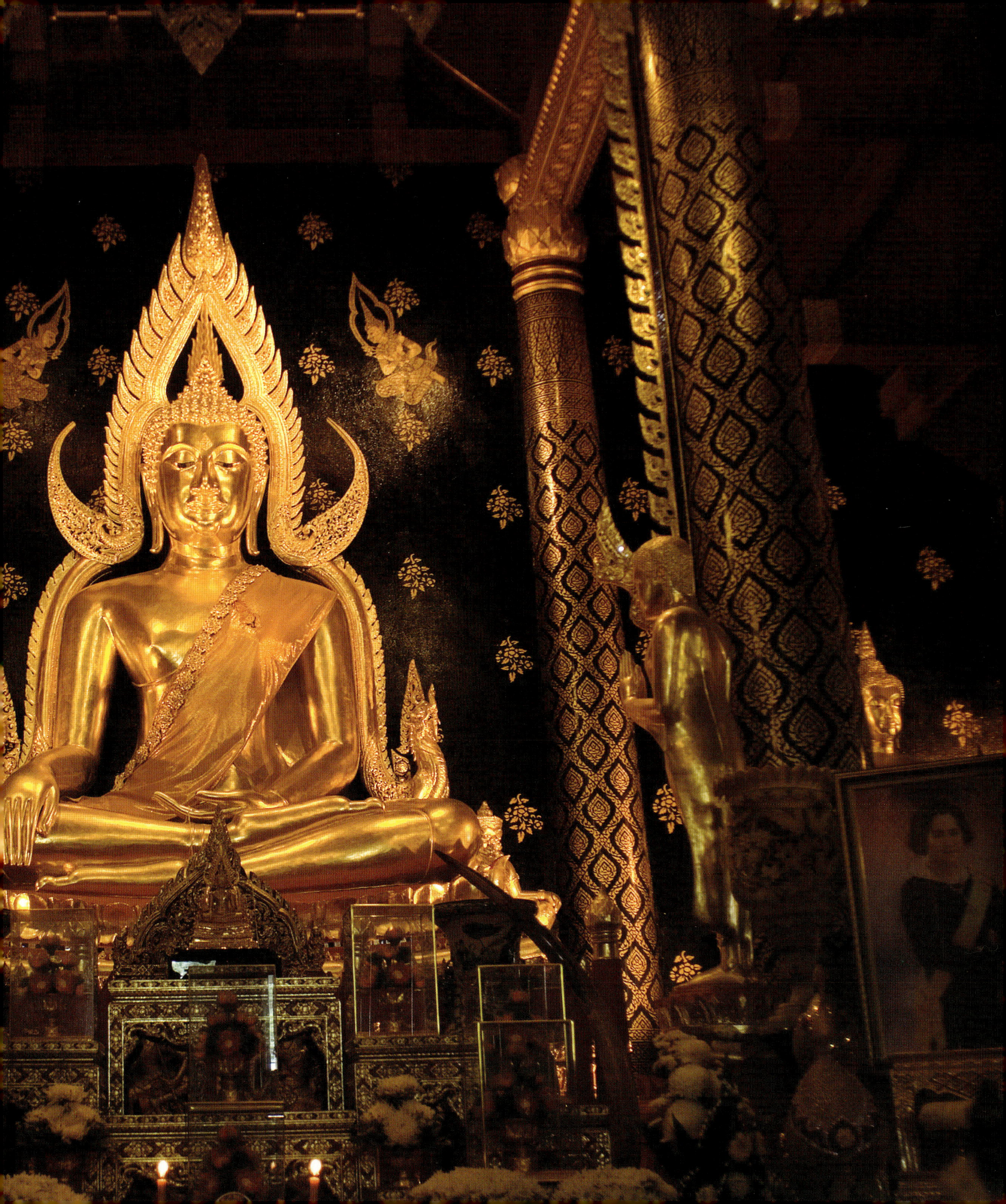

In the classic Lanna style, it features low walls, lacquered teak columns and a low-swept roof. Narrow slits in the walls toward the main altar are reminiscent of Lan Xang architecture in Luang Prabang, Laos. In the relatively small and dimly lit interior space, the famed image appears larger than it might in a grander *wihan*.

The doors of the *wihan* are inlaid with mother-of-pearl in intricate designs sponsored by King Boromakot in 1756, during a 27-year interval when Phitsanulok served as the capital of Siam. *Jataka* murals added in the 19th century feature the deep, jewel-like tones favoured in Ratanakosin-era Bangkok

Behind the *wihan*, a tall *prang* with complex reticulated lines and 'corncob' shape was added during the Ayuthaya era, probably replacing an earlier Lanna stupa.

Above: Seated Buddha images in the cloister.
Right: Entry to the main *wihan*.

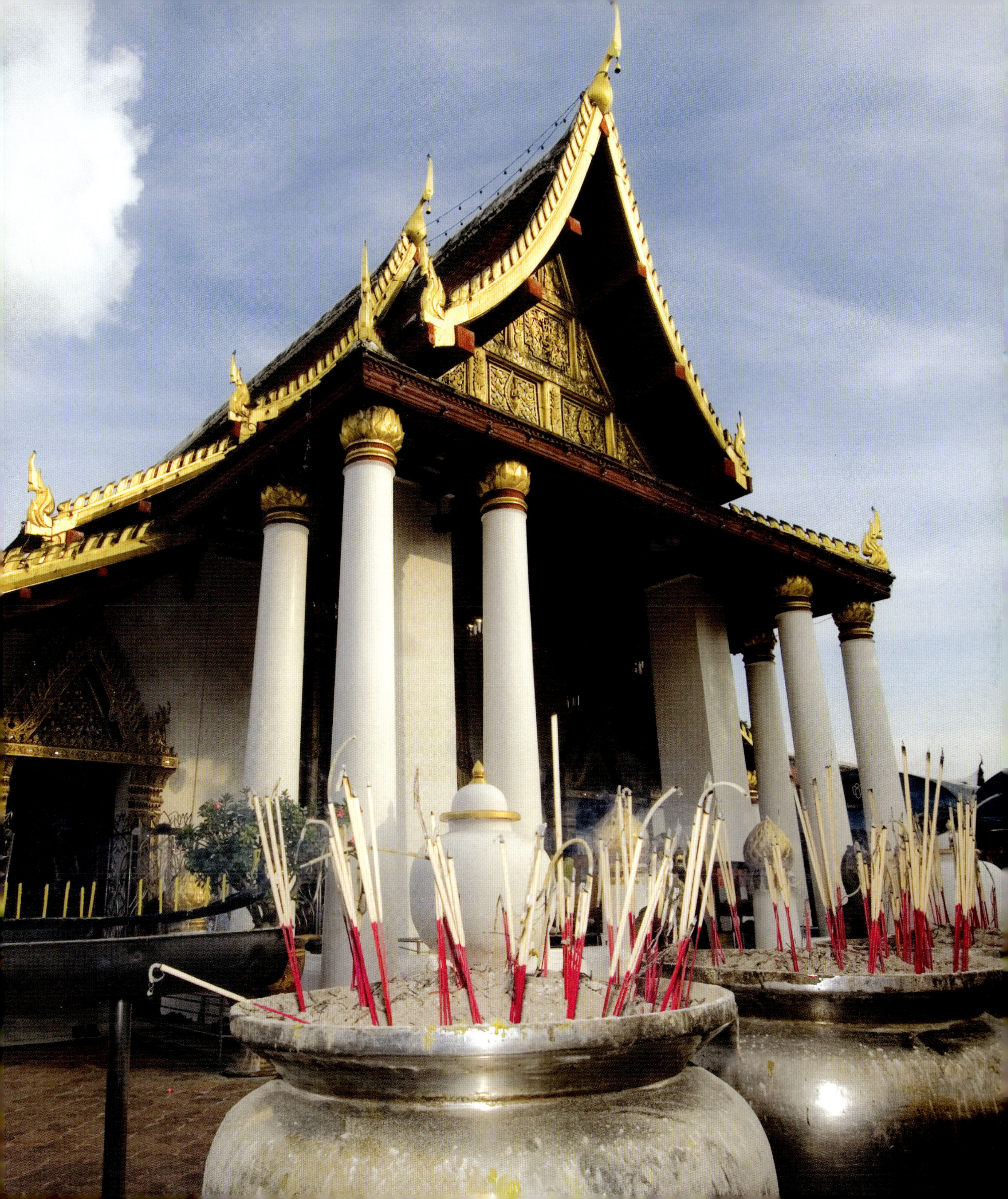

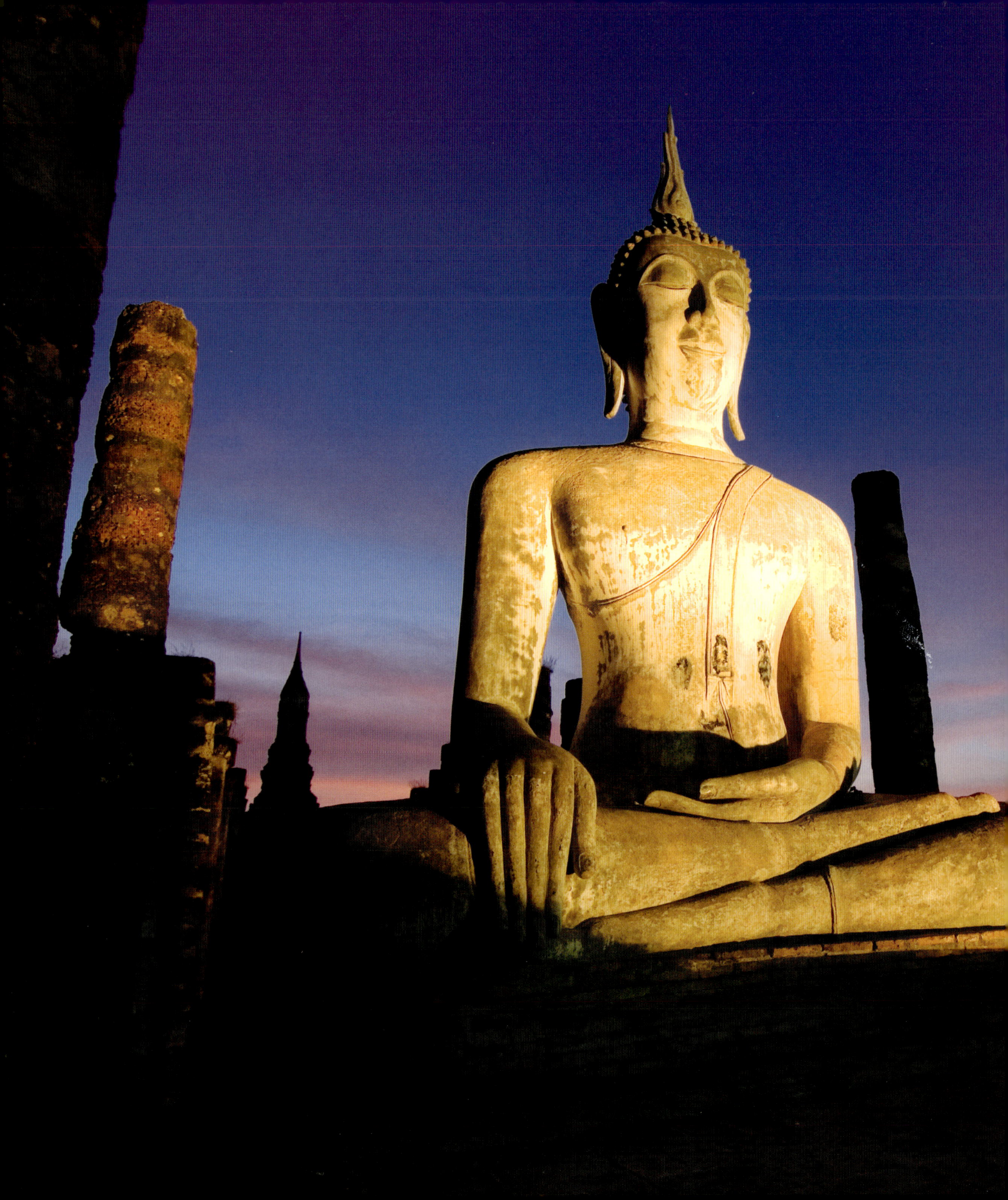

Wat Phra Si Ratana Mahathat

Sukhothai Historical Park

Wat Phra Si Ratana Mahathat, which translates as Monastery of the Great Sacred Royal Gem Relic, is one of the oldest and most significant Buddhist monastery ruins in Thailand. Once a far-flung Angkor satellite state, as the Angkor Empire's power waned in the early-13th century, the principality declared its independence under Thai chieftain Phaya Si Intharathit in 1238. Si Intharathit called the new Thai kingdom 'Sukhothai,' the Dawn of Happiness.

Sukhothai's third king, Ram Khamhaeng (Rama the Brave, 1279–1317), forged an important alliance with Lanna to the north, enabling him to expand the kingdom's influence to include most of present-day Thailand, western Cambodia, the entire Malayan Peninsula and Laos. The learned monarch also sponsored the codification of the Thai alphabet, and left behind the oldest known piece of Thai writing – a stone slab inscription dating to 1292.

Before Sukhothai was annexed to the Ayuthaya kingdom (Siam) in central Thailand in 1376, its scholars and artists had helped forge key components of the Thai national identity, including literature and architecture. Sukhothai temple art and architecture combined Khmer, Thai, Sinhalese and Mon influences to forge a distinct Sukhothai flavour. Unfortunately the kingdom's grand architecture was nearly forgotten as the centre of power moved to Ayuthaya and later to Bangkok and the neglected ancient site fell into ruin until a government restoration project was approved in 1976. In 1988, the old city site was opened to the public as Sukhothai Historical Park, and in 1991 UNESCO added the site to its World Heritage list.

Pages 186-187: The principal Buddha image, illuminated just after sunset.

Right: A series of restored Buddha sculptures line the base of the main stupa.

188 Buddhist Temples of Thailand

Region: Northern Thailand 189

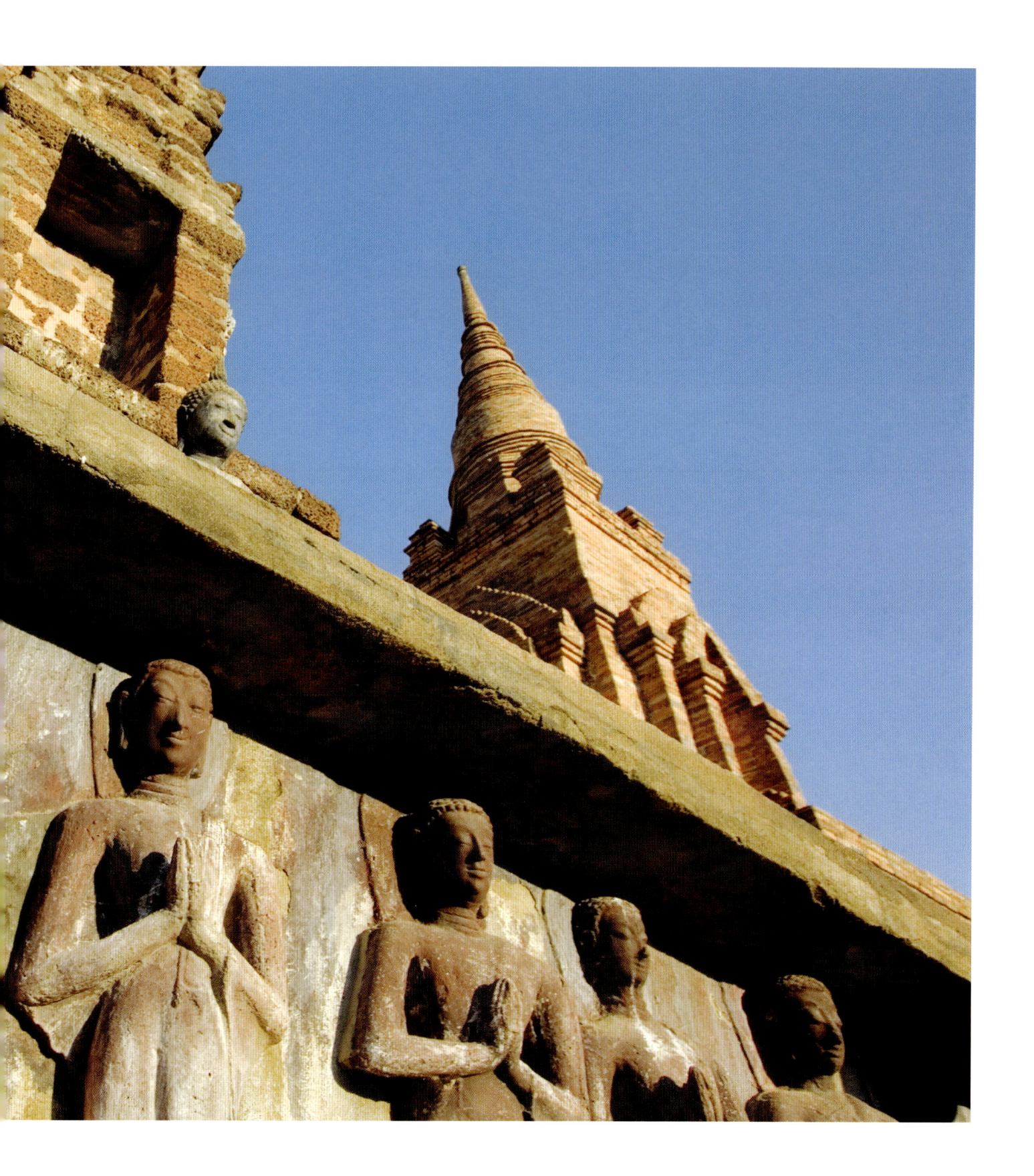

Above: Travelling Buddhist monks admire the partially restored temple.

Right: A sitting Buddha, a stupa and a pediment are all that remain of this *wihan*.

Pages 192-193: A collection of classic Sukhothai stupas.

The 70-sq-km park contains 193 ruin sites, including the remains of the royal palace and 26 monasteries, of which the largest is Wat Phra Si Ratana Mahathat. Surrounded by laterite walls and a moat roughly 200 metres on each side, the monastery features 198 stupas, a principal *wihan*, 10 secondary *wihan* and a *bot*. The main stupa, believed to contain Buddha relics, exhibits Sukhothai's characteristic lotus-bud finial, relic box, dome and three-tiered base. Some original stucco reliefs of animals, angels and demons remain visible.

Huge columns standing in front of the stupa, and their base, are the only remains of a large *wihan* which once contained a bronze sitting Buddha image cast in 1362 and now installed at Wat Suthat in Bangkok. A smaller brick *wihan* nearby contains an eight-metre high sitting Buddha.

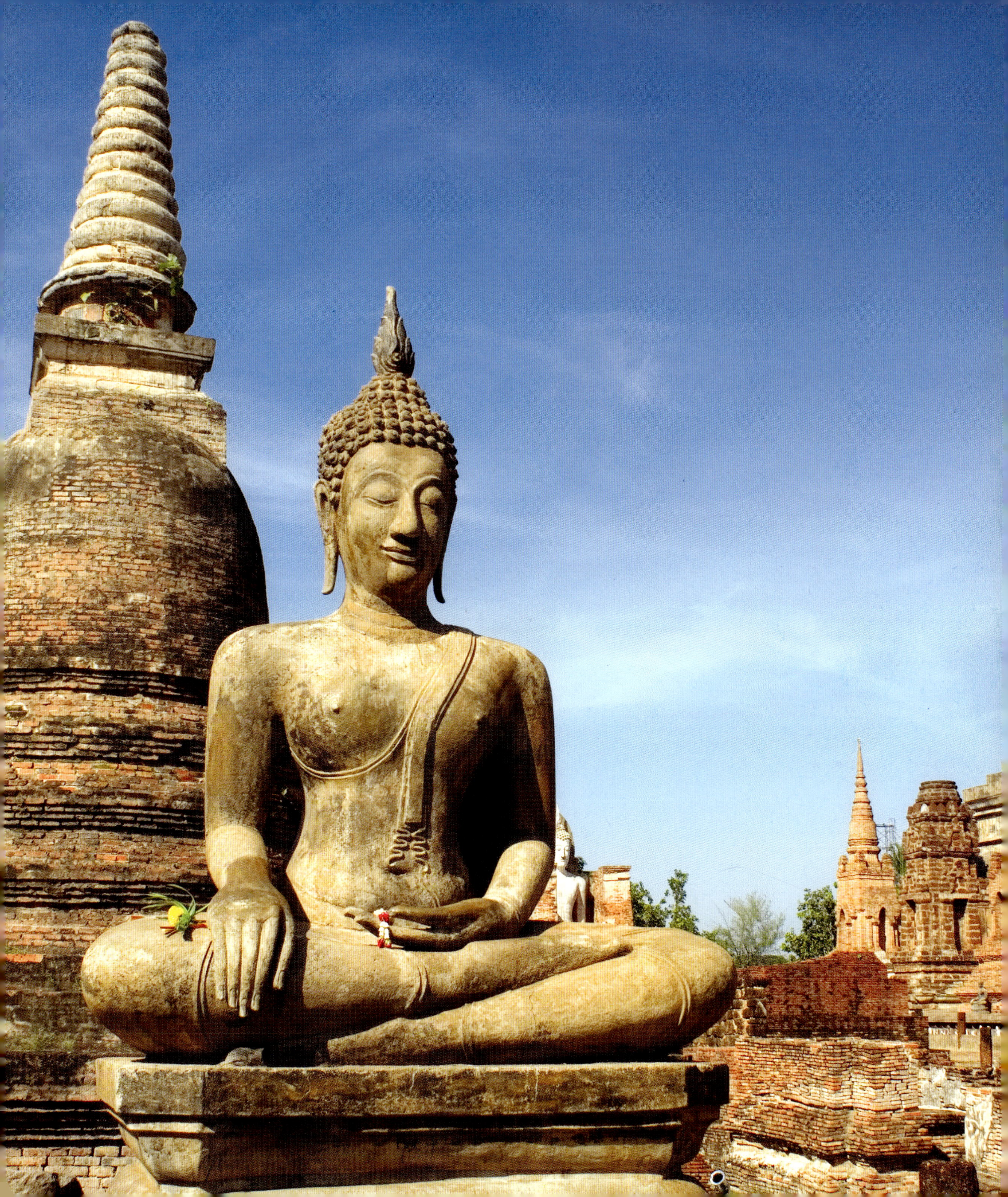

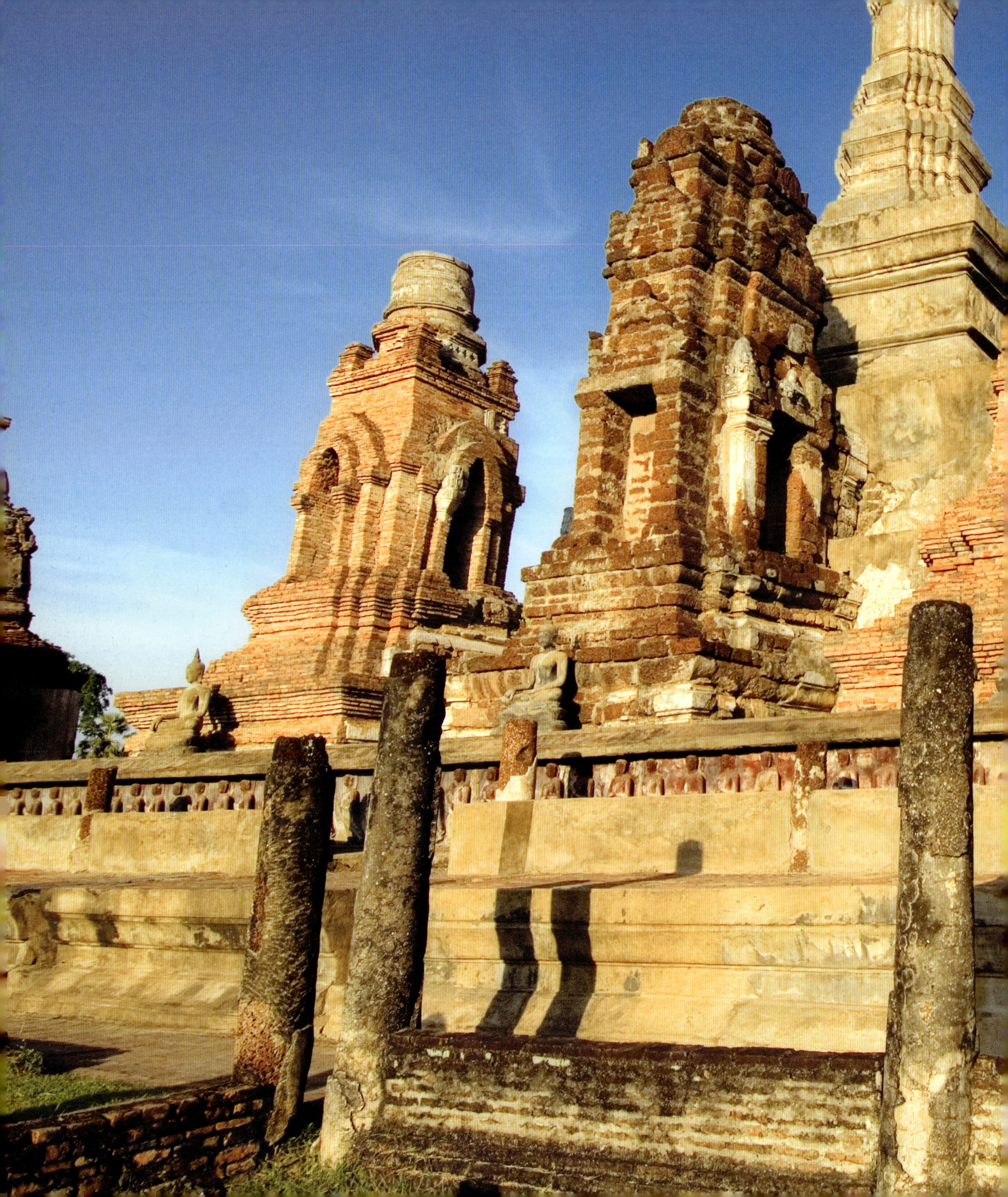

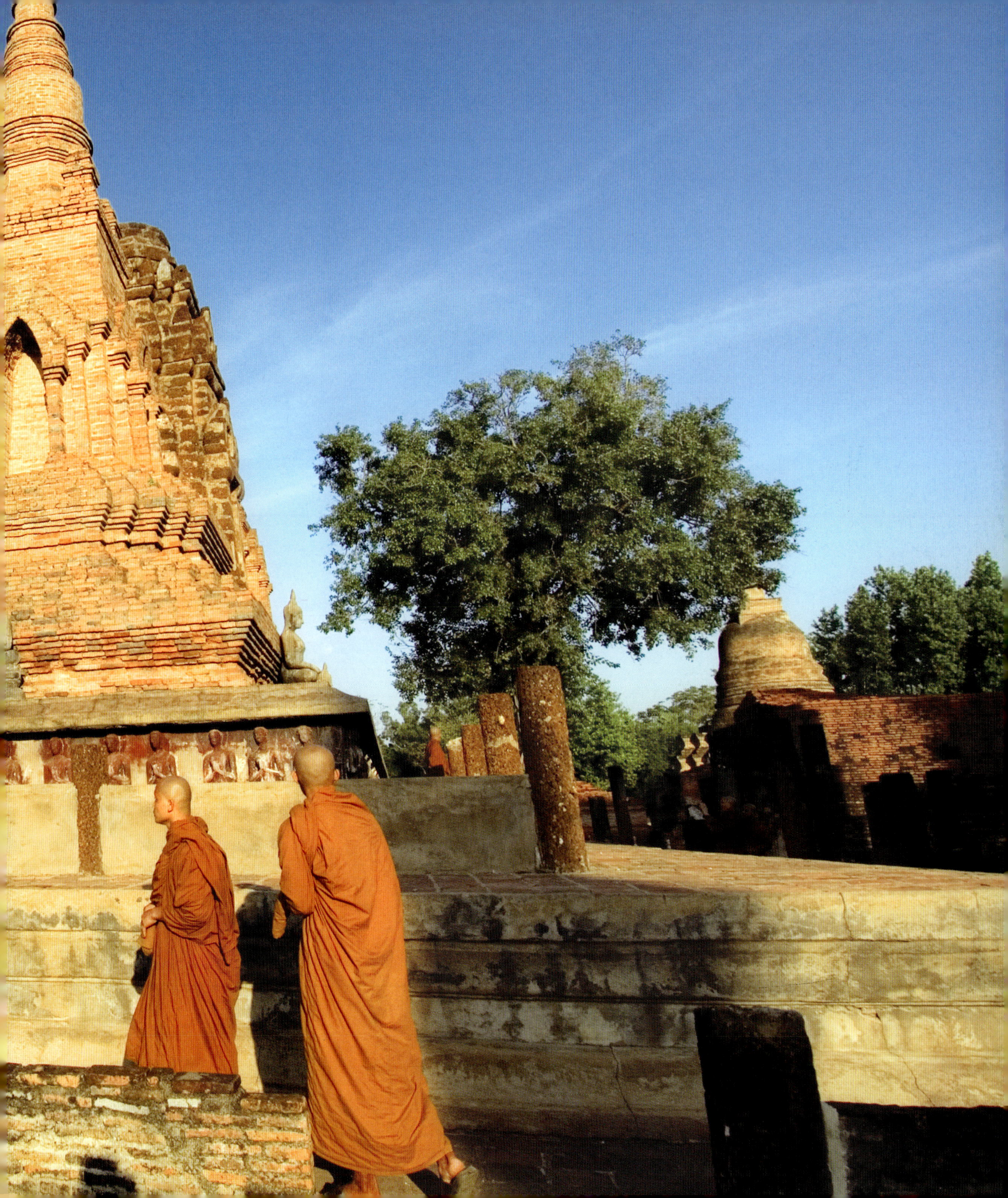

Wat Chao Chan

Si Satchanalai/ Chaliang Historical Park

The three semi-ruined monuments that comprise Wat Chao Chan form an important historical and aesthetic link in the early development of Thai temple architecture. One of over 200 sites conserved within the 81-hectare Si Satchanalai Historical Park (opened in 1988 and designated a UNESCO World Heritage Site in 1991), it occupies the oldest sector of the walled and moated city. While most monuments date to the 13th to 15th century Sukhothai era, Wat Chao Chan was part of Chaliang, an 11th century town originally developed as a satellite of the Angkor empire under King Jayavarman VII (1181–1220). Unlike his Brahmanist predecessors, who built temples devoted to Shiva or Vishnu, Jayavarman VII practised Mahayana Buddhism with particular focus on Lokesvara, a Bodhisattva dedicated to answering the prayers of all sentient beings. In addition to building numerous temples, most famously the 'third Angkor,' i.e. Angkor Thom, the pious king established a network of roads and more than a hundred resthouses and hospitals for travellers throughout his empire.

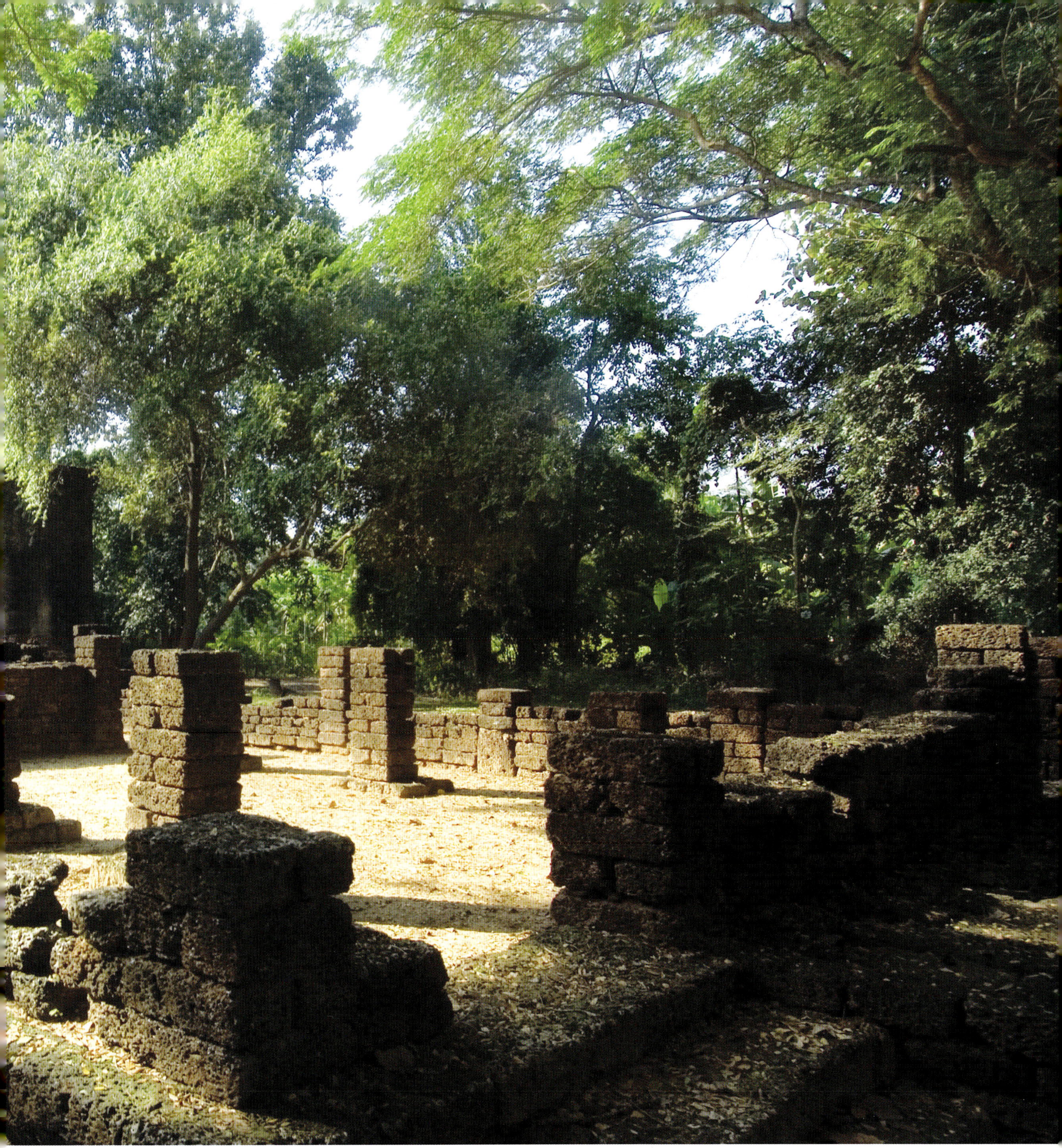

Pages 194-195: The use of laterite blocks instead of brick, as well as the architecture of the *prasat*, indicates that Wat Chao Chan was Khmer-built.

Above: The heavily weathered remains of a Buddha image sculpted from laterite blocks.

Right: The *prasat*, consisting of a shrine tower and entry chamber.

The centrepiece of Wat Chao Chan, the northernmost example of Jayavarman VII architecture, is a laterite-block *prasat* typical of the Bayon school of Angkor-period architecture, which in turn was directly influenced by classic Indian temple architecture as relayed via Buddhist kingdoms of central Java. Consisting of an entry chamber and tower, these were intended to enshrine a sacred image, in this case a small stupa containing a Buddha relic. The shrine chamber is accessible via an ornate portal facing east, while false doorways serving as niches for Buddha images occupy the other three cardinal points of the monument.

The shrine is topped by a beautifully proportioned Bayon *prang* with multiple reticulated corners curving inwards as the spire ascends, achieving the familiar 'beehive' profile found at temple sites in Bayon as well as in Lopburi and other sites once under Khmer rule but later taken over by the Thais. Judging from its size, the shrine was clearly part of an important temple and was likely renovated during the Sukhothai and Ayuthaya periods.

Beside the *prasat* stands a large *wihan* made of laterite blocks, of which only the foundation pediments and partial roof columns remain. Excavations have unearthed ceramic roofing tiles bearing decorative designs of the Bayon style. Behind the *wihan* a tall laterite shrine contains the elegant outlines of a large standing Buddha.

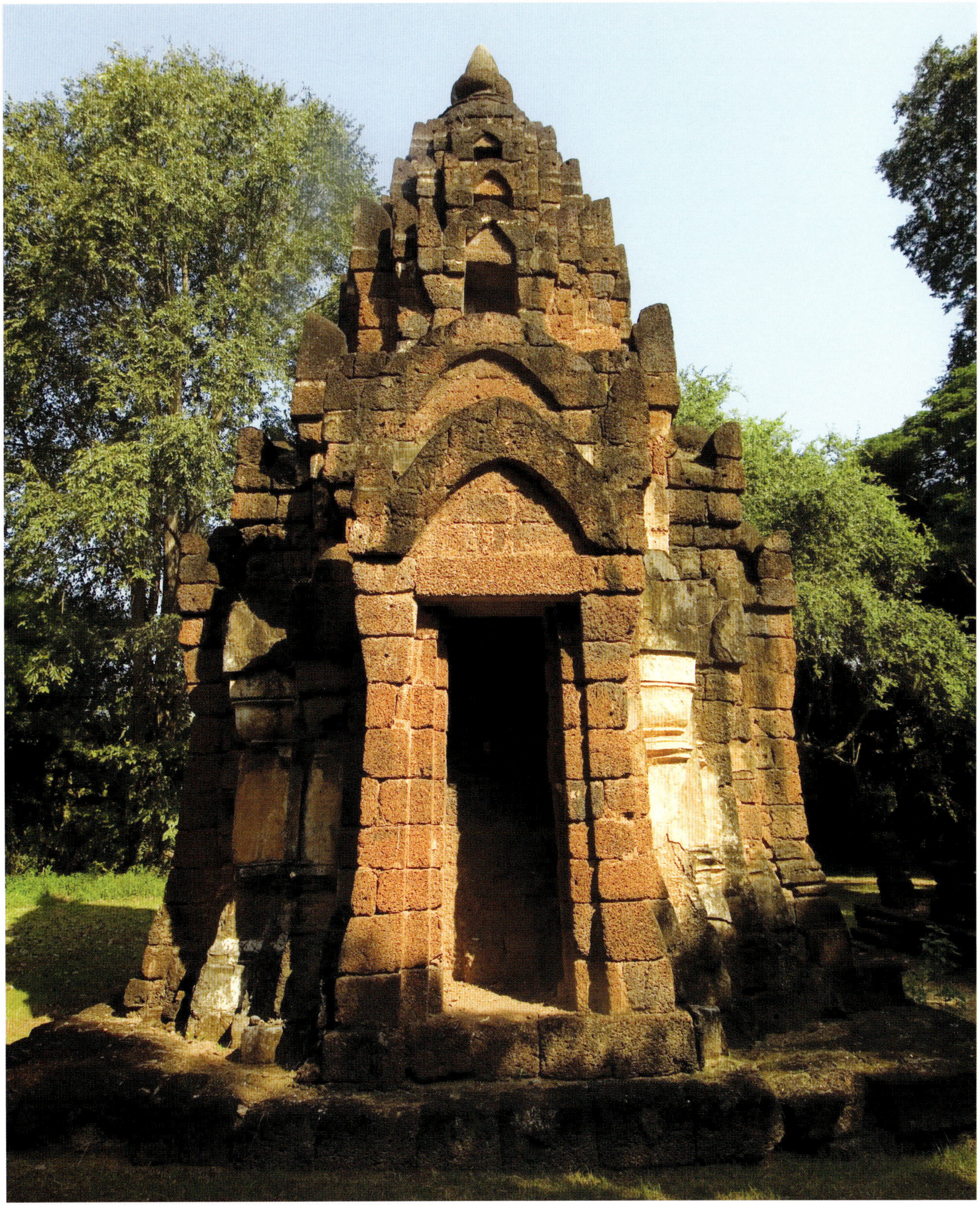

Wat Phra That Chae Haeng

Nan

Nan's cultural history is firmly linked with the Tai Lü, who inhabit a wide swath running from Phayao and Nan northward to Sipsongpanna (today's Xishuangbanna District in Yunnan Province, China). Of the many Buddhist temples in Nan showing Tai Lü heritage, Wat Phra That Chae Haeng is the oldest and largest. The main entry to the square, walled compound, which sits atop a hill overlooking the Nan River a few kilometres southeast of the current provincial capital, faces west. Although most Buddhist temples in Thailand face east, the original architects probably chose a western orientation because the road to the capital comes in from the west.

A 10-metre entrance promenade — added in 1806 by order of Chao Atthawon Panyo — is flanked by balustrades topped with undulating *naga*, the mythical water serpents believed to protect the Buddhist religion. While temple balustrades of this kind are common in Thailand, typically they terminate in multiple *naga* heads extruding from a *makara* (dragon) and raised a metre or two above the railing. By contrast here we see single, massive heads on each side, rising four metres into the air and angled slightly as if peering vigilantly across the plains below.

At the centre of the compound stands the monastery's namesake, a 55-metre high stupa erected on a large square base with reticulated corners and Lanna-style gilding. The slender dome and finial rise skyward in diminishing circlets, characteristic of Tai Lü stupa design. Local chronicles record that the stupa was constructed over a five-year period beginning in 1353 to enshrine a Buddha hair relic presented to Phaya Kan Muang, ruler of Phu Kha (also known as Nanthaburi, an early Nan kingdom), by the Sukhothai kingdom. Also of note within the main stupa enclosure is a very old reclining Buddha image cast in the Thai Yuan style.

198 Buddhist Temples of Thailand

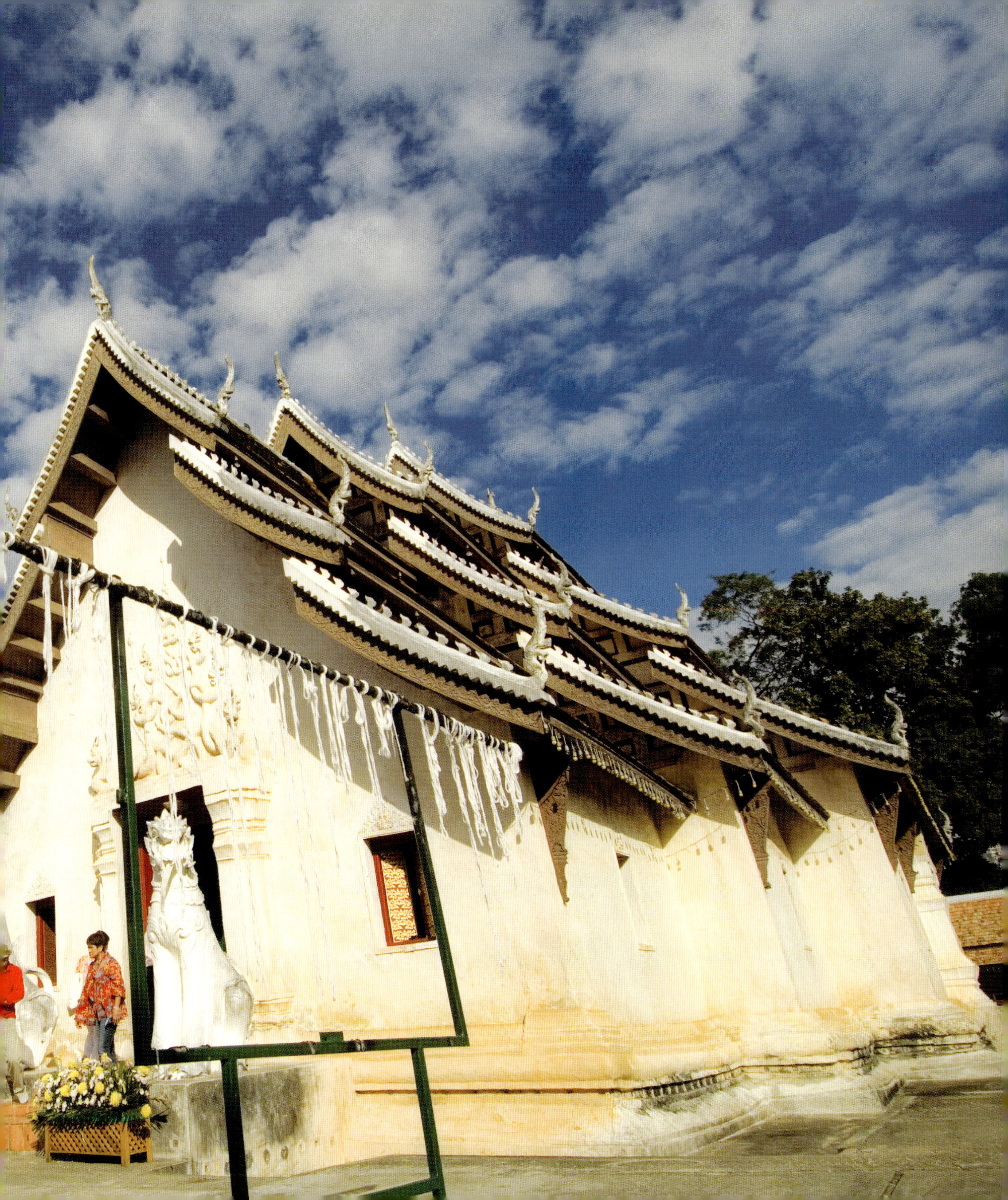

Pages 198-199: A temple-goer prays before sacred string to be used in a 'life-extending' ceremony. In the background one can see the entwined *naga* reliefs over the entry to the Wihan Luang.

Above: Local Buddhists make offerings inside the main cloister.

Right: Phra That Chae Haeng, a 55m high Lanna/Tai Lü-style stupa, is one of the most venerated in Thailand.

Pages 202-203: Sacred lengths of cotton string to be tied around laypeople's wrists to bind the spirits of their vital organs.

Featuring thick walls of brick sealed with plaster and punctuated with tiny windows, the Wihan Luang sits outside the stupa compound and is one of the finest examples of Tai Lü Buddhist architecture found anywhere in Thailand, Laos or China. In an exquisite stucco relief over the western doorway, eight *naga* intertwine in soft geometric patterns. The triple-tiered, open-gabled roofs with carved wooden eaves — where the naga motif is repeated — are also worth noting.

Behind the compound to the east, an open-sided shed stores longboats carved from solid logs and painted in colourful designs. A few of the boats are 150 years old. Every year, teams of 40 to 50 rowers per craft race the longboats in the nearby Nan River to mark the end of the Buddhist Rains Retreat. The event is usually held in September or October.

200 Buddhist Temples of Thailand

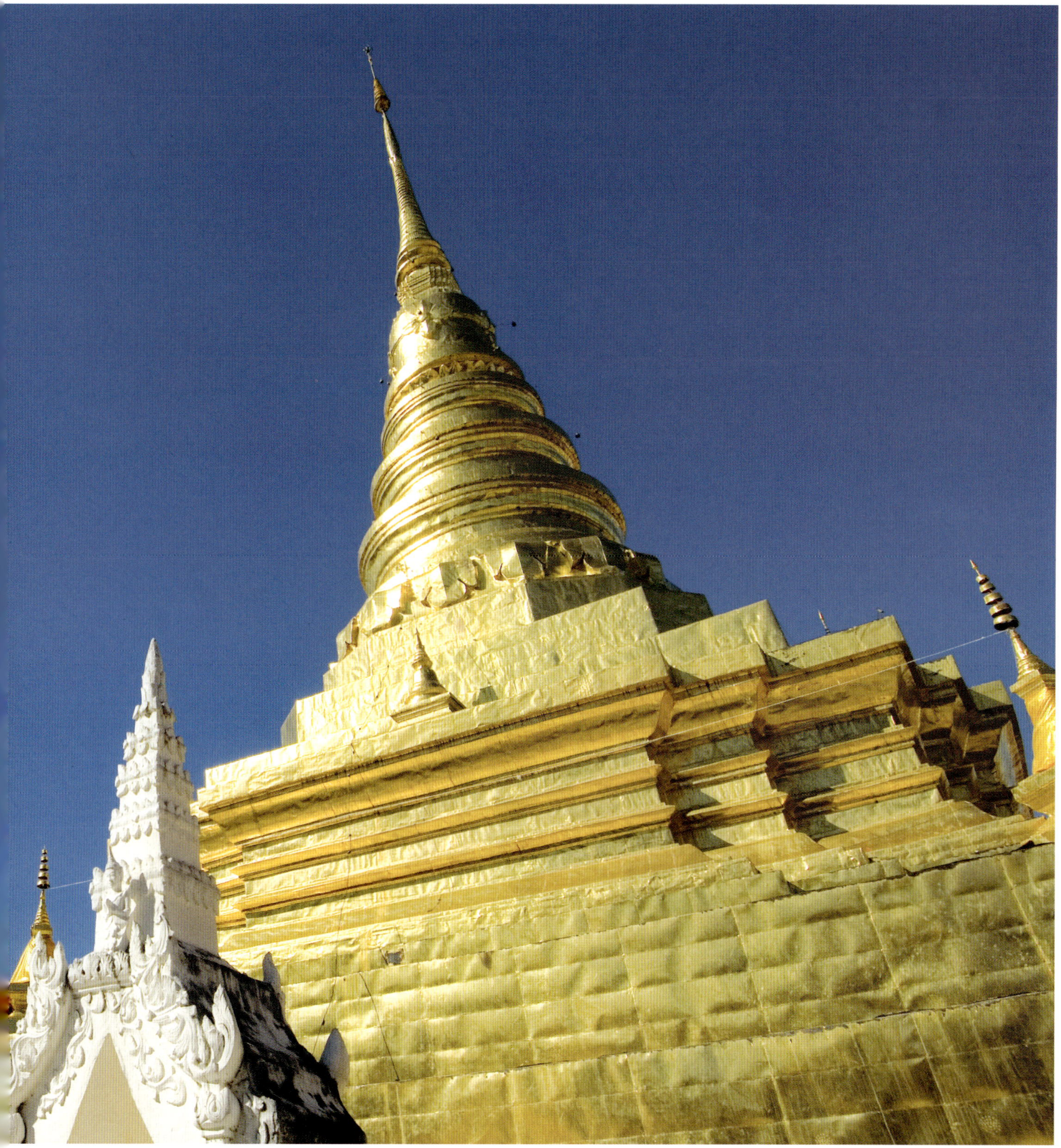

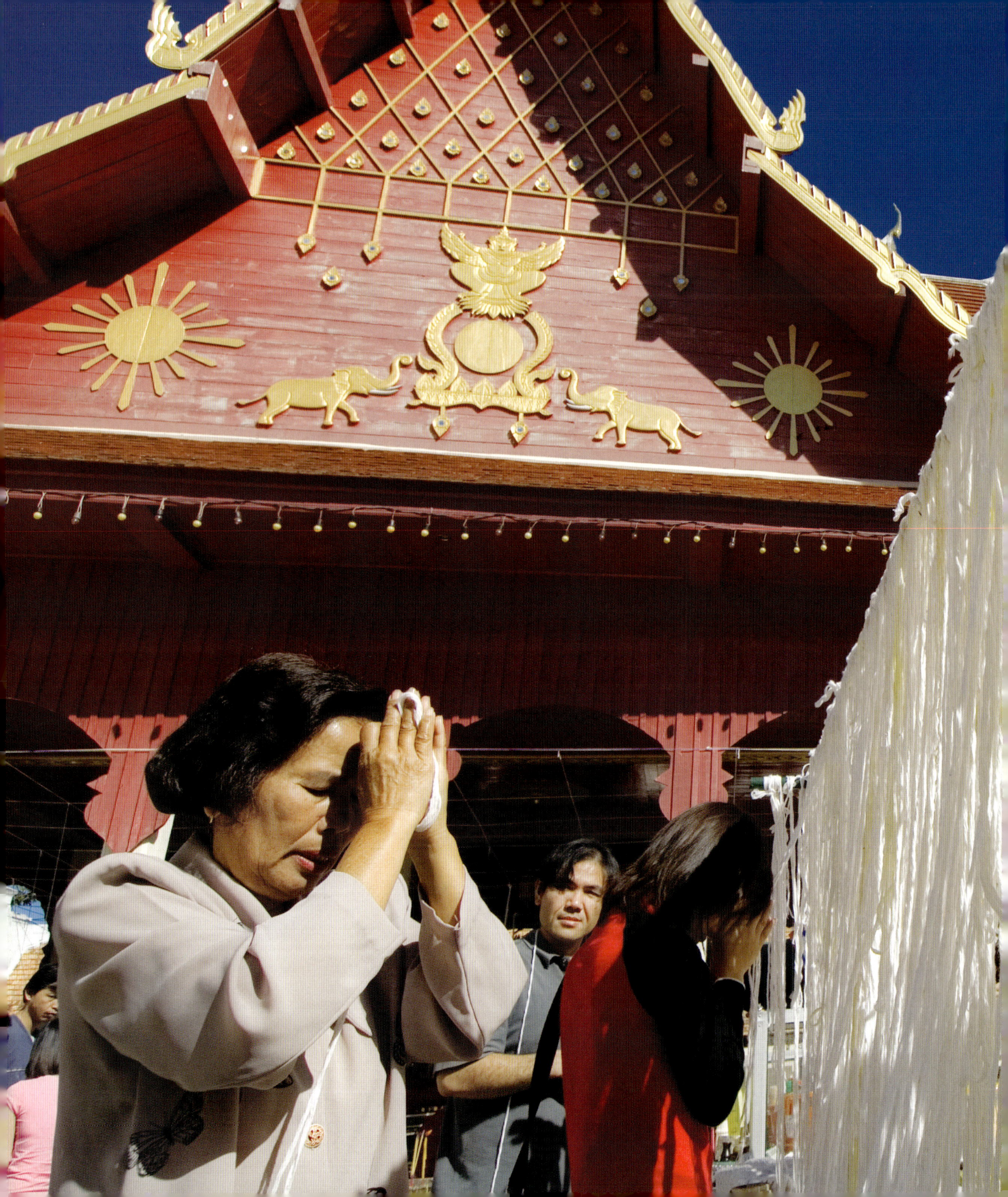

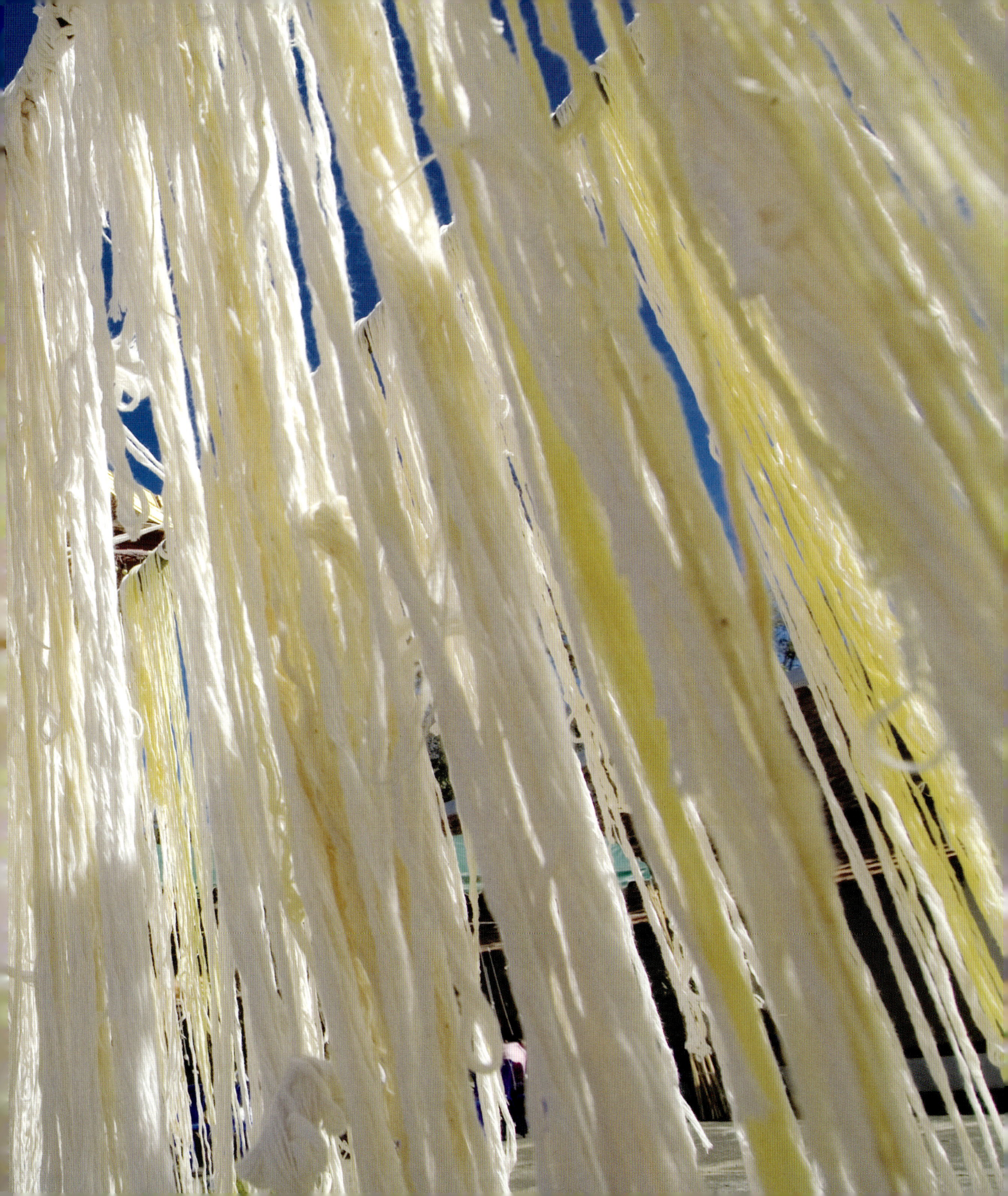

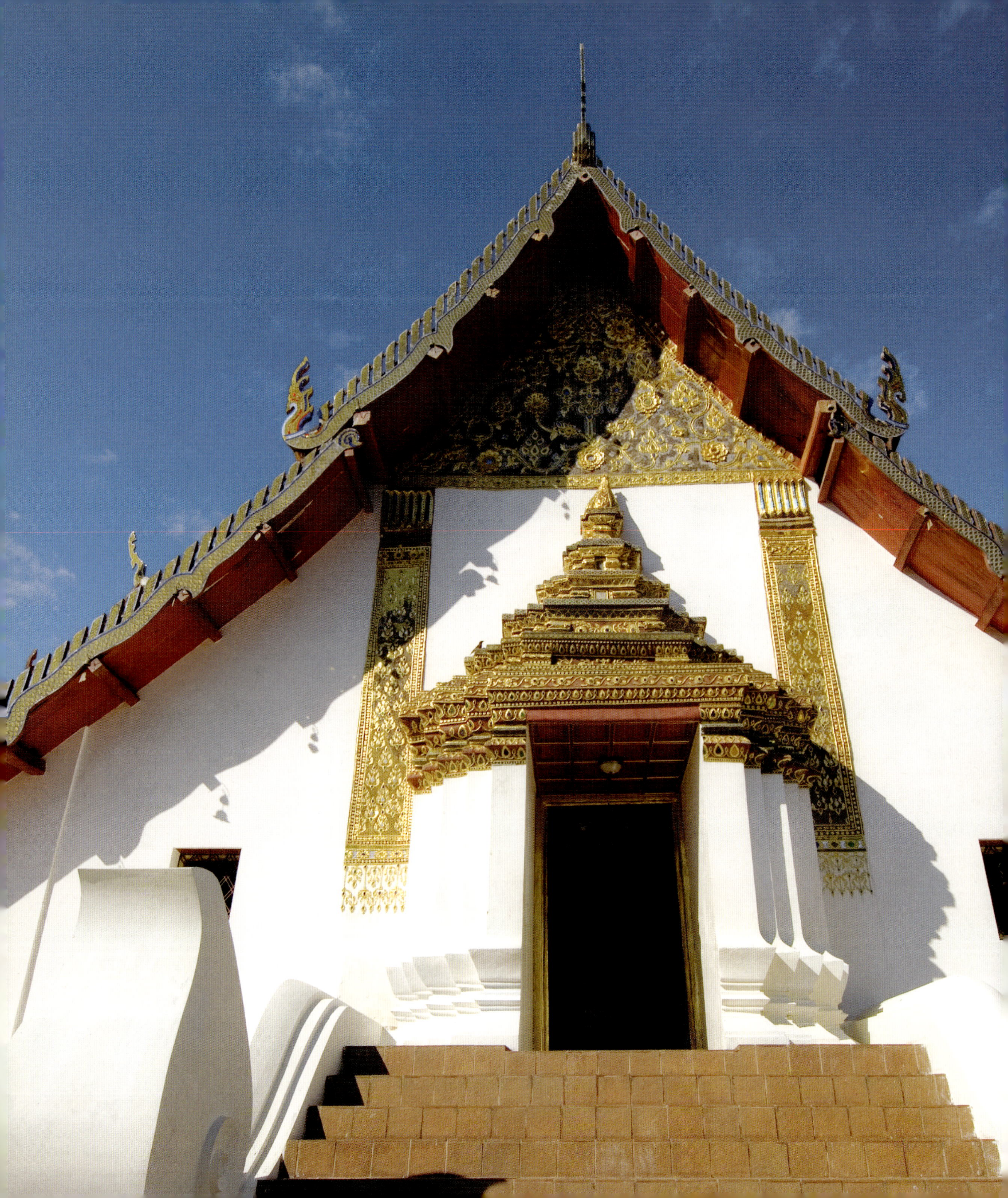

WAT PHUMIN

NAN

One of the most distinctive temples in northern Thailand, Wat Phumin was originally built in 1596, and its name may have derived from 'Prohmin' the name of the Nan monarch who sponsored the construction. The unusual cruciform floor plan most likely dates to a reconstruction undertaken between 1867 and 1875 during the reign of Chao Anantaworaritthidej. Serving a dual function as both *wihan* and *bot*, the main structure features north and south porticoes flanked by oversized, *naga* balustrades, single-headed in a Tai Lü tradition unique to Nan. For the smaller east and west entries, balustrades end in whitewashed nautilus patterns that have become a major element in the modern renaissance of Lanna design in the north.

The sumptuous interior features 12 large teak pillars supporting the roof and decorated in rich *lai kham*. The centre of the hall is dominated by a cluster of four Buddhas in the *bhumisparsa* mudra sitting back to back and facing the four directions. The figures represent the four Buddhas of the past — Gautama, Kakusandha, Konagamana and Kassapa — an uncommon motif seen in early Mon or Dvaravati art in Myanmar and Thailand, but rarely in Lanna or post-Lanna Buddhist art. According to northern Buddhist sculpture expert Carol Stratton, they are Nan III Period (1558–1796) images, meaning Thai Yuan in

Left: One of the side entries to the *wihan* at Wat Phumin, with classic Lanna nautilus-motif balustrades.

style but incorporating native or folk characteristics from late Lanna, Lao and Myanmar influences as well. These probably date to the 1596 construction of the original temple.

Wat Phumin is most famous for housing Thailand's finest and best preserved Lanna-style murals, which cover nearly all the interior walls and add to the structure's overall sense of symmetry. Painted by Tai Lü artists during the *wihan*'s 19th century restoration, these murals have historic as well as aesthetic value since they incorporate scenes of local life from the era in which they were painted, along with scenes from Khattana Kuman Jataka and Nimi Jataka. Some of the patterns seen in the wraparound skirts worn by female figures in the murals still find favour among northern Thai women today. Life-sized portraits to either side of the entryways and at the top of the pillars may represent well-known Nan residents of the time. The figure in the red cape on the east wall is thought to portray the Nan governor who ordered the restoration of the temple. On the west wall, next to the door, the tattooed male figure shown whispering to his female companion is believed to be a portrait of the artist himself.

Above: One of the four sitting Buddhas facing the cardinal directions inside the *wihan*.

Right: Another, smaller representation of the four sitting Buddhas.

Pages 208-209: Both the *lai kham* (gold patterns on lacquer) and the flowing pastel murals at Wat Phumin are second to none in Thailand.

206   Buddhist Temples of Thailand

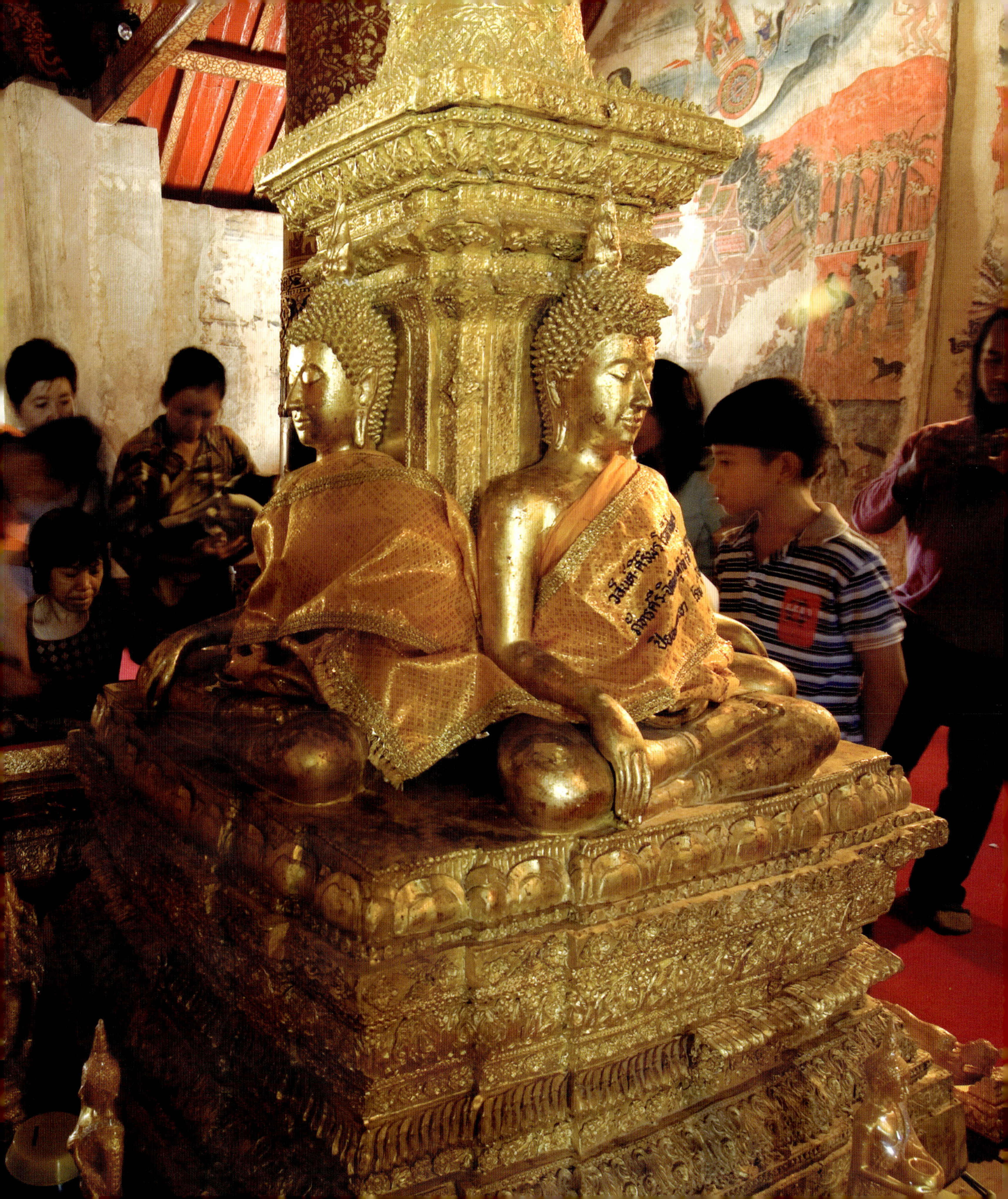

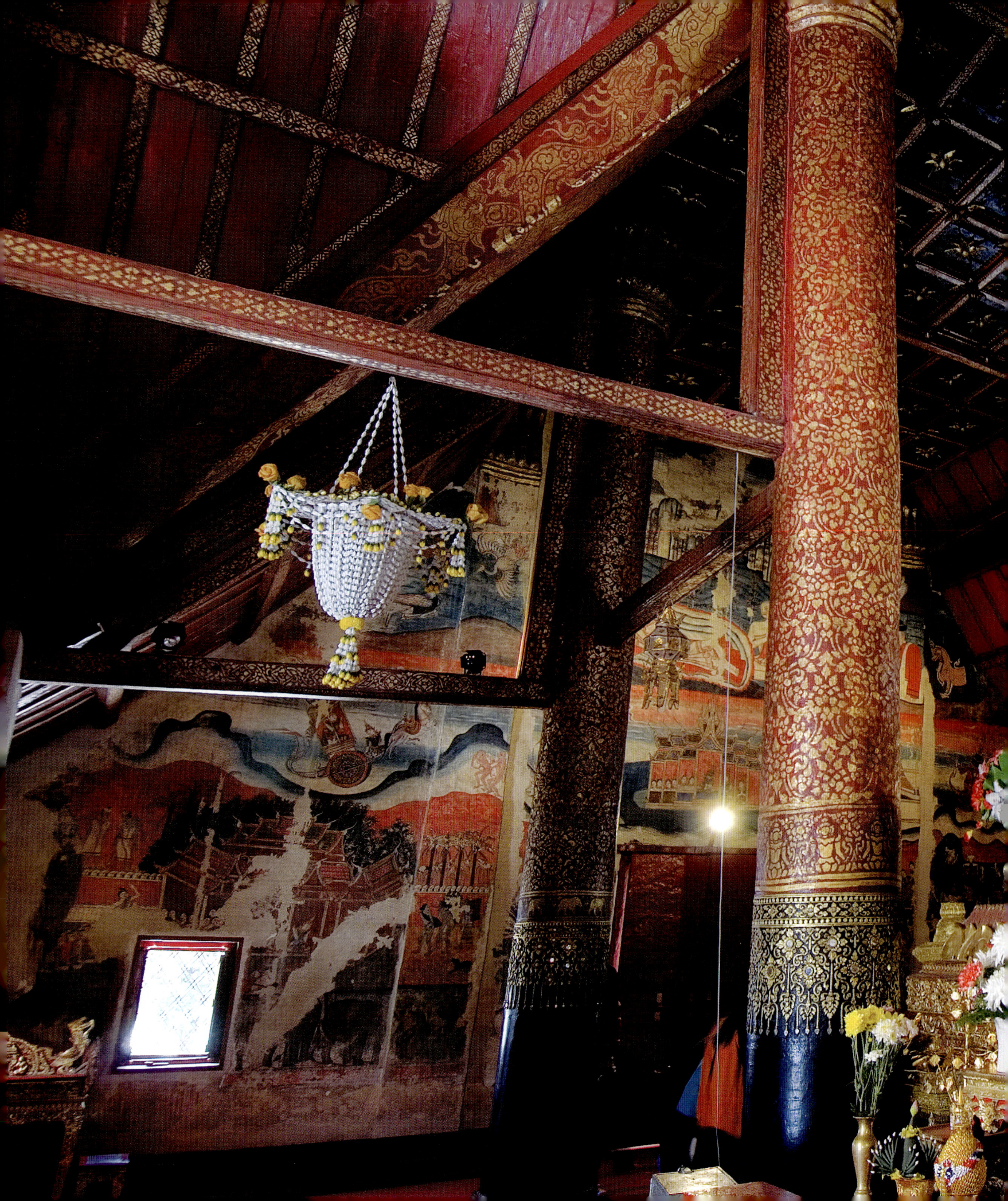

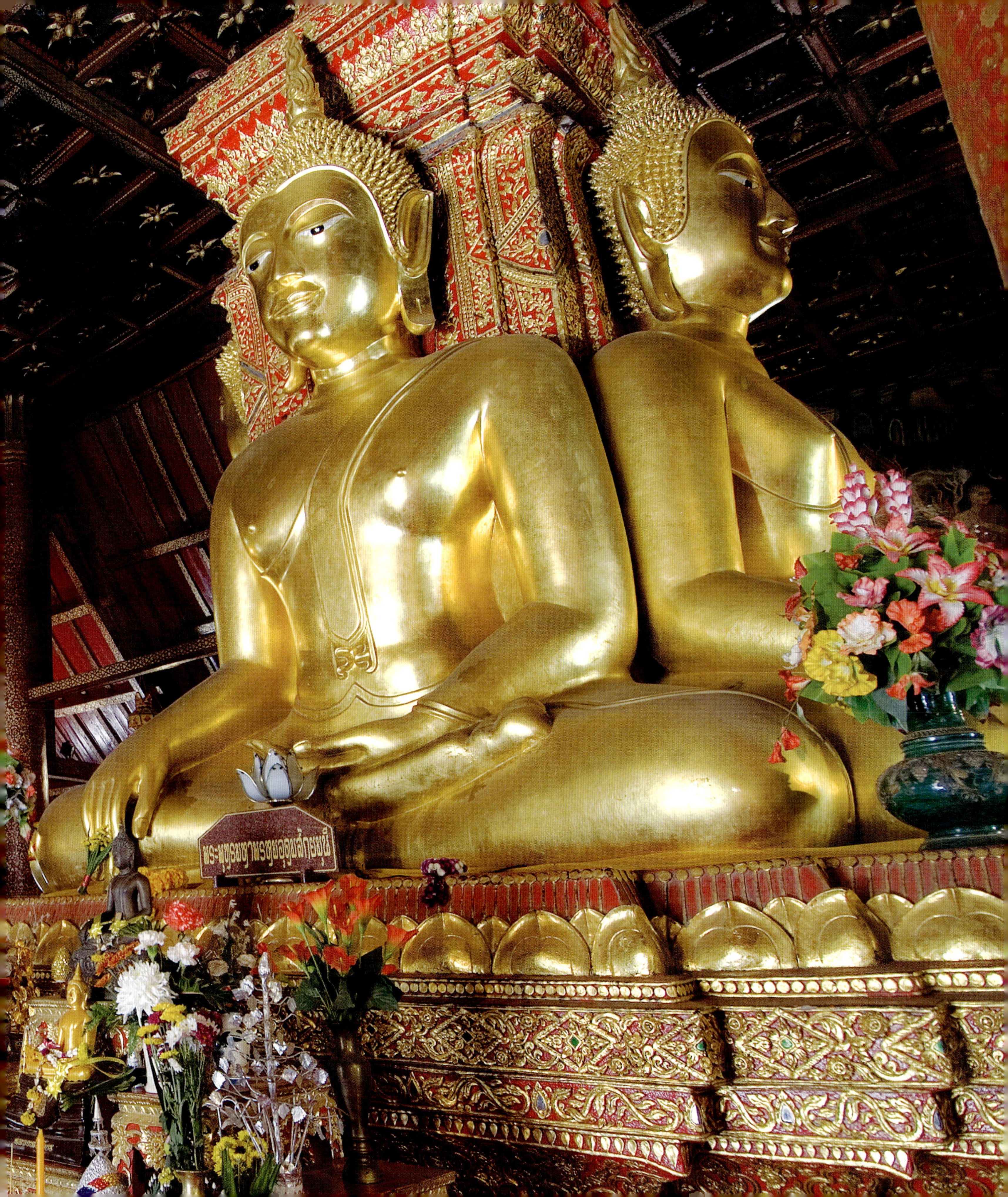

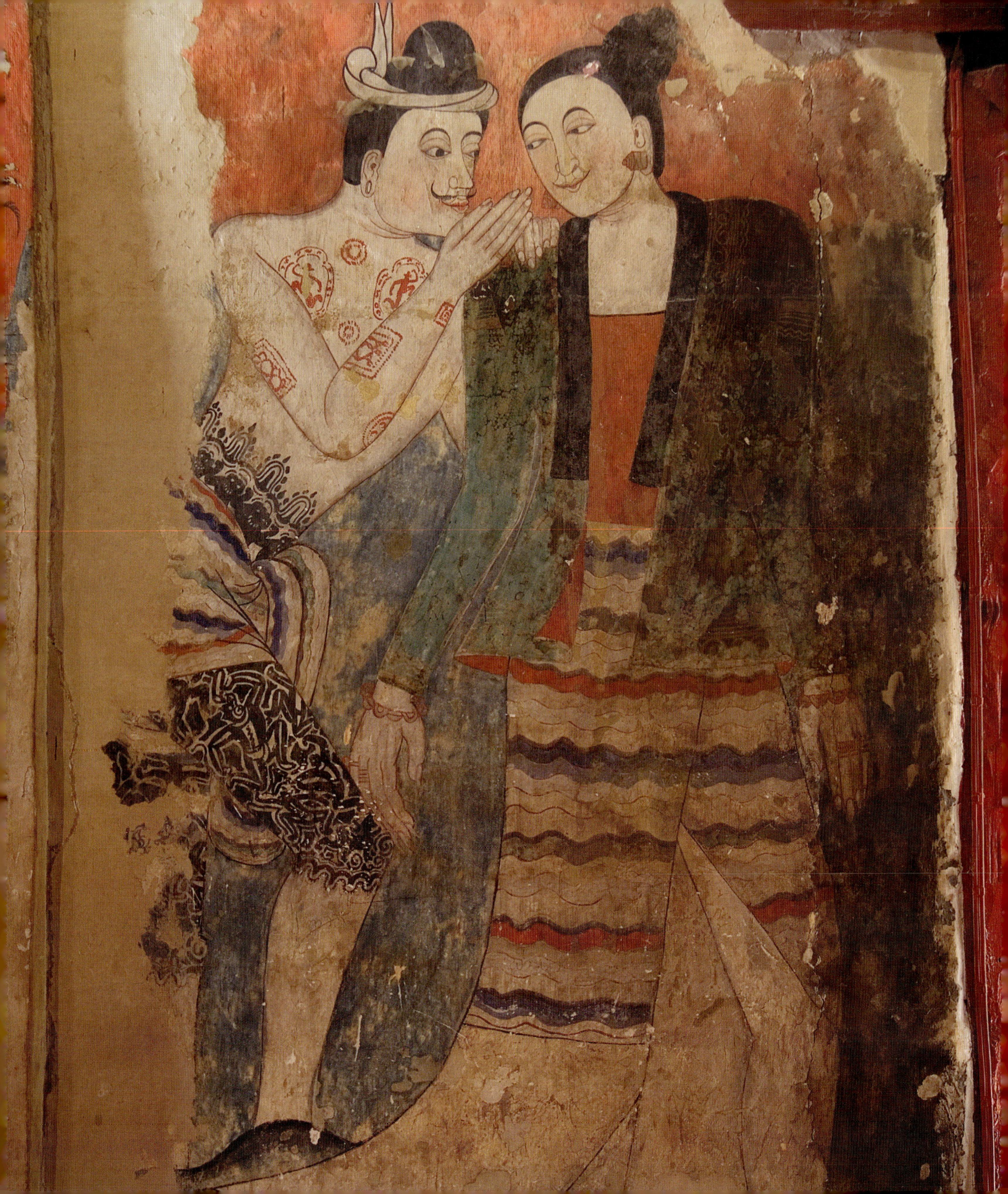

Left: Northern Thailand's most famous temple mural shows a heavily tattooed Tai Lü man flirting with a well-dressed woman.

Above: This scene depicts a traditional weaving loom and Lanna-style costumes.

Region: Northern Thailand 211

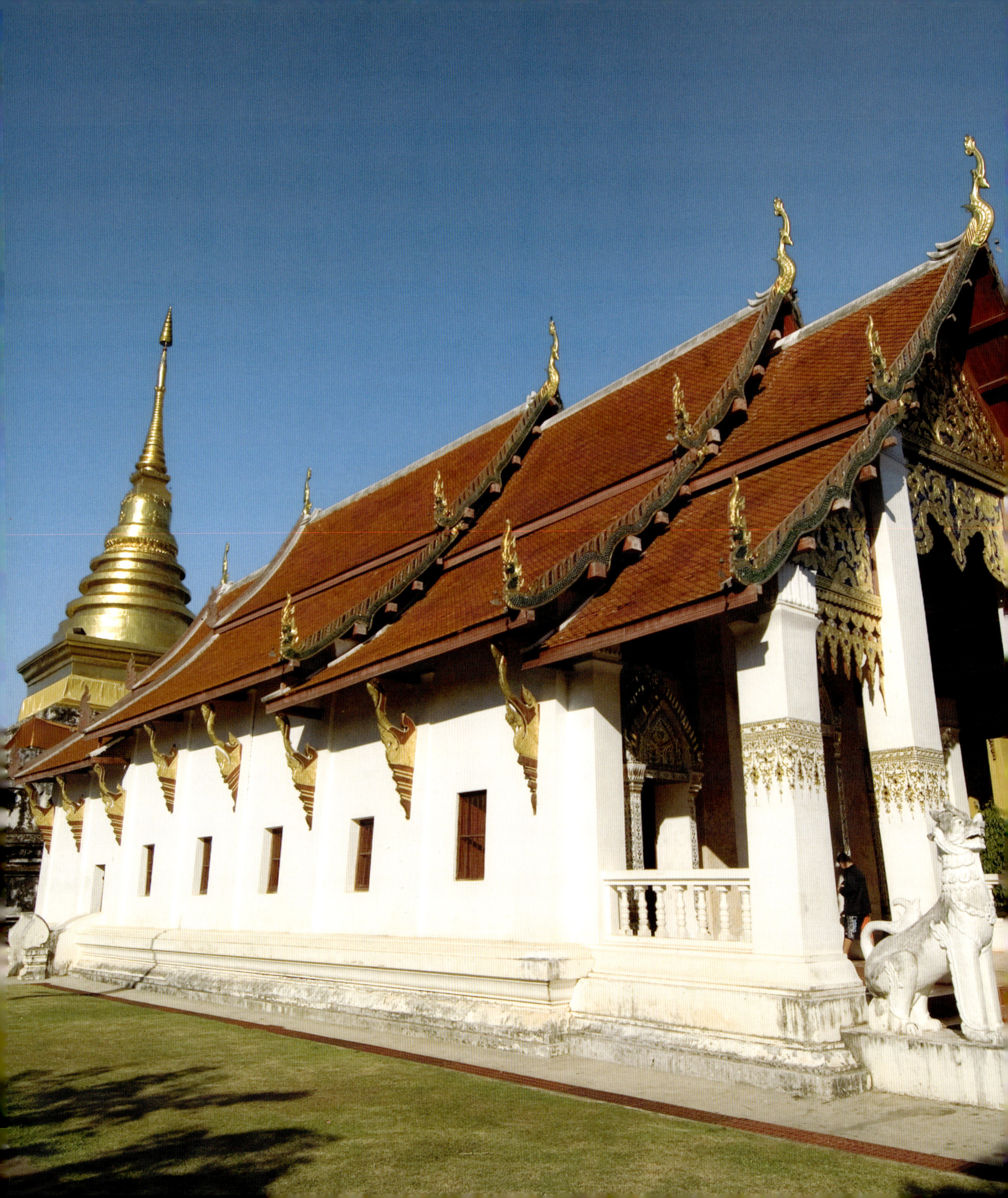

Wat Phra That Chang Kham

Nan

After Wat Phra That Chae Haeng, this is the most important temple in Nan. A large stupa dating back to 1406 exhibits Lanna influence in the round, gilded tower and Sukhothai influence in the square base 'supported' by 24 elephant sculptures, six on each side, from which the *wat* derives its name (Monastery of the Elephant-Supported Stupa).

Wihan Luang, the main *wihan*, was reconstructed in 1458 and holds a huge sitting Buddha called Phra Chao Luang and cast in the Lanna style. Two smaller images on display belong to a set of five images made locally in 1427 by skilled Sukhothai-trained artisans. Cast in the late classic Sukhothai style, they are among the finest examples of walking and standing Buddha images in the north. Two of the others can be found at nearby Wat Phaya Phu. Faint 19th century murals can be seen

Left: The main *wihan* at Wat Phra That Chang Kham shows Tai Lü influence in its small windows and *naga* bargeboards.

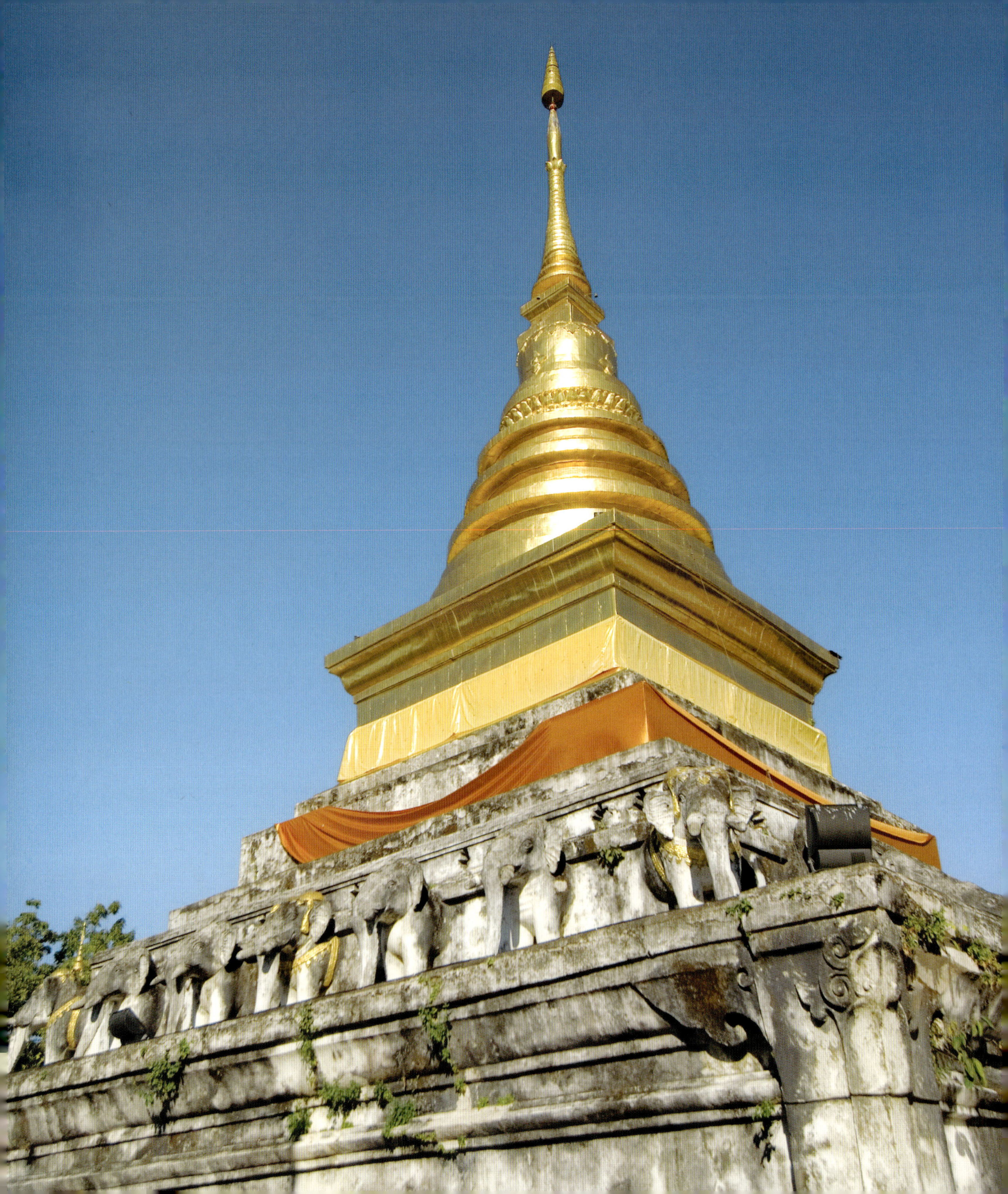

on the walls of the *wihan* through a layer of whitewash added in the 20th century by an abbot who found the art distracting.

The *wihan* also contains a collection of palmleaf manuscripts written in Lanna script that include texts on history, astrology and law according to King Mangrai, in addition to Buddhist scriptures. They were once kept in the adjacent Ratanakosin-era *ho trai*, which was the largest library of its kind in Thailand and now stands empty.

Next to the stupa stands a small, undistinguished *wihan* dating to around the same time as the stupa and known as Wihan Phra Chao Thum Jai. In 1955 art historian A. B. Griswold found a 184-cm tall walking Buddha, crudely moulded of plaster, inside. As Griswold began removing the image from the building, it fell and the plaster around the statue broke away to reveal an original Sukhothai Buddha of gold alloy underneath. Known as Phra Phuttha Nanthaburi Si Sakayamuni, the striking image is now kept on display inside an ornate cabinet of glass and gilded wood in the temple library.

Left: The stupa features a typically Lanna dome but the base, with its elephant sculptures, is designed in the Sukhothai style.

Above: The immaculate entry to the *wihan* has been heavily restored.

WAT HUA KHUANG
NAN

Believed to have been constructed around 1525, Wat Hua Khuang was restored in 1882 and again in 1927. The compound is relatively small and today just three of the original structures are still standing. Typical of Tai Lü and some Lanna temples, one the chapel serves as both *bot* and *wihan*. The style of the building is Tai Lü, with thick walls and small windows. The main entry stairs are flanked by huge single-headed *naga,* raised high as at Wat Phra That Chae Haeng. *Naga* encompass the bargeboards and appear in stucco reliefs over the side entrances as well, confirming the building's Tai Lü origins. A large but simply carved wooden eyebrow-shaped pelmet, similar to those found among temples in Luang Prabang, Laos, hangs over the entry veranda. Heavily decorated window frames – possibly added later – are topped by a hemispherical sun-ray pattern similar to the front gable decoration found at Wat Ton Laeng, a provincial Tai Lü temple much farther north in Nan province.

Inside, teak roof pillars that probably once displayed *lai kham* ornamentation or wood-and-glass-mosaic rosettes are now plain and whitewashed. The large principal Buddha image, fashioned in the Thai Yuan style, sits at the back on a huge *naga*

Right: The Lanna/Lan Xang-style stupa, likely the oldest structure in the compound.

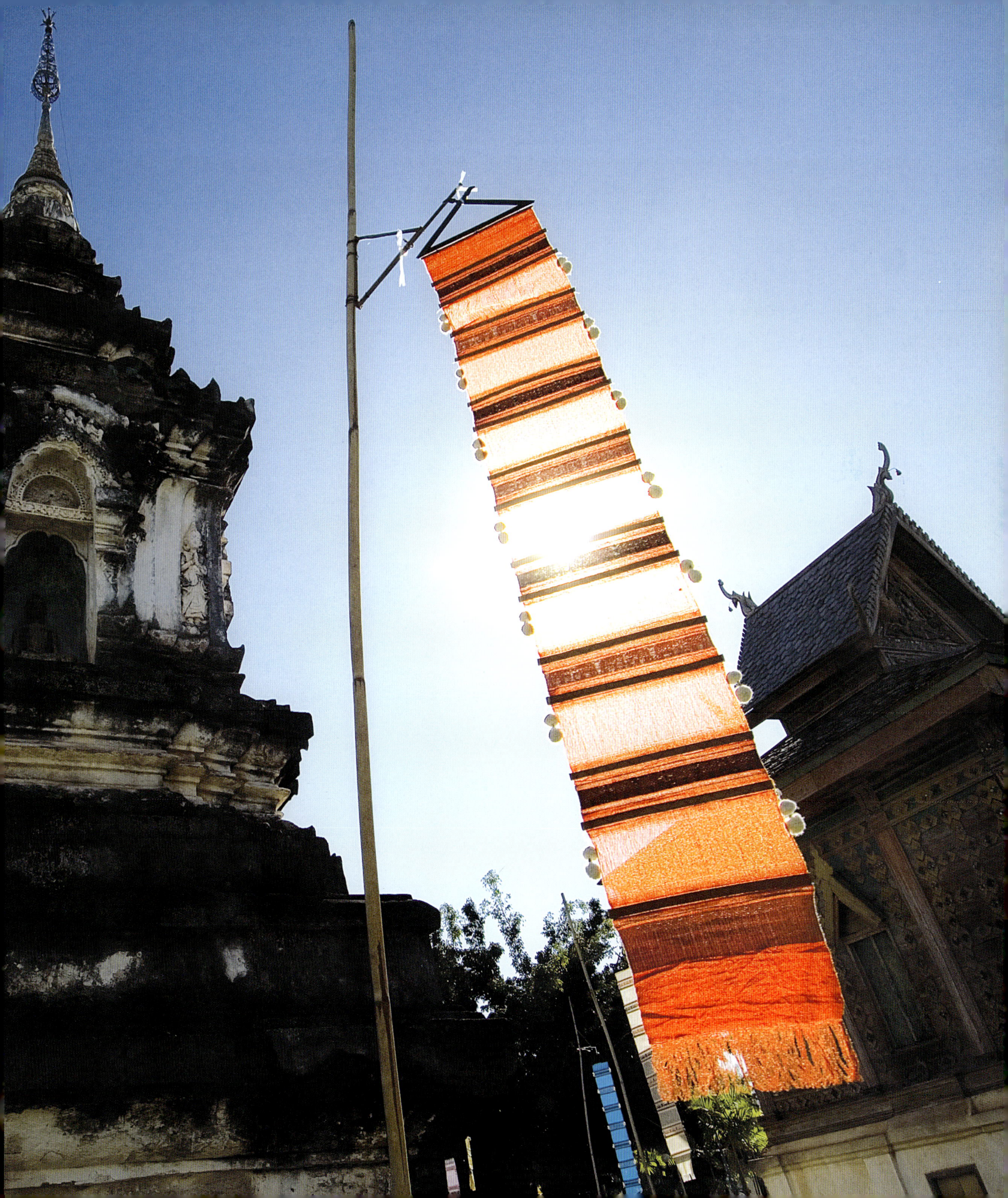

throne decorated with coloured ceramics. This is also reminiscent of Wat Ton Laeng, where the principal image sits on a wooden *naga* throne, and it may be that the same artisans worked on both temples. On the upper left and right walls behind the image are lively, pastel-hued Tai Lü murals of Buddha figures.

A uniquely square (rather than rectangular) *ho trai* nearby features all-wood architecture on its upper storey, the exterior walls festooned with carved wood-and-glass mosaic rosettes. The stacked, wood-shingled roof follows classic Lanna form, as do the gable panels carved in floral patterns and *thewada*. The lower storey consists of a brick-and-stucco pedestal. The library is now used as a monastic residence.

The third structure of note at Wat Hua Khuang is a complex late Lanna/Lan Xang-style stupa with multiple levels and heavily reticulated corners showing more sophistication than the other two buildings. It is likely the stupa is the oldest element here, and that *naga* lintels over Buddha niches facing the four directions were added later.

Above: Delicate carved wooden floral motifs in the eyebrow-shaped pelmet of the veranda.

Right: The *naga* heads on the balustrade are unusually tall at Wat Hua Khuang.

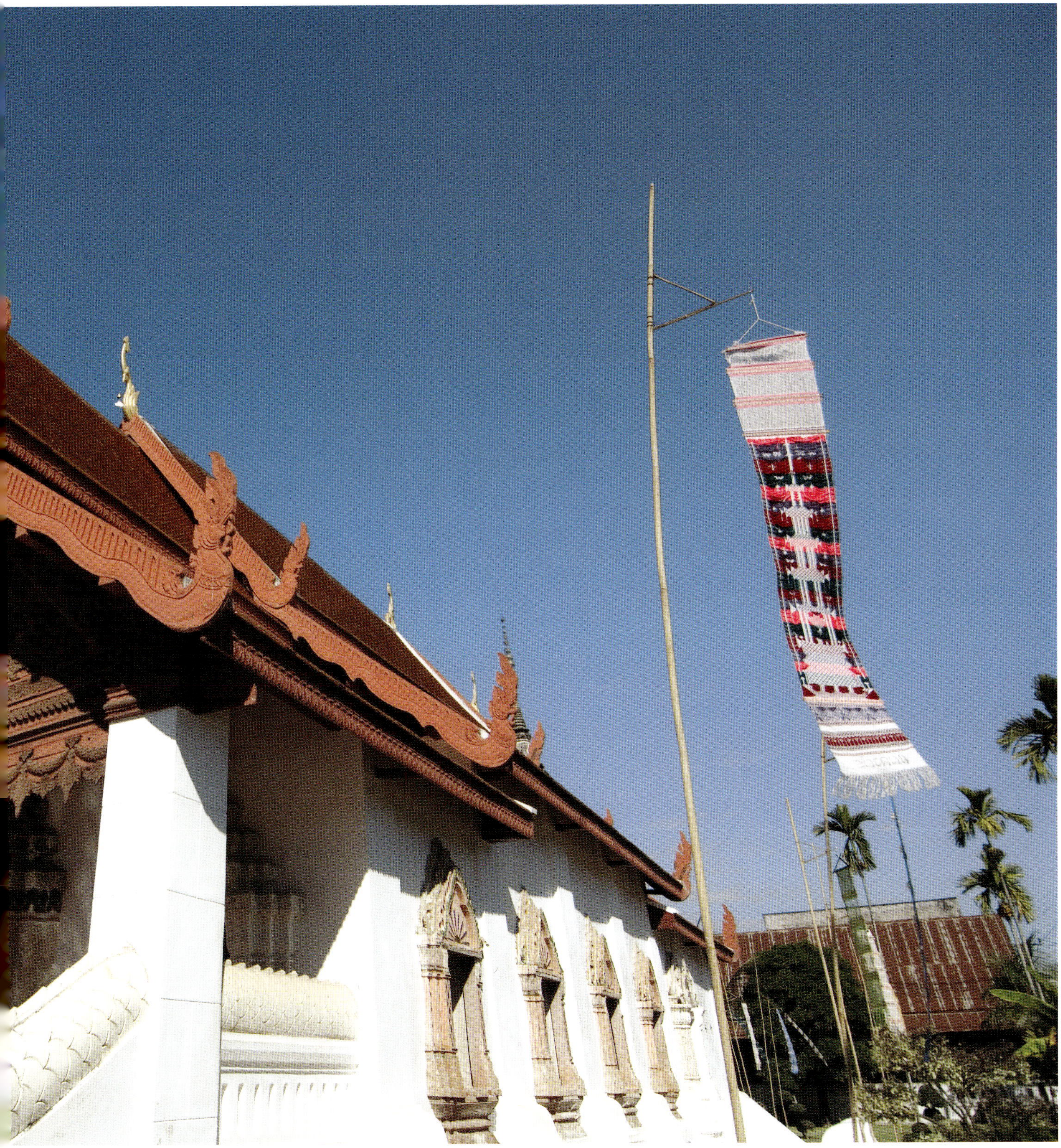

Wat Jong Klang & Wat Jong Kham

Mae Hong Son

The visual centrepiece of Mae Hong Son, indeed serving as so strong a symbol that any visual rendering immediately brings the province to mind, Wat Jong Klang and its 'mate' Wat Jong Kham occupy the southern banks of serene Nong Jong Kham, a small natural lake.

Wat Jong Klang is the larger of the pair but Wat Jong Kham is actually the older of the two monasteries, having been constructed by Shan artisans from Mandalay in the early- to mid-19th century. Much of Wat Jong Kham was destroyed by fire in 197. It was allegedly intended to serve as a way-station for monks travelling between Myanmar's Shan state and the teak centres of Chiang Mai, Lampang and Phrae. As the migration of Shan merchants and timber workers increased in the late-19th century, Wat Jong Klang was added between 1867 and 1871. Today around half of the local population are Shan, and unlike Shan-built monasteries in Chiang Mai, Lampang or Phrae, the Shan character of the buildings and interior art has been preserved. *Jong* (sometimes transliterated as chong) in the temple names derives from the Shan word for monastery.

Both compounds contain stupas in the classic Shan style, resembling stupas found in today's western Shan state (for example, at Indein or Katku) more than those in the eastern Shan state (Chiangtung/Kengtung). When maintaining the stupas, the local community chooses to alternate whitewashed levels with gilded levels.

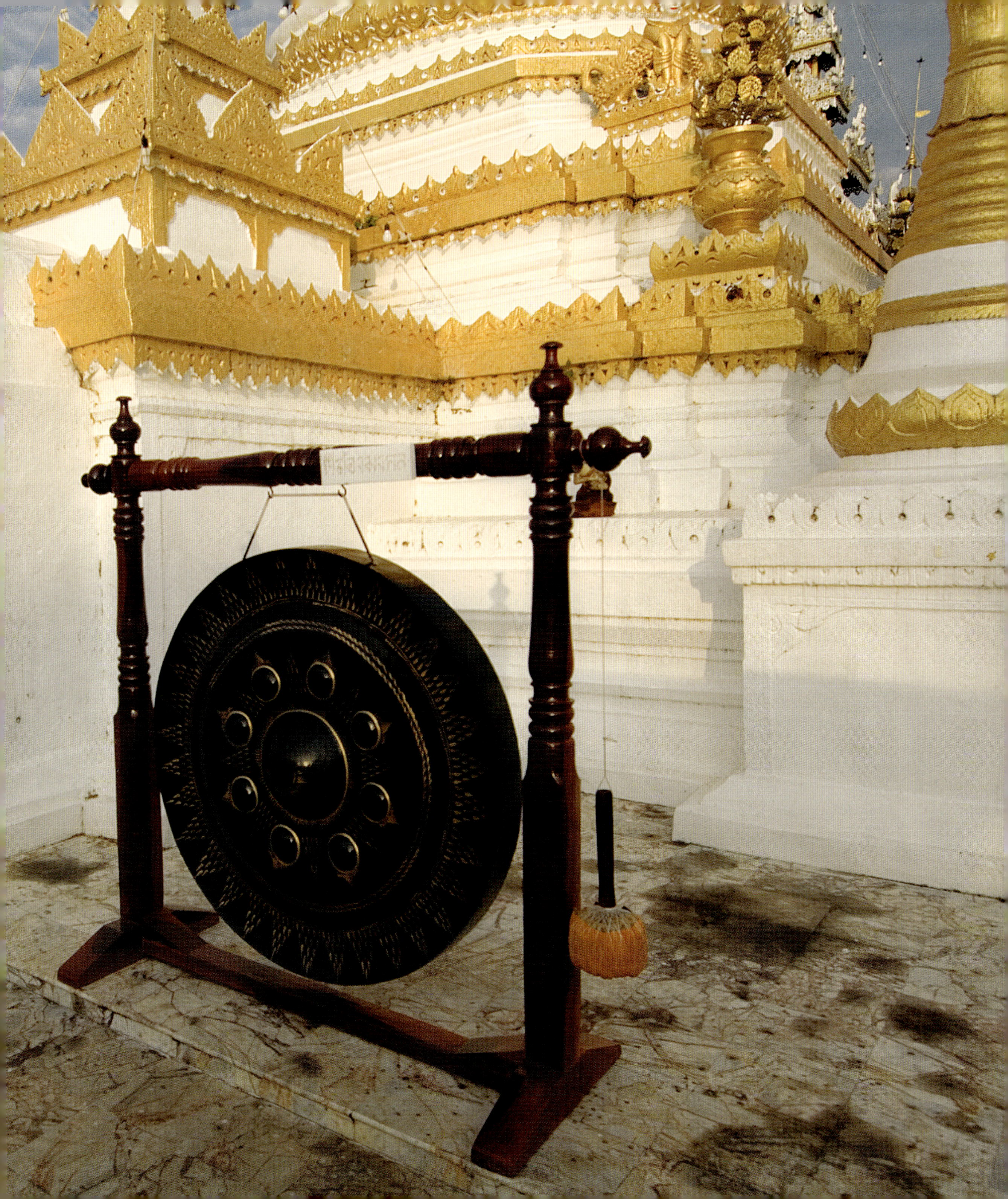

Pages 220-221: The Shan-style stupa at Wat Jong Klang features eight Buddha niches around its base.

Above: The layered rooftops with tin filigree along their bargeboards show Shan influence.

Right: Rooftops and mountains form an inspiring skyline.

A sprawling wooden *wihan* with 36 roofs trimmed with metal fretwork at Wat Jong Klang contains a display of glass panels painted with *Jataka* scenes and carved wooden figures depicting characters in the *Vessantara Jataka* (a popular tale in which the Buddha-to-be develops the Perfection of Giving). Also found in the *wihan* are arcade-like games with Buddhist themes, offering visitors a little amusement in exchange for their donations. A replica of the Phra Phuttha Sihing sits on an altar.

Wat Jong Kham also contains a wooden *wihan* decorated with fretwork and multiple rooflines. Next to the *wihan*, a more modern building contains a revered Mandalay-style Buddha image known locally as Luang Pho To. An unusual *bot* is the large rectangular slab with several smaller stupas on the roof.

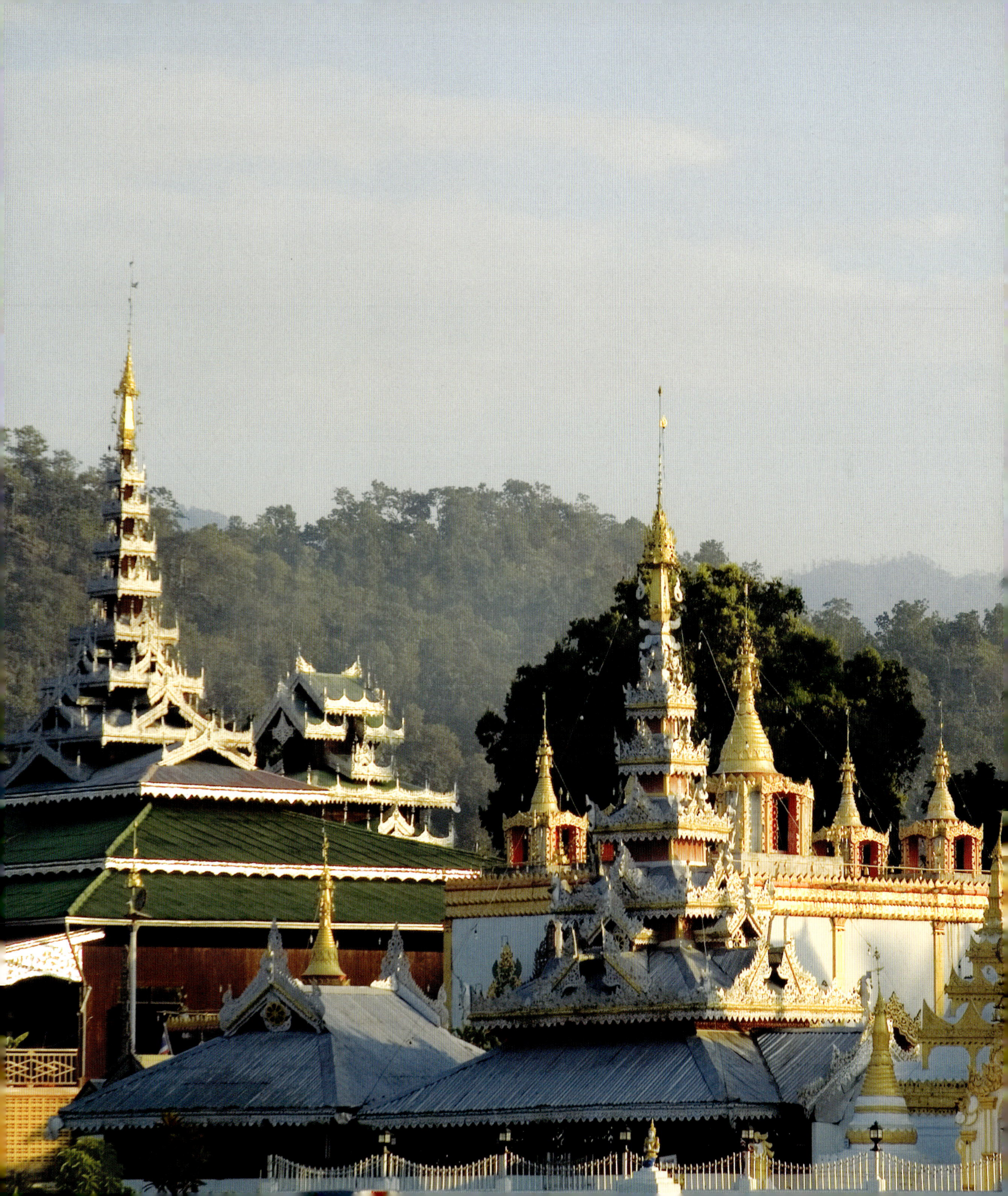

Northeast Thailand

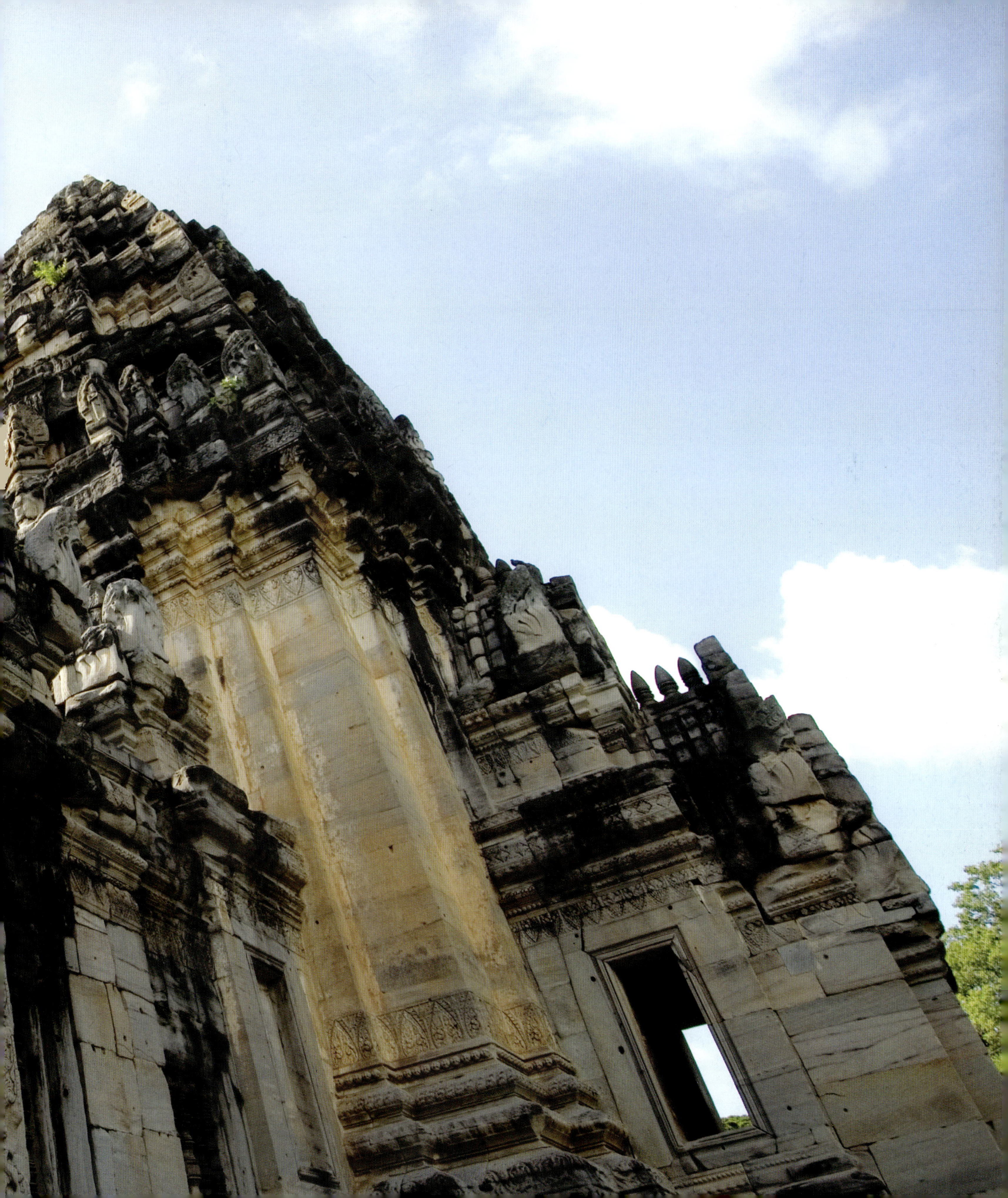

Prasat Hin Phimai

Prasat Hin Phimai Historical Park, Nakhon Ratchasima

From Asia's earliest bronze-age culture 4,000 years ago to present-day Thai nationhood, Isan – northeastern Thailand – has played a role in virtually every key historical transition mainland Southeast Asia has seen. Of these important cultural phases perhaps none has captured the world's imagination as much as the Angkor civilisation, which flourished in northeastern Thailand and northwestern Cambodia from the 9th to 13th centuries.

Inspired by the Hindu-Buddhist architecture of central Java, where he was educated, King Jayavarman II became the first ruler of Angkor in the 9th century and was the first in mainland Southeast Asia to sponsor the building of religious monuments bearing brick or stone towers. Over the next 350 years, this style of architecture evolved into a sophisticated set of walled and moated temple complexes extending from northwestern Cambodia, across northeastern Thailand and as far west as Kanchanaburi in central Thailand.

Connected to 12th century Angkor Wat by a sacred 'superhighway' lined with ceremonial shrines, Prasat Hin Phimai bears key architectural milestones in the development of Angkor design and ritual. It is considered the most significant Angkor site in Thailand. Started by King Jayavarman V in the late 10th century and finished by King Suriyavarman I in the early-11th century, the complex predates Angkor Wat by a hundred years or so, but it nevertheless shares a number of features with its more famous cousin, including the design of its *prasat*, the temple's most prominent feature. The original Sanskrit term *prasada* applied to cube-like religious structures, but in Thai and Khmer contexts such sanctuaries are elaborate monuments of brick, sandstone or laterite, richly carved with religious themes empowering the shrine for ritual use.

Featuring a cruciform floor plan and a 28-metre, *prang*-topped shrine chamber, the *prasat* at Phimai represents a masterpiece of white sandstone

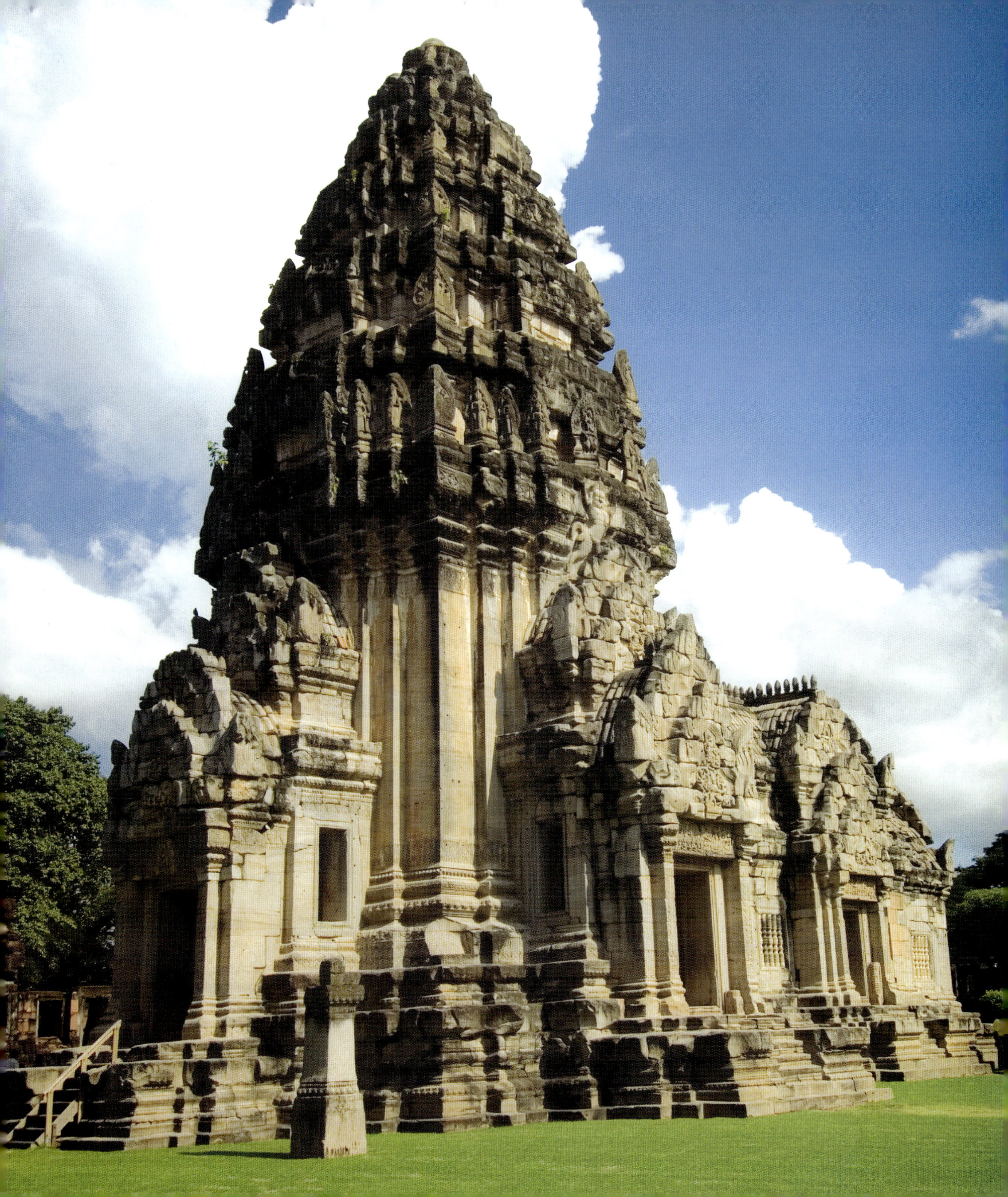

228 Buddhist Temples of Thailand

Pages 224-225: Prasat Hin Khao Phanom Rung, Buriram.

Pages 226-227: Tower shrine and antechambers in the Angkor style.

Left: Roofless galleries.

Region: Northeast Thailand

Above: A Mahayana Buddhist deity, possibly Avalokitesvara.

Right: Monks approach a restored *prang*.

sculpture, with every cornice, lintel, pediment, and pilaster carved to depict scenes from Hindu or Buddhist mythology. The presence of Mahayana Buddhism at Phimai at the beginning of the 12th century was unusual since in Cambodia at this time the principal religion was still Hinduism. However it is likely that at Phimai a mixture of animism, Buddhism, and Hinduism was practised — not unlike mainstream Thai Buddhism today.

The most important relief carvings are almost always found on lintels, the assemblage of stone or brick along the tops of doorways. The southern lintel at the main shrine bears a sandstone relief of Buddha meditating beneath a seven-headed *naga*. Meanwhile the eastern portico is topped by a relief depicting Krishna defeating the demon Kamsa. Adjunct shrines on the grounds, made of pink sandstone, are equally impressive.

230 Buddhist Temples of Thailand

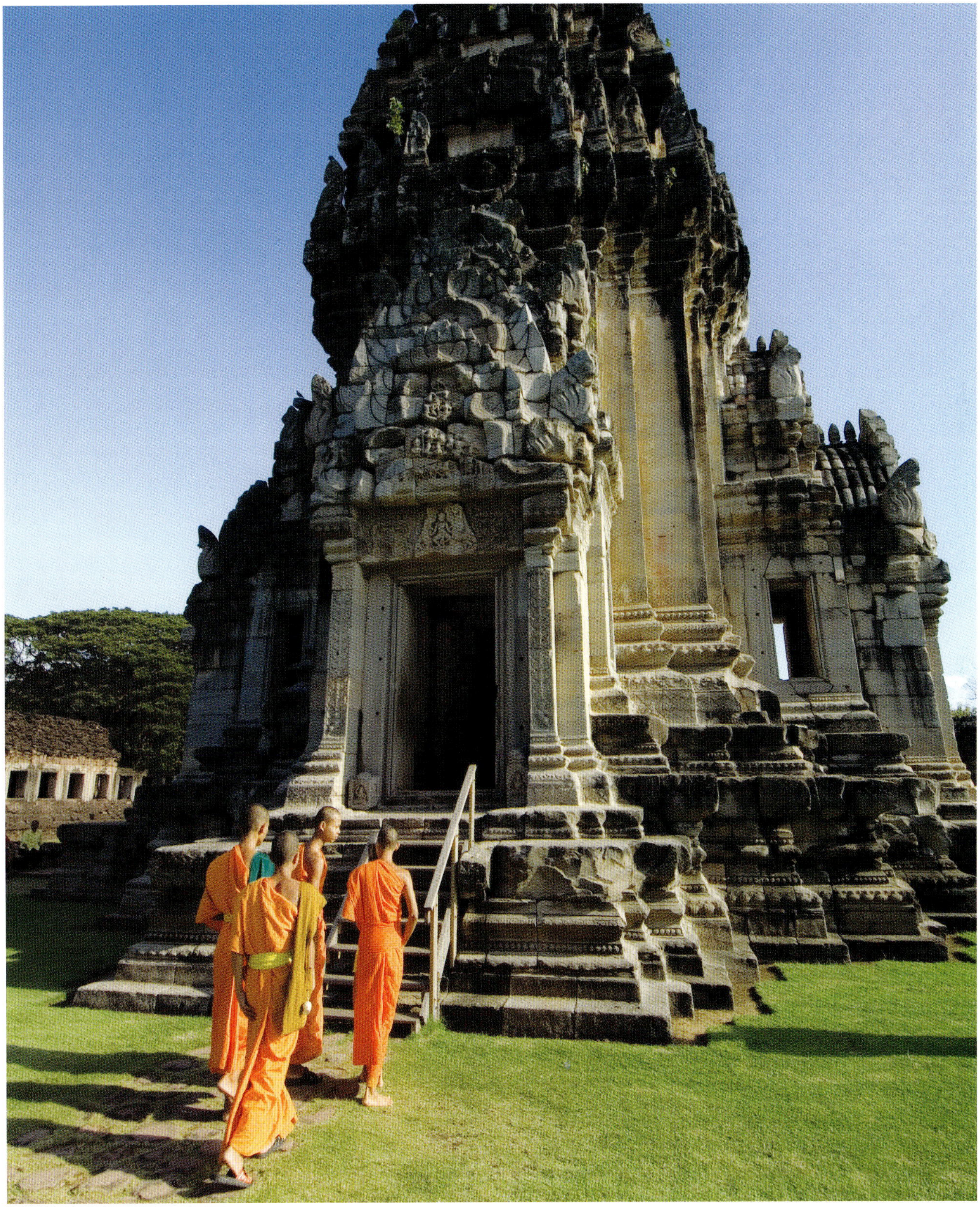

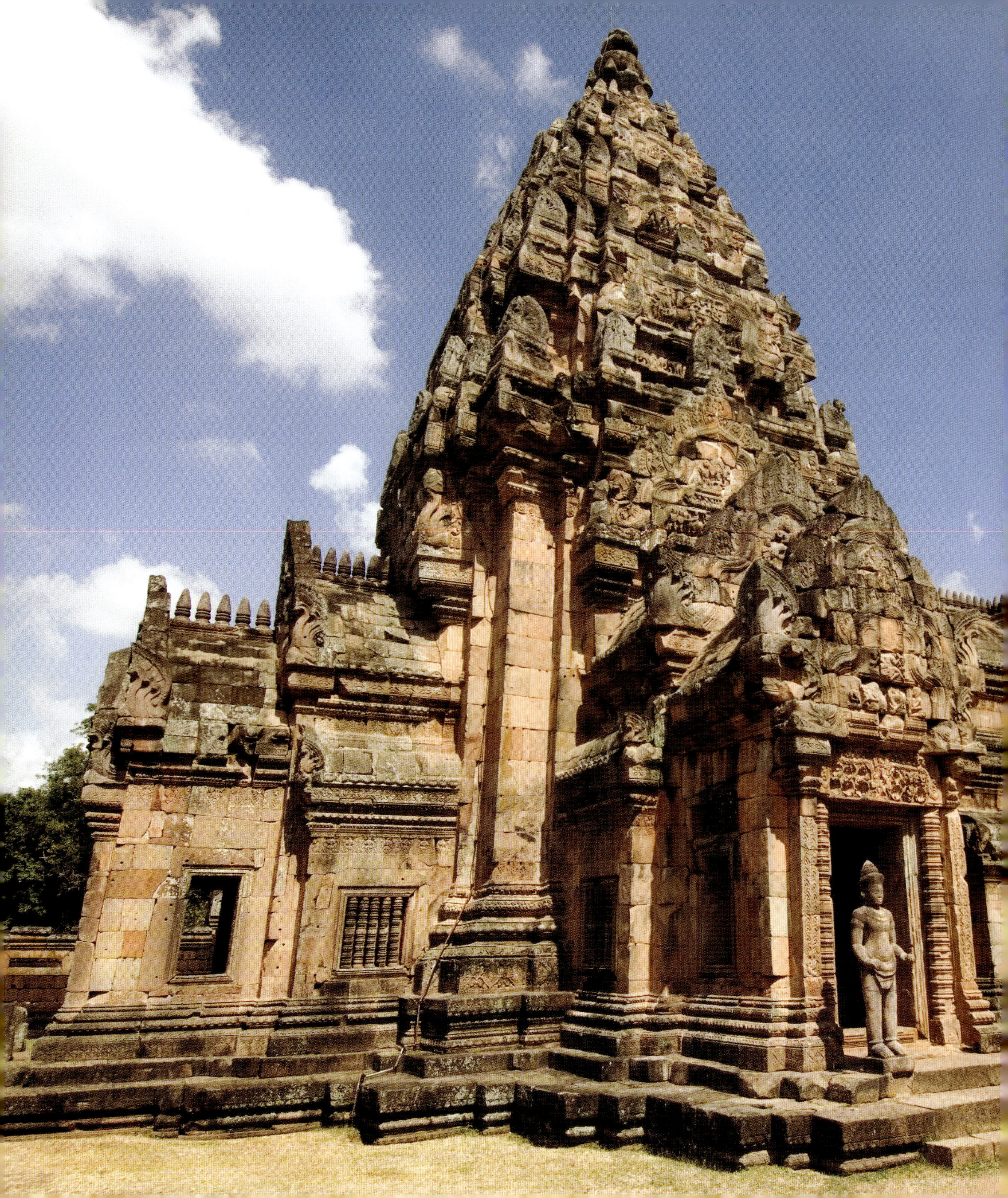

Prasat Hin Khao Phanom Rung

Prasat Hin Khao Phanom Rung Historical Park, Buriram

This striking temple sanctuary crowns the summit of an extinct volcano, 400 metres above sea level and overlooking flat paddy fields below. To the southeast one can clearly see Cambodia's Dongrek Mountains, beyond which the capital of the Angkor empire once lay. In both animist and Hindu belief systems, hills and mountains were often believed to be abodes for gods and the temple was built between the 10th and 13th centuries as a religious sanctuary dedicated to the Hindu god, Shiva, whose Himalayan abode was the mythical Mount Kailash. According to stone inscriptions in Sanskrit and Khmer found at the site, the original name of the temple complex was Phanom Rung, Khmer for 'big mountain,' to which the Thais have added their own word for mountain, *khao*. With Prasat Hin Phimai to the southwest, Phanom Rung was formed as the pinnacle of a triangle route connecting both temples with Angkor Wat. As with many other Angkor-era temples in northeastern Thailand, Thai Buddhists 'colonised' the abandoned remains of Phanom Rung by filling them with Buddha images, by establishing Buddhist monasteries next to them and by using them to host Buddhist festivals. Angkor Wat itself was occupied in the 19th century by Thai Buddhist monks.

Phanom Rung was built between the 10th and 13th centuries, most of it during the reign of King Suriyavarman II (1113-50), a period representing the apex of Angkor architecture. The Department of Fine Arts thoroughly restored it over a 17-year period in the 1970s and 1980s and today it is the largest and best restored of all major Khmer monuments in Thailand.

One key design feature is the promenade leading to the main gate, beginning on a slope 400m east of the main tower, and ascending a system of earthen terraces meant to reinforce the impression of height and evoke a humbling effect on visitors as they prepare to worship on a higher plane. To the north

Pages 232-233: This adjunct *prasat* bears the classic traits of Angkor-period temple architecture: tower shrines linked to antechambers; corbelled roofs; and uniquely Khmer Brahmanist sculpture.

Right: The *prasat* and extended gallery at Prasat Hin Khao Phanom Rung is a masterwork of Angkor satellite architecture. Along with Beng Mealea in Cambodia, it may have served as a prototype for Angkor Wat.

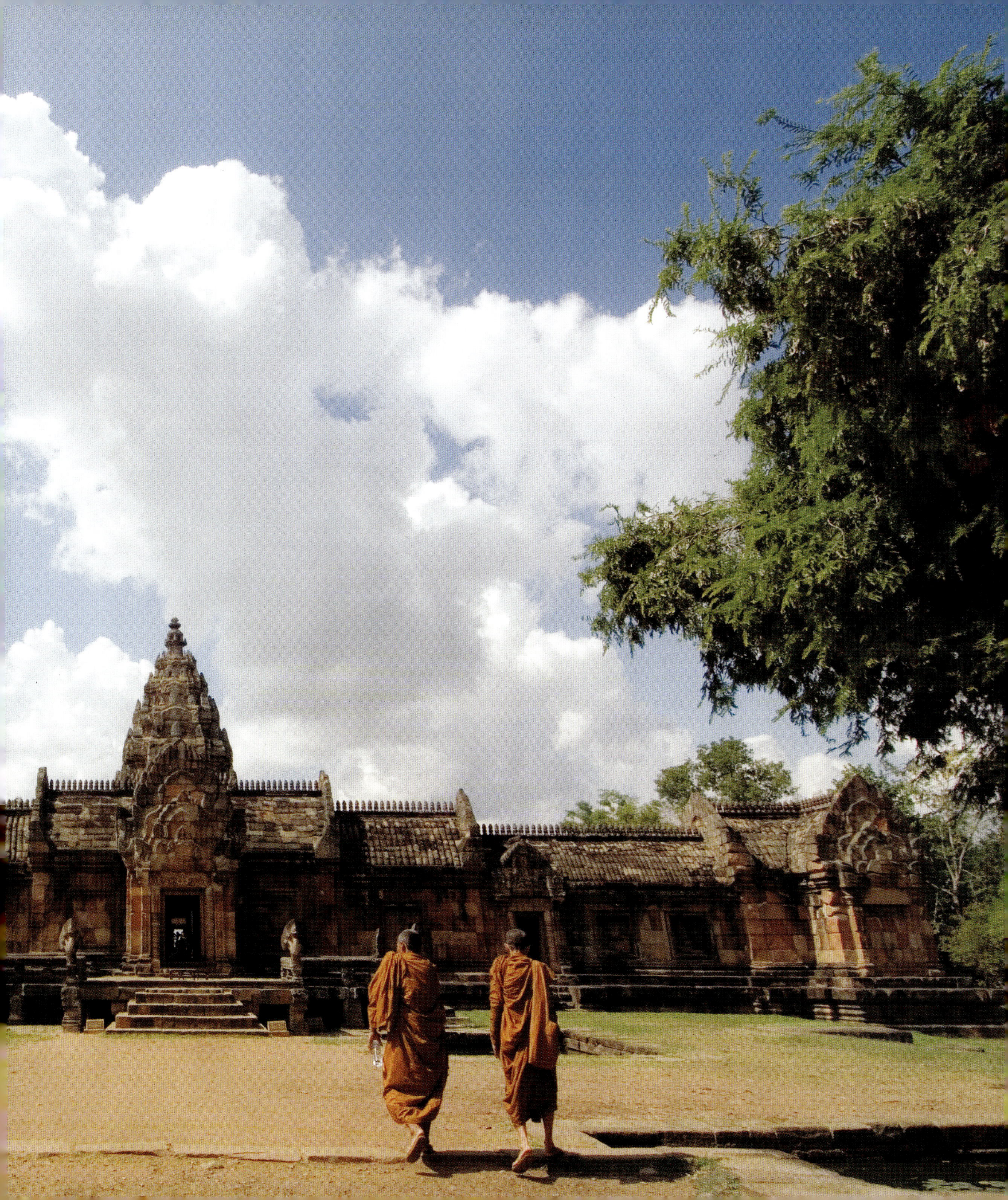

Above: The middle portion of the eastern *gopura* carries a figure of Shiva in ascetic form, surrounded by celestial nymphs. Below this the main lintel depicts Indra, king of the gods, sitting atop the head of Kala, the god of time and death.

Right: Exquisite stone carvings decorate door frames and lintels while Brahmanist statuary stands guard.

side of the approach lie two *baray* or pools which worshippers once used for ritual ablutions before entering the temple complex. This is followed by a 160-metre avenue paved with laterite and sandstone blocks, and flanked by sandstone pillars with lotus-bud tops, ending at the first and largest of three *naga* bridges. These are the only Angkor-period *naga* bridges that have survived in Thailand. The first is flanked by 16 five-headed *naga* which are identical to those found at Angkor Wat. A stairway then leads to the magnificent east gallery of the main sanctuary, topped by curvilinear stone roofs and ventilated with false-balustrade windows.

Inside the temple walls, the sculpture of the *prasat's* stone lintels represents the pinnacle of Khmer artistic achievement. Above the east portico of the *mondop* stands a Nataraja (Dancing Shiva), carved from sandstone in the late Baphuan style. Below this relief is the temple's most beautiful and most famous lintel, depicting a reclining Vishnu (Narayana) in the Hindu creation myth. Growing from his navel is a lotus that branches into several blossoms, on one of which sits the creator god Brahma. On either side of Vishnu are heads of Kala, the god of time and death. He is asleep on the milky sea of eternity, here represented by a *naga*. This architectural treasure made headlines when it mysteriously disappeared in the 1960s, then reappeared at the Chicago Art Institute. After 16 years of protests it was finally returned to its rightful place. Meanwhile the south entrance carries a lintel relief of Shiva and Uma riding their bull mount, Nandi. The central cell of the *prasat* itself contains a venerable Shivalingam (Shiva phallus). Several sculpted images of Vishnu and his incarnations, Rama and Krishna, decorate various other lintels and cornices.

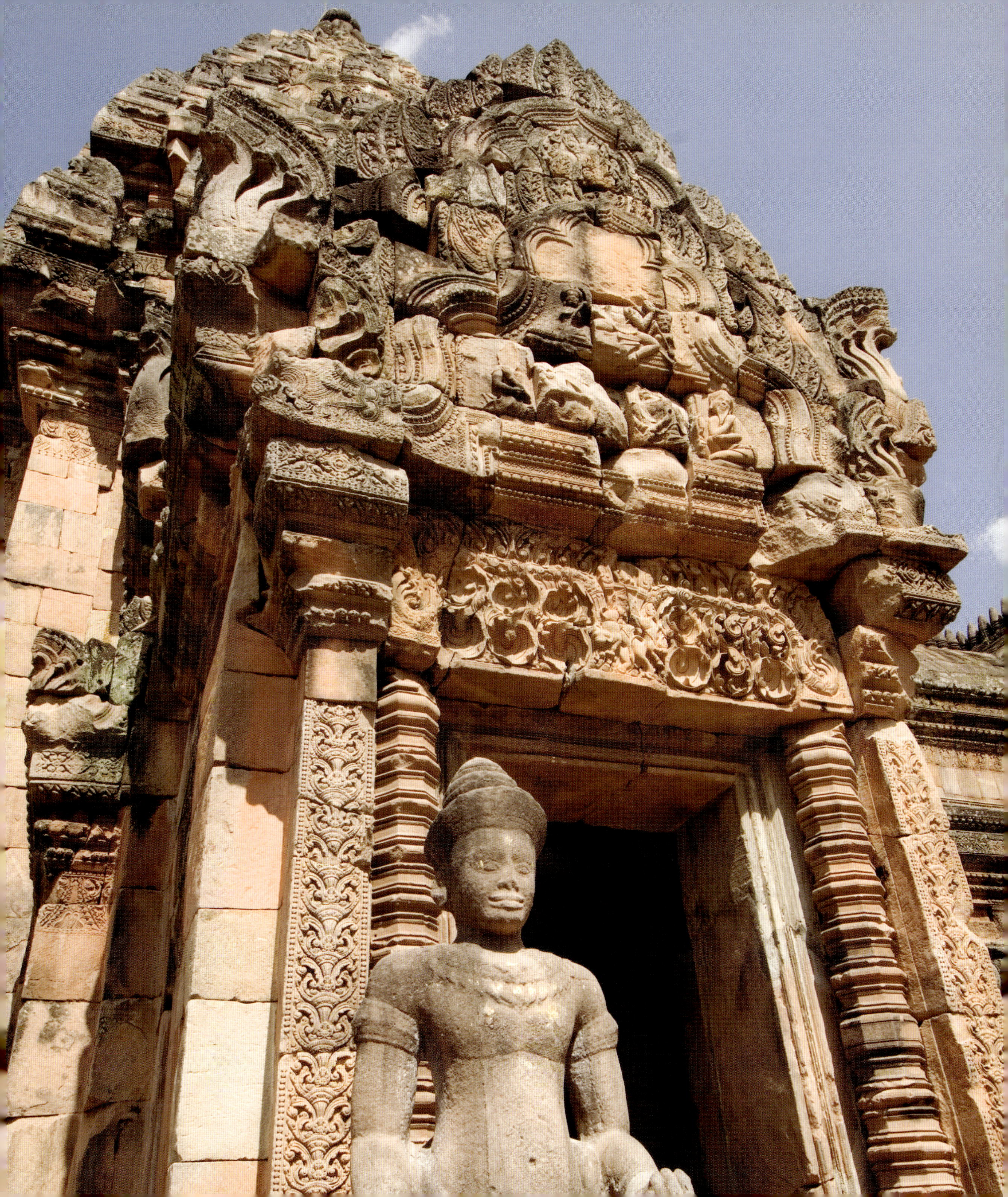

Wat Phra That Phanom

That Phanom, Nakhon Phanom

The most sacred Buddhist pilgrimage point in all of northeastern Thailand, Wat Phra That Phanom is believed to occupy the site of a much older temple dating to the late Chenla or early Angkor era, circa 6th to 10th centuries. No traces of the original structures, which would have been Mon-Khmer in style and Hindu in function, are visible today.

The central feature of the monastery, the highly revered Phra That Phanom, the stupa for which the monastery is named, dominates the skyline and is surrounded by its own large square enclosure. It is believed the stupa was built by a Lao king ruling over Vientiane in the 15th or 16th century. The 57-metre high monument, which is said to enshrine a breastbone of the Buddha, is designed in the classic Lao way, featuring a four-sided, curvilinear superstructure standing on a multi-tiered base. The artistic impact is enhanced by dramatic vine-like decorations made from solid gold — 110kg in all — on all four sides. Surrounding the stupa is a cloister filled with Buddha images.

The monument collapsed during unusually heavy rains in 1975 (an event many locals equated with the fall of Vientiane to the communist Pathet Lao) and was restored by the Department of Fine Arts in 1978. Amid the ruins of the fallen stupa, restoration workers found golden Buddha images, gold ingots, large rubies and jewellery that had been the personal possessions of royalty who had enshrined them as Buddhist offerings. There were also shrine compartments where commoners placed their offerings, which included family heirlooms such as betel nut scissors. All were carefully replaced in their original locations.

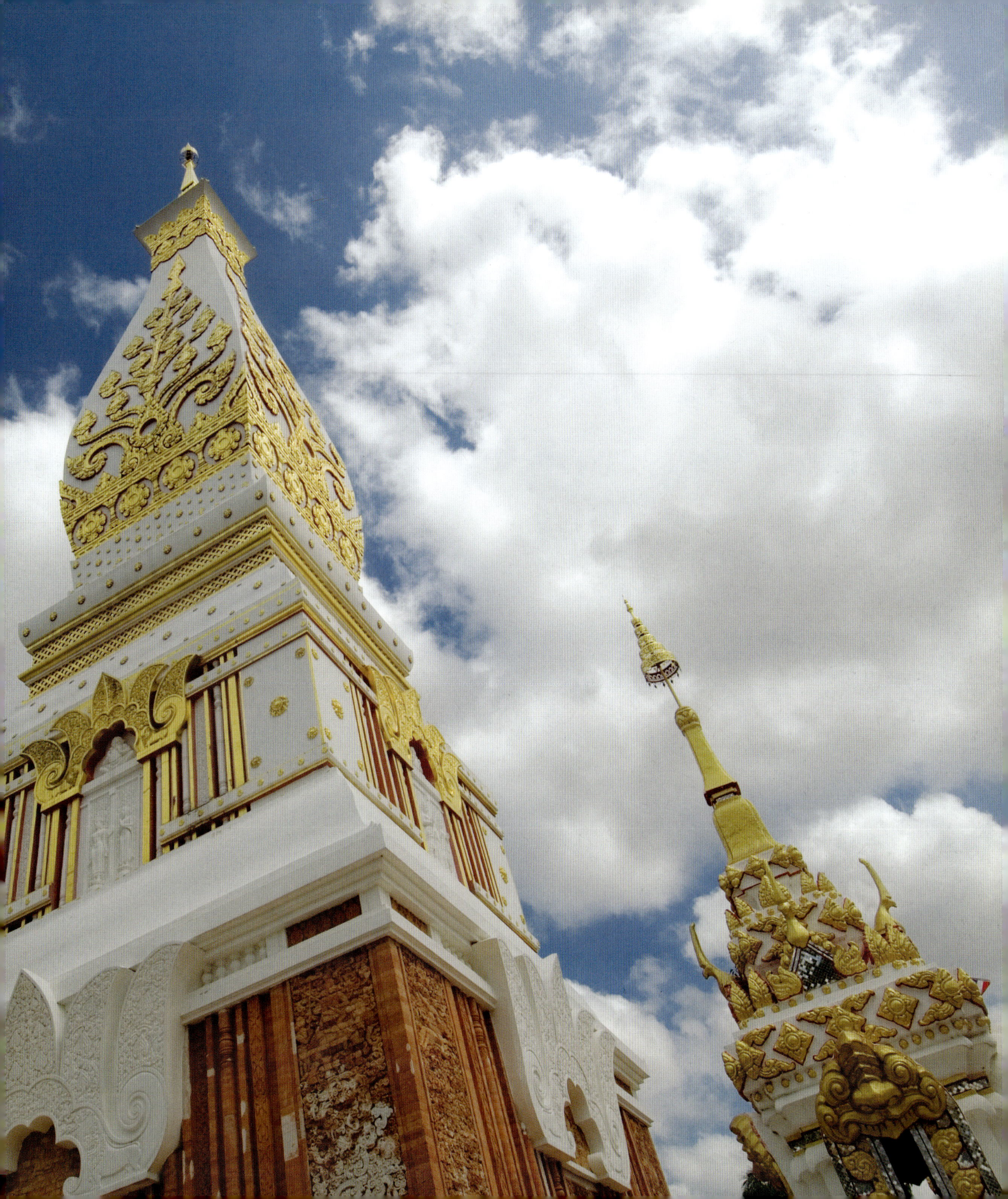

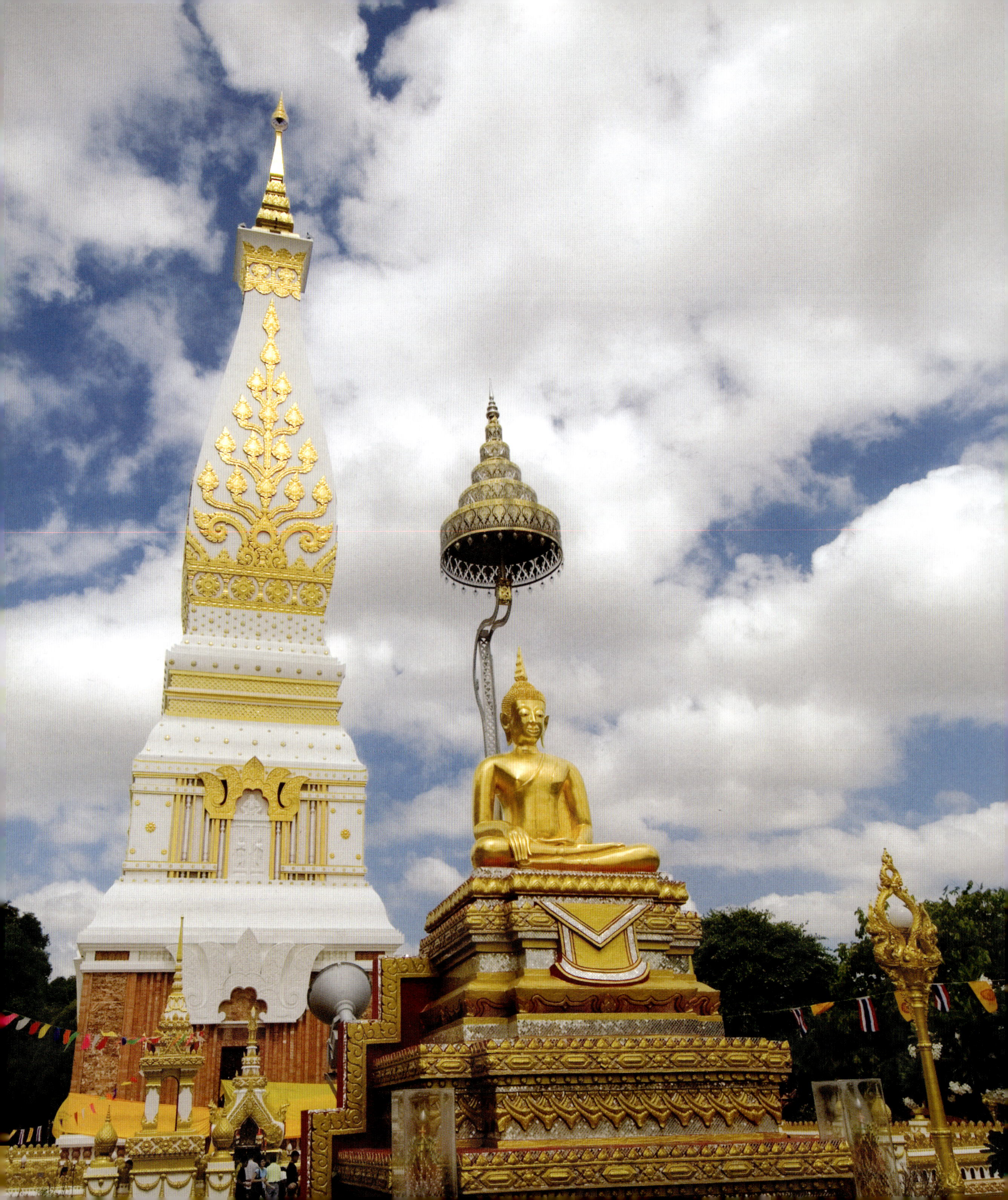

Today Wat Phra That Phanom is a popular 'wish-fulfilling place,' and virtually every Thai visitor will perform a minimum of three circumambulations of the stupa, stopping at Buddha shrines along the way to pray. Some pilgrims will purchase a sparrow kept in a small bamboo cage from a temple vendor, then carry the caged bird with them while walking round the temple. At the end of the circuit, worshippers free the bird to the skies in the belief its release will speed the pilgrim's prayers to heaven.

While pilgrims visit Phra That Phanom all year round, the most popular time of year to visit is during the annual week-long Phra That Phanom Festival. Held in late January or early February, depending on lunar phases, the festivities can draw several thousand pilgrims.

Pages 238-239: Phra That Phanom.

Left: The main stupa is decorated with 110kg of solid gold.

Above: Visiting monks make offerings.

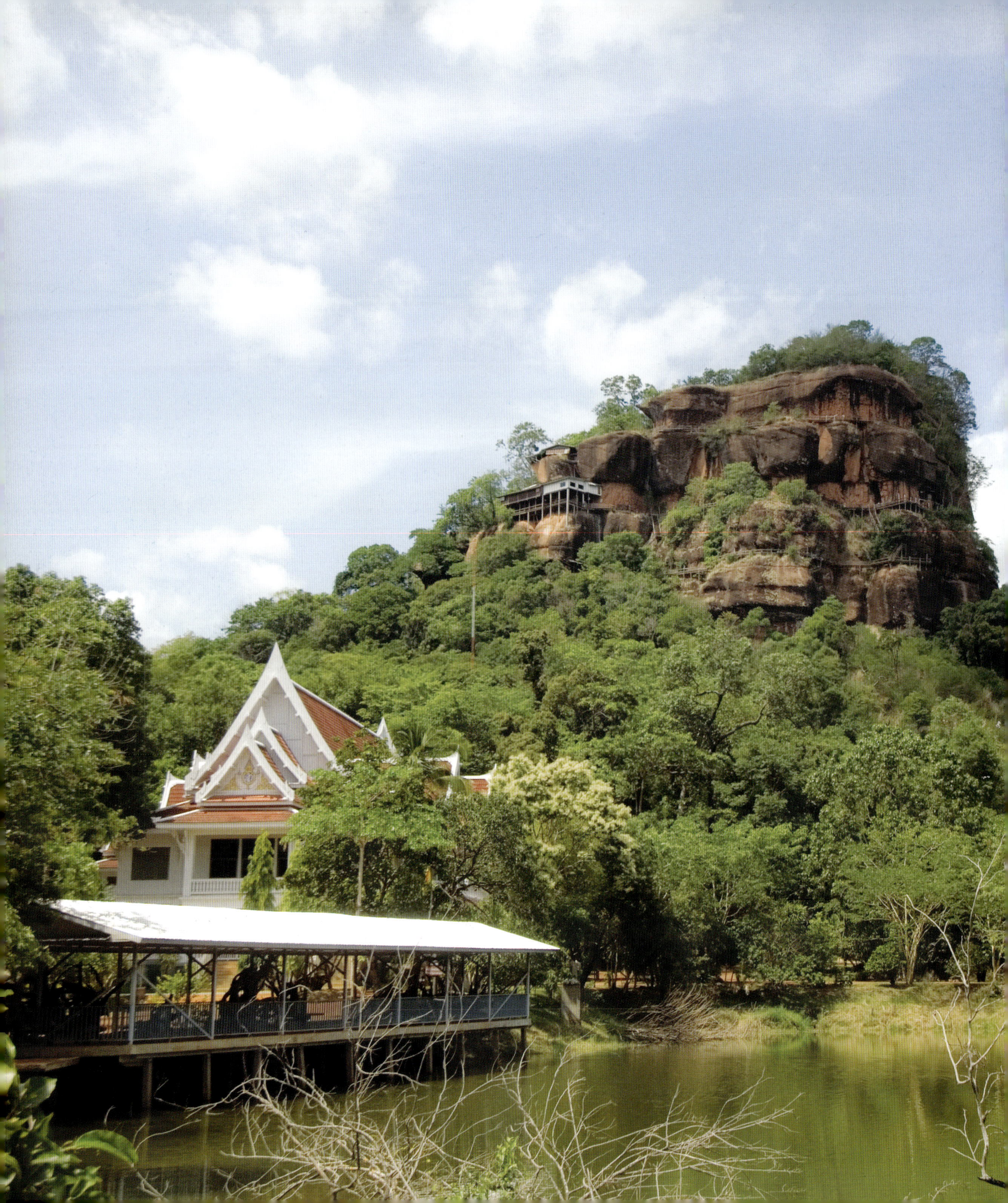

Wat Chedi Khiri Wihan (Wat Phu Thok)

Beung Kan, Nong Khai

Wat Chedi Khiri Wihan is one of Thailand's most unique Buddhist monasteries, not by virtue of age or artisanship, but because of its position atop a massive sandstone outcropping overlooking the plains of northeastern Thailand. The 200m-tall rock formation, too steep for roads or footpaths, is scaled via a rickety system of wooden ladders, stairs and walkways. More commonly known as Wat Phu Thok – named for its perch, Phu Thok ('Isolated Mountain' in local Isan dialect) – the *wat* was established by Phra Chuan Kunlachettho, a Thai monk who came across the lonely peak during his ascetic wanderings in the 1960s. A disciple of the late Ajahn Man, a renowned early-20th century meditation master who inspired the tradition of forest monasteries through the northeast, Phra Chuan saw that the tranquil surroundings and natural shelter provided by cool, mosquito-free caves were well-suited for a meditation centre. Construction on the walkways began in 1969, and it took five years to complete the spiralling route through rocky, forested terrain.

On the ascent to the summit, the paths link seven levels, representing the seven stages of Buddhist enlightenment. Each level is cooler and provides more breathtaking views than the previous level, making the strenuous climb an allegory for the path to nirvana. The first, second and third walkway sections wind around the mountain through dense forest and past large boulders. At the end of the third level, the circuit splits into two alternate routes, one proceeding to the fourth level and the other offering a steep shortcut direct to the fifth. Resident and visiting nuns are lodged at the fourth level, where the walkway wraps around the outcropping for a half kilometre, providing expansive views of forested Phu Langka to the west and a picturesque zone of rolling hills along the way.

A variety of Buddha pavilions, *kuti*, meditation caves and cliff rest areas occupy the fifth level. A natural stone bridge here also leads to a *wihan* enshrining Buddha relics. Most visitors walk no further than the fifth level, where they consult with monks, make offerings, enjoy the views and return to the plains below. The sixth level is not for the faint of heart as it consists of a long section of walkways and bridges suspended alongside high, steep cliffs. The challenging route leads to the shady, windswept summit, the seventh and final level.

Pages 242-243: Phu Tok, the 200-metre sandstone outcropping on which Wat Chedi Khiri Wihan is built.

Right: The interior of a natural rock cave *wihan*.

Far right: A memorial stupa to the late Ajahn Chuan.

244   Buddhist Temples of Thailand

Region: Northeast Thailand

Southern Thailand

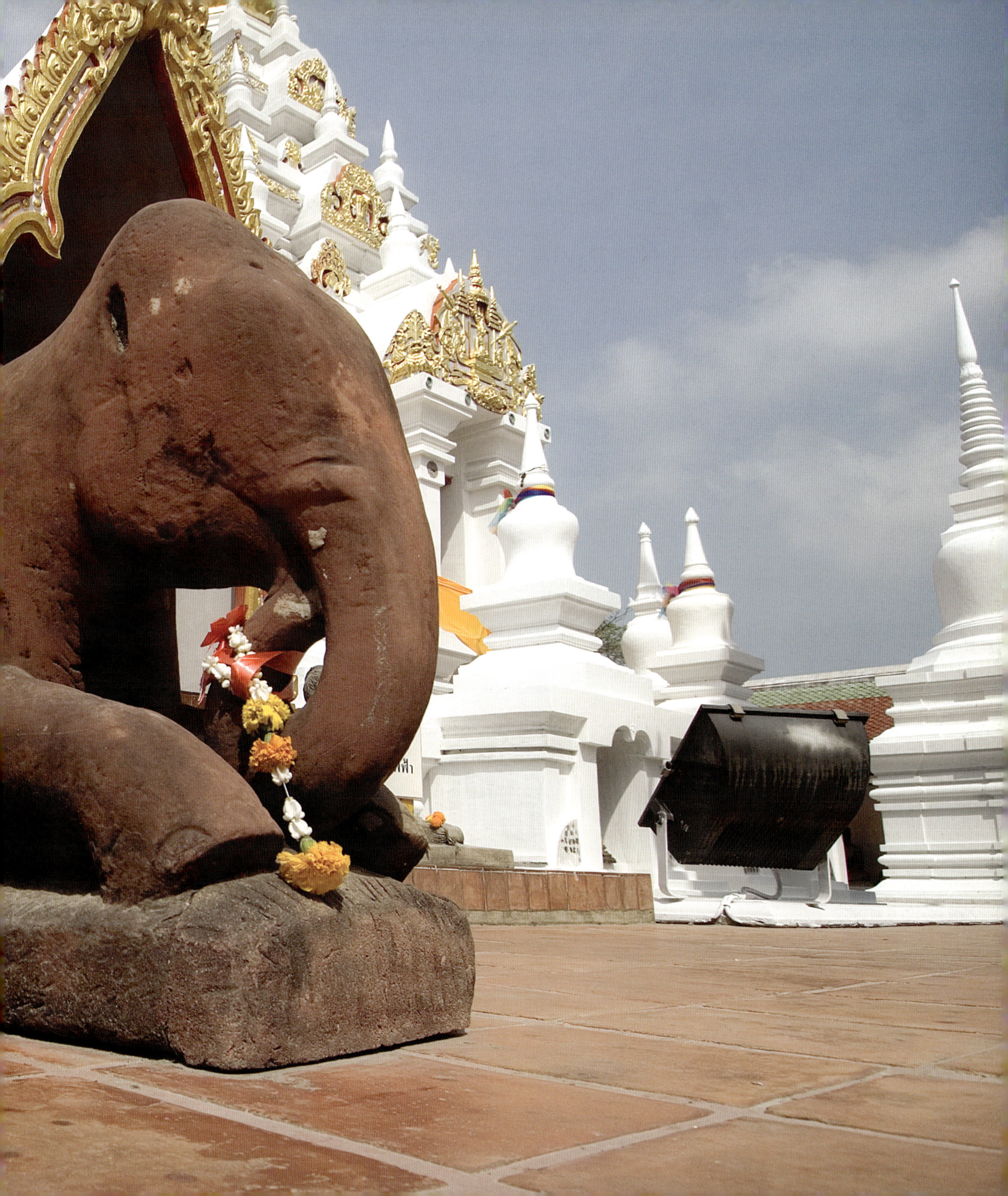

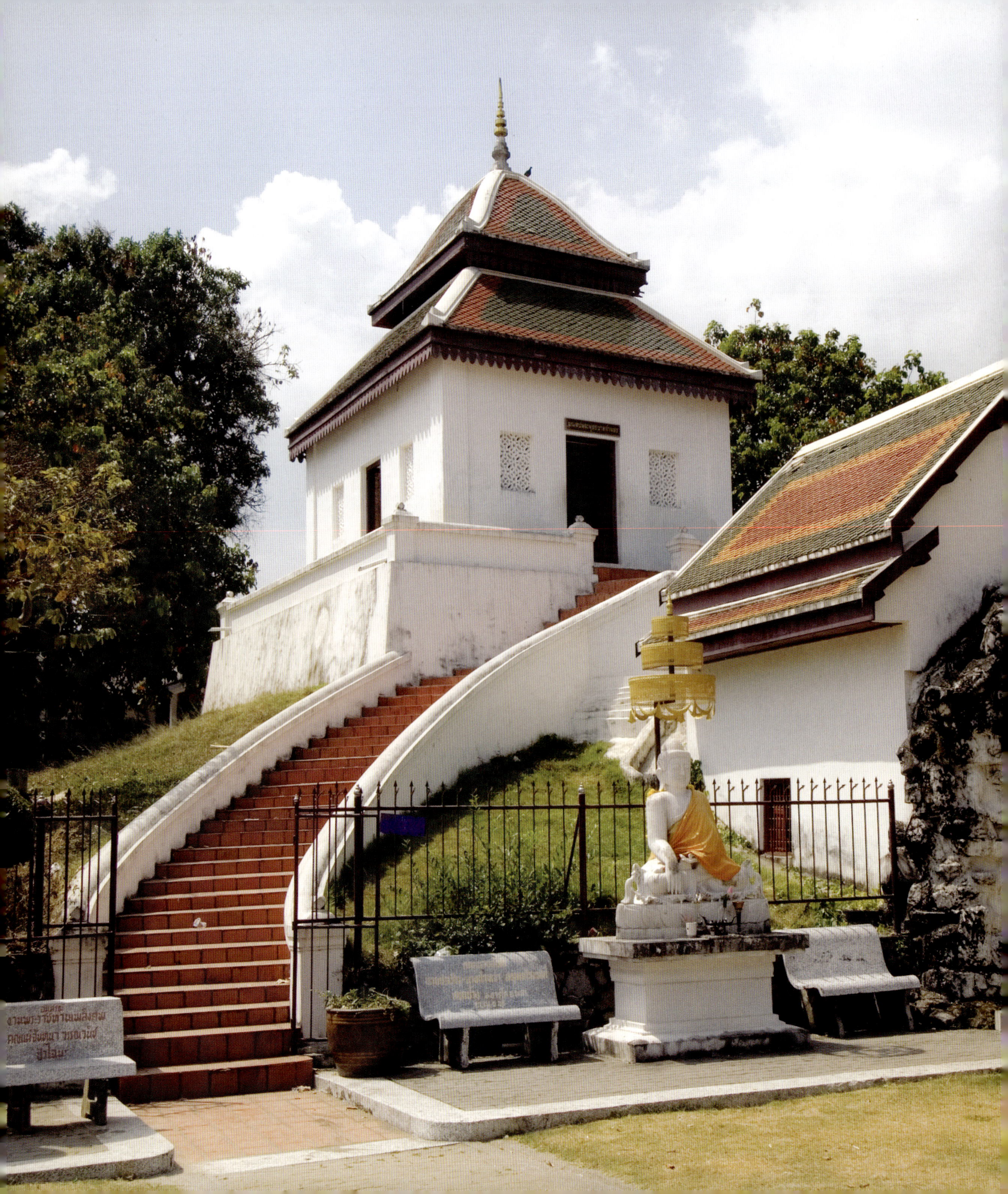

Wat Phra Mahathat

Nakhon Si Thammarat

Nakhon Si Thammarat was once the capital of the kingdom of Tambralinga. Also known as Ligor, it is one of the oldest towns in Thailand. Little is known about this early kingdom, which, along with the entire Thai-Malay Peninsula, was subjugated by the Srivijaya empire from the 8th to 11th centuries. After Tambralinga had achieved independence again in the 12th century, Sri Lankan-ordained Buddhist monks established Wat Phra Mahathat and the city name was changed to the Pali 'Nagara Sri Dhammaraja' (City of the Sacred Dharma-King), rendered in Thai phonetics as Nakhon Si Thammarat. An overland route between the western port of Trang and eastern port of Nakhon Si Thammarat became a major trade link between Thailand and the rest of the world, as well as between the western and eastern hemispheres and the city flourished.

A pronounced Sinhalese influence is immediately visible at Wat Phra Mahathat in the simple dome-box-cone design of the stupas, which were built in the mid-13th century and inspired by the great stupas of Sri Lanka. Looming over the entire compound is the 78-metre high main stupa, said to contain a Buddha tooth relic and crowned by a solid gold spire weighing several hundred kilograms. Local historians claim it was built over an earlier Srivijaya-era stupa. The central stupa is surrounded by 173 smaller satellite stupas in typical mandala configuration. Every year during the third lunar month (February to March) the city hosts the colourful Hae Pha Khun That festival, in which a lengthy saffron cloth is ceremonially wrapped around the main stupa.

Pages 246-247: A stone sculpture of a kneeling elephant at Wat Phra Mahathat may have originated from an earlier monastery site.

Pages 248-249: The roof of this *mondop* may have been influenced by Sumatran-style mosque architecture.

Right: The 13th century stupas at Wat Phra Mahathat were inspired by the great stupas of Anuradhapura in Sri Lanka.

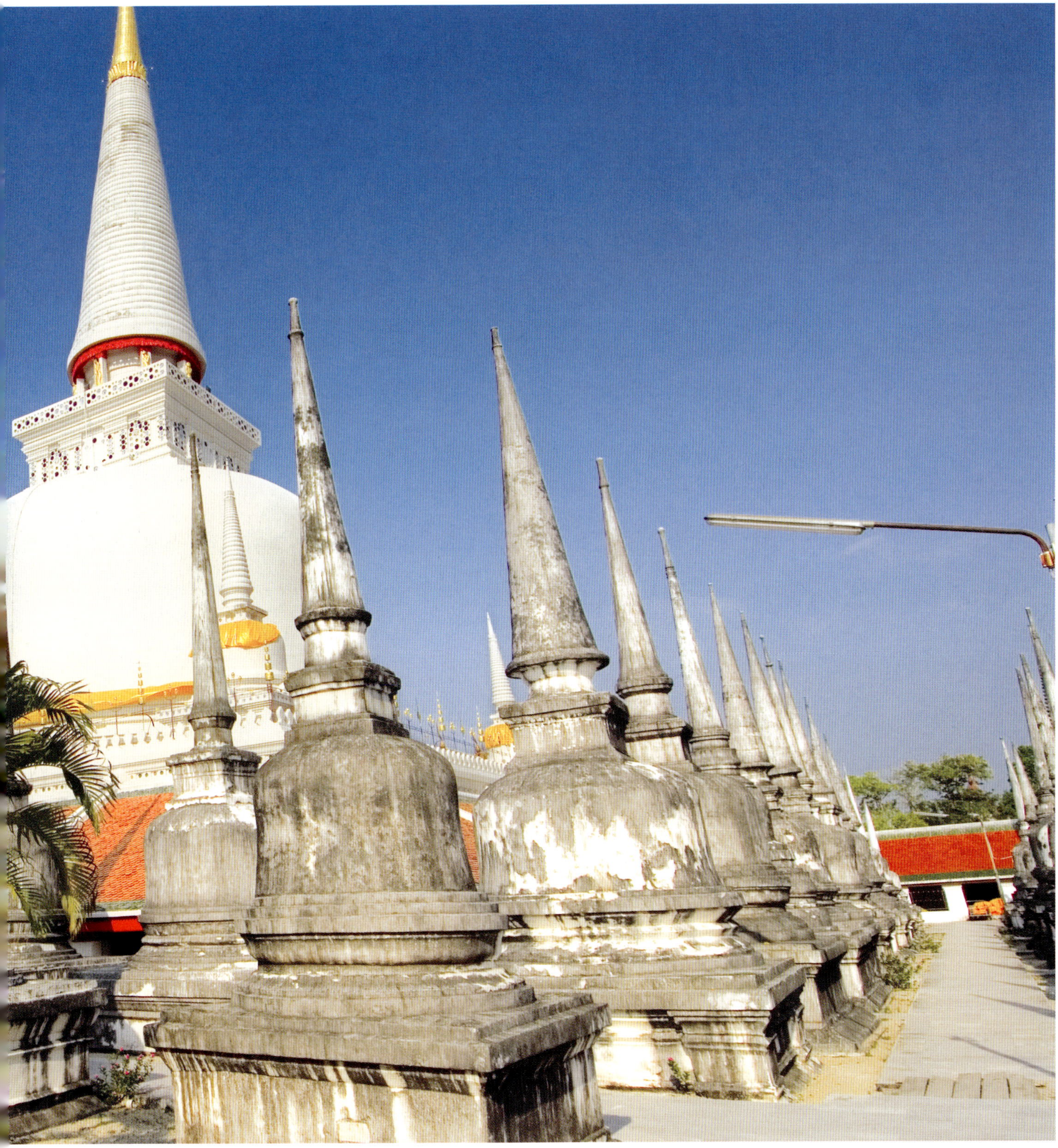

Above: Detail of a Jatukham Ramathep amulet.

Right: A vendor wears a necklace made up of Jatukham Ramathep amulets to entice visitors to the *wat* to buy a souvenir.

Four intricately designed *wihan* occupy positions next to the stupa's four cardinal points. Wihan Khian contains a museum displaying valuable Nakhon Si Thammarat- and Ayuthaya-style Buddha images. A large *bot* can be found to the south of the grand stupa, and towards the northern end of the temple grounds, a thick-walled *mondop* with a fortress-like appearance holds a Buddha footprint shrine. Monks quarters for the monastery are not found in this compound but instead across the road at Wat Na Phra Boromathat.

Since 1987 Wat Phra Mahathat has been famed for selling Jatukham Ramathep amulets, said to invoke the power of two Tambralinga princes, Jatukham and Ramathep, whose spirits protect the city. On the grounds are two bronze statues said to represent the princes. Some scholars believe the statues depict the Brahman deities Skanda and Vishnu and were brought to Nakhon Si Thammarat from Sri Lanka.

Region: Southern Thailand 253

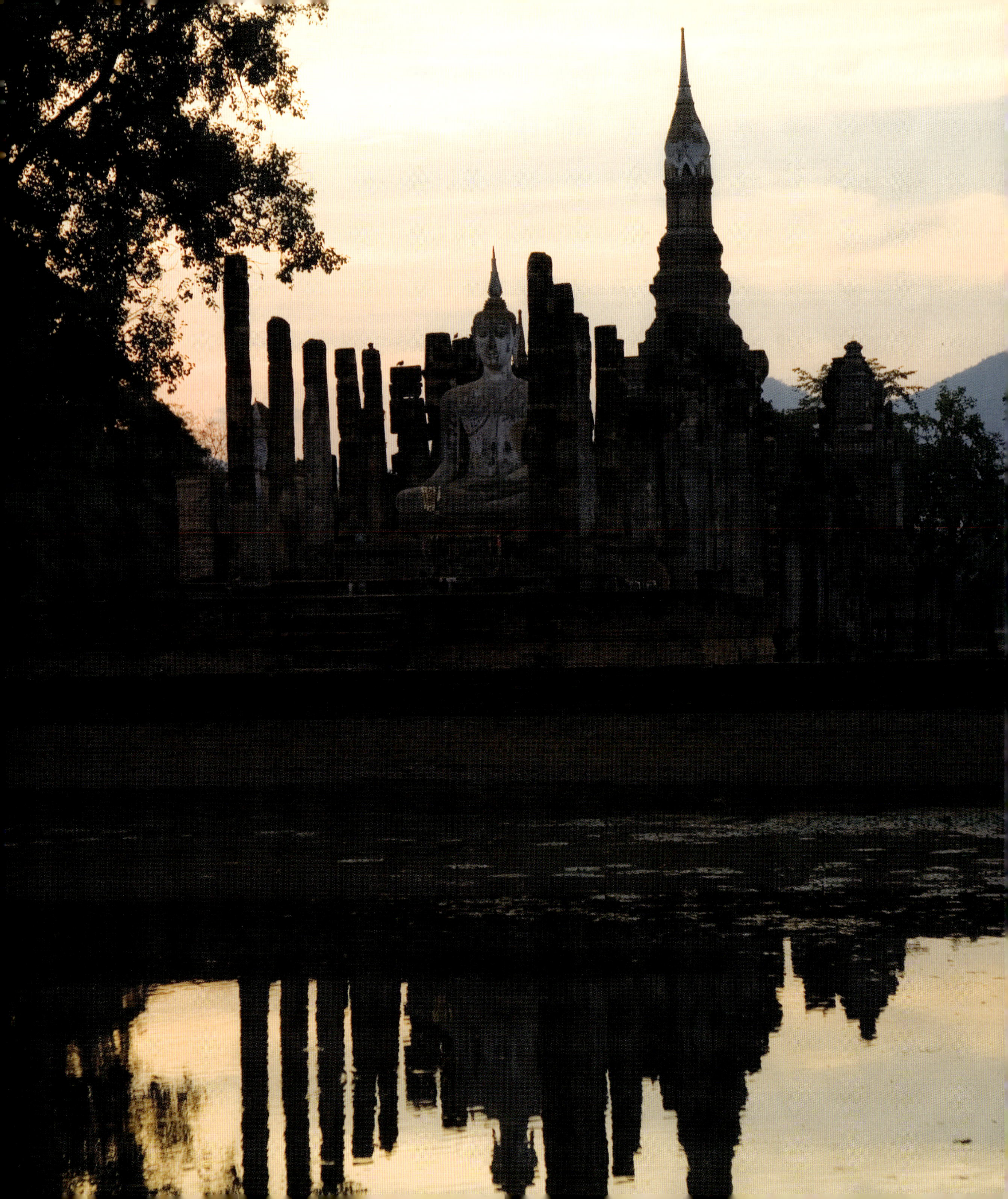

Further Reading

Aasen, Clarence, *Architecture of Siam: A Cultural History Interpretation*. New York: Oxford University Press, 1998.

Bechert, Heinz and Richard Gombrich, eds., *The World of Buddhism: Monks and Nuns in Society and Culture*. London: Thames and Hudson, 1984.

Bhirasri, Silpa, *Thai Buddhist Art (Architecture): Thai Culture, New Series No. 4*. Bangkok: Fine Arts Department, 1961.

Chihara, D., *Hindu-Buddhist Architecture in Southeast Asia*. Leiden: E.J. Brill, 1996.

Coomaraswamy, Ananda K., *Elements of Buddhist Iconography*. Cambridge, Mass.: Harvard University Press, 1935.

Cummings, Joe, *Buddhist Stupas in Asia: The Shape of Perfection*. Lonely Planet Journeys, 2001.

Dallapiccola, Anna, ed., *The Stupa: Its Religious, Historical, and Architectural Significance*. Wiesbaden: Franz Steiner Verlag, 1980.

Döhring, Karl, *Buddhist Temples of Thailand: An Architectonic Introduction*. White Lotus, 2000.

Freeman, Michael, *Khmer Temples in Thailand and Laos*. Bangkok: River Books, 2009.

Ginsberg, Henry, *Thai Manuscript Painting*. Honolulu: University of Hawai'i Press, 1989.

Lester, Robert C., *Theravada Buddhism in Southeast Asia*. Ann Arbor: University of Michigan Press, 1973.

Ringis, Rita, *Thai Temples and Temple Murals*. New York: Oxford University Press, 1990.

Smitthi, Siribhadra and Elizabeth Moore, *Palaces of the Gods: Khmer Art and Architecture in Thailand*. Bangkok: River Books, 1992.

Stratton, Carol., *Buddhist Sculpture of Northern Thailand*. Chiang Mai: Silkworm Books, 2003.

Swearer, Donald K., *The Buddhist World of Southeast Asia*. Albany: State University of New York Press, 1995.

Wells, Kenneth E., *Thai Buddhism, Its Rites and Activities*. Bangkok: Christian Bookstore, 1960.

Woodward, H., *The Art and Architecture of Thailand*. Leiden: E.J. Brill, 2003.